Governance and Complexity in Water Management

Governance and Complexity in Water Management

Creating Cooperation through Boundary Spanning Strategies

Edited by

Hans Bressers

Kris Lulofs

CSTM, Institute for Governance Studies, University of Twente, the Netherlands

Edward Elgar

Cheltenham, UK • Northampton, MA, USA

Published by
Edward Elgar Publishing Limited
The Lypiatts
15 Lansdown Road
Cheltenham
Glos GL50 2JA
UK

Edward Elgar Publishing, Inc.
William Pratt House
9 Dewey Court
Northampton
Massachusetts 01060
USA

A catalogue record for this book
is available from the British Library

Library of Congress Control Number: 2009937928

ISBN 978 1 84844 955 8

Co-published by IWA Publishing, Alliance House, 12 Caxton Street, London SW1H 0QS, UK
Tel. +44 (0) 20 7654 5500, Fax +44 (0) 20 7654 5555
publications@iwap.co.uk
www.iwapublishing.com
ISBN 1843393298
ISBN13 9781843393290

Printed and bound by MPG Books Group, UK

Contents

Figures

Tables

Contributors

Hans Bressers is professor of policy studies and environmental policy at the University of Twente and founder and first director of the CSTM, the center for studies in sustainable development of that university. In over three hundred publications he published on public policy and governance, mostly applied on environmental policies and water management. He has been project leader of numerous projects, including several studies in water management sponsored by European and national research programmes.

Jaap Evers holds a Masters degree in irrigation and water engineering from Wageningen University (August, 2006). Since November 2006 he has been a PhD candidate at the School of Management and Governance of the University of Twente (unit CSTM). His research is on the effectiveness of implementation of integrated water management plans and aims to test the principles of interactive implementation.

Simone Hanegraaff holds a Masters degree in environmental social science from Utrecht University. At the School of Management and Governance of the University of Twente (unit CSTM) she researched the boundary spanning behaviour of water managers in the Netherlands. Her research interest is in the analysis of responses to social issues from governmental actors, market players and civil society.

Wim van Leussen works for the Dutch State Water Authority and the Dutch Ministry of Transport, Public Works and Water Management. Over many years he held several positions in varying fields, including recently flood management and the implementation of the European Water Framework Directive. As professor of river basin management, he is also attached to the University of Twente (unit CSTM).

Kris Lulofs is senior research associate at the School of Management and Governance of the University of Twente (unit CSTM). His research interest is in policy analysis and especially in governance strategies for sustainability. For over twenty years he has been researcher and project leader of numerous projects in the fields of water management, climate change and corporate social responsibility, and teaches in undergraduate and postgraduate programmes. He is a senior member of the Dutch interuniversity research School for Public Administration and Political Sciences.

Jan van der Molen works at the water board Velt and Vecht as a consultant in the field of policy and strategy. As a water manager he is involved in different projects on transboundary water management. In addition he is undertaking a PhD at the School of Management and Governance of the University of Twente (unit CSTM). In his PhD the focus is on the way transboundary regional cooperation can be developed. He teaches in some postgraduate programmes and is a certified member of the Dutch management consultancy council (Ooa).

Katharine Owens is assistant professor in politics and government at the University of Hartford in Connecticut, USA. Her research interests include policy implementation analysis and natural resource decision making. Empirical fields of focus include water and campus sustainability. She incorporates service- and applied-learning methodology in teaching and also conducts research on the effectiveness of these methods.

Aysun Özen Tacer is a PhD candidate at the School of Management and Governance of the University of Twente (unit CSTM). Her research interest is in the human dimension of public participation within the domain of sustainable water resources management, especially decision-making and social learning processes. She has been working as a senior consultant at Deloitte Consulting and has conducted several public sector projects.

Mirjam van Tilburg is a PhD candidate at the School of Management and Governance of the University of Twente (unit CSTM). Her PhD thesis focuses on the use and usability of science knowledge in decision making in water management projects. She attempts to identify the conditions which stimulate or obstruct knowledge transfer and utilization. Mirjam worked at the regional water authority Regge and Dinkel as a policy maker and for a political party in the Parliament of the province of Overijssel. Her research interests are knowledge utilization, policy analysis and decision-making processes in environmental policy.

Abbreviations

AWM	Adaptive Water Mangement
CFC	Considerations of Future Consequences
CIT	Contextual Interaction Theory
EC	European Commission
EIS	Environmental Impact Statement
EU	European Union
GLTO	Agricultural Organization
IPCC	Intergovernmental Panel on Climate Change
IRMA	Interreg Rhine Meuse Activities (European Interreg programme)
IWM	Integrated Water Management
IWRM	Integrated Water Resource Management
MNP	Netherlands Environmental Assessment Agency
NBW	National Administrative Agreement on Water
NGO	Non-governmental Organization
NIMBY	Not in my back yard
UNDP	United Nations Development Programme
WB21	Committee Water Management for the 21st Century
WFD	(European) Water Framework Directive
WV21	Water Safety 21st Century
WWF	World Wildlife Fund
ZTPI	Zimbardo Time Perspective Inventory

Preface

Within natural resource management water issues have always been in a prominent position. The reasons for that are obvious. Events like flooding of land, extreme droughts, shortage of drinking water, spread of infectious diseases and long-term problems such as inefficient irrigation and bad water quality cannot be ignored. These water-related issues reflect social challenges that had to be met centuries ago as well as today.

Recently both climate change, and its impacts on water systems, and raised ambitions within the European Union (EU) caused water issues to rapidly re-enter the priority agenda. Large-scale flooding in several European countries as well as severe periods of droughts caught public attention. Serious contemporary water management challenges now have to be addressed. These include realizing huge storage locations to buffer excess water, improving irrigation works, disconnecting urbanized and rural water systems for improving water quality and restoring the ecological and natural quality of water systems.

The resources for water management have not increased relative to elevated problem pressures and ambitions. Meeting the challenges requires substantial interference in society and claims on society's resources. Water managers have to adapt to these new challenges. For the last few decades water managers were perfectly equipped to solve single water issues in a technological manner without being intrusive on other sectors of society. Now they enter into processes of negotiation and even risk conflict between water management and vested interests in society. Water managers have to reconsider their position and strategies. Often dependencies exist and this inevitably implies joining forces with other sectors in order to cope with contemporary water issues while minimizing sacrifices within society. Problem-solving capacity in modern and democratic societies is dispersed over many actors that hold ownership rights, user rights and management rights. Synthesized solutions based on pooling of ambitions and resources are called for. This leads to increasingly complex multi-purpose projects.

Water managers now have to learn a new art of juggling multiple actors, multiple preferences, multiple problem perceptions and multiple institutional rule settings. They have to engage in all kinds of collaboration across sector and organizational boundaries, enter into political and strategic alliances, and seed social capital in those networks. This requires opening up, becoming receptive and adaptive to other sectors and actors in society.

Dealing with barriers in society implies seeking cooperation, searching for well-equipped coalitions that have the necessary resources in place. If actors act in a purposeful manner while linking across subjective demarcation lines in the social world we label this as boundary spanning. Boundary spanning of water managers encountering complex water challenges is therefore defined by us as: *adaptive governance of activities by linking their sector, scales and timeframes to other previously independent sectors, scales and timeframes.*

In this context the message of this book is that a careful reconsideration of strategies to achieve water ambitions, together with a more in-depth knowledge of the theories and practices of boundary spanning, could thus make solutions for contemporary water problems become closer to fruition. The content of this book incorporates conceptual, theoretical and practical foci that deal with complexity and conflict by boundary spanning in adaptive water management. The conceptual and theoretical frameworks dominate the majority of Chapters 1–4. In Chapters 3–10 empirical cases of boundary spanning issues are presented and analyzed with the help of these frameworks. Guidance for boundary spanning in practice is given, among others, in Chapters 10 and 11. In several chapters storylines of important contemporary water management themes are included. These contemporary water management themes are flooding and flood policy (Chapters 3, 5 and 6), water depletion (Chapters 4 and 8), water (restoration) and nature (Chapters 6, 8 and 9), acceptance and use of scientific models and information (Chapter 8) and international cooperation on water basins (Chapter 10).

Chapter 1 starts with a historical perspective on the role of water management in society, then describes three memorable water management innovations that occurred during the last decades. In the context of adaptive water management the concepts, forms and applications of dealing with boundaries are described: often strategies for spanning boundaries, but sometimes also emphasizing boundaries or even creating boundaries.

In Chapter 2 the concept of boundary judgements and its sector, scale and time dimensions are introduced. An explanatory framework is presented for analyzing their role in social interaction processes within a layered context and to illustrate the points of intervention to apply change strategies.

Chapter 3 elaborates boundary spanning in flood policies. It deepens the understanding of the roles of boundary spanners across sectors, scales and time in a longitudinal perspective. The analysis is related to the conceptual framework presented in Chapter 1.

Chapter 4 deepens the conceptual and theoretical understanding of the time perspective within the explanatory framework, with an example of resource depletion by irrigation. It describes the impact of the time perspective on the likelihood of conflict, rivalries, problem recognition and adaptive action taken. It ends by indicating the implication for actors that want to be boundary spanners. The elaboration is related to the theoretical perspective presented in Chapter 2.

Chapter 5 uses the theoretical framework introduced in Chapter 2 to analyze a case in which an inhabited area was prepared for use as water buffering storage in case of threatening river water levels. The multi-functionality of land use that was partially realized after a complicated process shows many of the boundary issues that have to be dealt with in contemporary water management. It ends with reflections on managing complexity with boundary spanning.

Chapter 6 is another case study using the same format as Chapter 5. In this case of building a new river to reconnect a natural creek system to the tributary river basin it once belonged to, the multi-functionality aimed for is even more unavoidable and challenging.

Chapter 7 concentrates on the implications of a certain institutional setting of multi-sector cooperation for boundary spanning. Two processes of wetland restoration are analyzed with the help of one of the theoretical tools described in Chapter 2. The degree to which an institutional setting is helpful for boundary spanning is shown to be dependent on the details of the context.

Chapter 8 focuses upon spanning the boundary between natural science-based knowledge and its use in decision-making processes. The position of scientific models is discussed, a case analyzed and lessons presented with regard to exchange of natural science knowledge and policy processes.

In Chapter 9 two approaches towards project implementation are discussed: serial and parallel implementation. Often there is no single solution in the sense that one approach is always better than the other. What is offered is guidance on when to apply which approach.

In Chapter 10 boundary spanning across national borders of sovereign countries is analyzed and four guidance schemes for boundary spanning in practice are presented. The process conditions and circumstances that need attention are addressed.

Chapter 11 finally presents our conclusions from both the scientific perspective and from the perspective of boundary spanning in practice.

Acknowledgements

Most of the theoretical and empirical chapters in this volume are based on studies that received support from various research programmes. A very important contributor is the Dutch national research programme 'Living with water'. Three projects in this programme are represented in this volume. The focus of the volume itself is very much related to one of them: administrative coupling, in which creating linkages across sector boundaries is central. Acknowledging the role of boundary judgements and the way they influence policy innovations is also at the core of the EU FP6 project 'Integrative systems and the boundary problem' that has supported part of this work. We also thank the Institute for Governance Studies, a social science-based interfaculty research centre of the University of Twente, for the opportunity offered to span several of our research projects and to integrate the results into this book. We thank water managers from, among others, the water boards Regge and Dinkel and Velt and Vecht for the opportunities to cooperate on water management and learn from their experiences as practitioners. Finally, we thank Ada Krooshoop for her editing and layout efforts on the text.

Hans Bressers and Kris Lulofs, Enschede, 30 April 2009

1. Innovations in water management requiring boundary spanning: roots and concepts

Kris Lulofs and Hans Bressers

1.1 INTRODUCTION

This chapter starts with a historical outline of the role of water and water managers in society. Three eras of water management will be described that present the largest common dominators in the landscape of water management's history. In the preamble to the third era of water management new and renewed issues call for new approaches. During the last decades some innovative strategies were developed which will be outlined. Taken together these steps describe the context in which the conceptual foci of this book are explicated and embedded.

The chapter structure is as follows: the historical landscape of the role of water management in society, as briefly touched upon in the Preface, is elaborated in Section 1.2. In Section 1.3 the innovative approaches in water management as they developed during the last decades will be outlined (in Section 1.3.1). The underlying contrasting principles of parsimony and redundancy are discussed in Section 1.3.2. This leads to a role and task model for craftsmanship of twenty-first century water managers. In this context, concepts such as dealing with boundaries, dimensions of boundaries and boundary spanning strategies are introduced and explained in Section 1.4. Section 1.5 summarizes the chapter.

1.2 THREE WATER MANAGEMENT ERAS

Starting early in history quantitative water management had played an essential role in societies. Water was often the single most important factor for communities to grow and prosper. Alongside seas, rivers and other water bodies people settled and started economic and social activities. Growth and welfare of these settlements depended on the availability of water. Several functions of water were exploited, for instance, irrigation for agricultural purposes, for shipping and transport in order to facilitate trade and for creating employment. Water as a defence strategy covered everything from the conscious flooding of polders to chase off intruders to the castle-moats all over Europe. In times of external threats water thus offered short-term possibilities to manage non-water-related crises. This being said, phenomena such as unanticipated meandering of rivers, floods and occurring droughts played destructive roles. The economic and social activities alongside the sea, rivers and water courses were frequently threatened by the very thing that made them come alive: water. In larger communities water pollution from a sanitary nature led to infectious diseases that sometimes almost disrupted, if not destroyed, local societies.

Given these water-related opportunities and crises, efforts in the field of institutionalized water management started early. For instance, more than 800 years ago the first Dutch local water boards were established. They still exist as some of the oldest public institutions although they changed and merged over time. In the early days water boards were more or less private initiatives of citizens, businessmen and farmers who all had a stake in the water system. Sometimes governments were also attached to the water boards. These early institutions can often be considered as hybrid public–private organizations.

Developing societies and growing cities and learning by doing led to continuous innovation in water management. Especially between 1800 and 1900 water managers became more capable, among others, with regard to the drainage of bogs and polders, the control of groundwater levels, and between 1900 and 1950 in the field of establishing drinking water facilities and sewage systems (Kuks, 2004). Of course regional differences can be observed within European countries in accordance with local characteristics and circumstances. In some countries the emphasis was, for instance, on keeping the water out and in others on getting water in by irrigation (Juuti and Katko, 2005).

Meanwhile European societies developed, populations grew and society industrialized further in the twentieth century. Having become more skilled and capable, water managers gradually developed their sector into a routine and engineering-based approach. Risks of flooding were more and more contained, water courses navigable, the supply of drinking water secured, irrigation to a large extent under control and even the successful containment of large-scale water-related infectious diseases was within sight. Water managers more and more became a sort of smooth operating footman of society. Almost unnoticeable and at reasonable costs issues were now dealt with in most cases. Also uninterrupted supply of water for water-dependent purposes such as agriculture and industry became more or less obvious in the twentieth century (Van Leussen and Lulofs, 2009).

When, in the 1960s and early 1970s, water quality deteriorated due to extreme economic growth, water quality management emerged as a sub-sector within water management. Large-scale systems of sewage treatment plants were built. In a couple of decades the problem of organic water pollution was under control (Bressers and Lulofs, 2004). Also comprehensive water quality and quantity policies were introduced; subsequently this also occurred in the field of fighting water depletion (Kuks, 2004). Water managers thus delivered many success stories in the twentieth century and facilitated economic growth. However, on their journey to glory, water managers and water management lost their significant and central position. This prominent position was gradually replaced by a bleached subordinate image and position as a service sector. Water management evolved into one of the footmen of society. And from footmen a lot is asked and little is expected to be given in return.

Then, in the late twentieth century the first signals emerged from all over Europe that water managers might not be in control to the extent previously thought. The issue of water pollution re-entered the agenda. Emissions from both point sources and diffuse sources of heavy metals and toxic substances, including chemicals, pesticides and herbicides, were now perceived as particularly harmful for the ecosystems. Increasing understanding led to more ambitious goals and standards.

Water managers responded Pavlovian style to these new ecological challenges. Applying easy one-dimensional and first order technological solutions mirrored the approach to water quality issues in the 1970s and 1980s. Such first order measures included the further physical separation of water courses and agricultural activities; for instance, by increasing artificial works or issuing more user-oriented regulation aimed at reducing the rinse off of pollutants from the banks into the water courses. Also measures to separate urban and rural water resources or water systems were frequently observed.

Although such measures on a case by case base might be rational, seen from a systems perspective this is far from the case. A more sustainable situation would benefit ecologically from the restoration of water courses into meandering ecological sound water, both from a chemical and a biological perspective. This solution also increases the resilience of the water system. Other signs of the times that announced a crisis in water management included, among others, a series of international and inter-regional incidents that emphasized that upstream countries or regions did not necessarily take into consideration the interests of downstream countries or regions. This kind of water conflict is not restricted to the Middle East or Africa but is also easily traceable in Europe (Verwijmeren and Wiering, 2007).

The European Commission (EC) was also against the large-scale application of first order solutions and against the ignorance about the water basin as the logical unit of water management. The European Union (EU) interpreted the signals referred to as a lack of rationality in water management. The first European Water Framework Directive was developed that considerably raised the ambitions in the field of ecological quality of water courses and water quality, both chemical and biological (2000/60/EC). In this regulation the EC adopted the lesson that efforts to manage ecosystems should be followed by viewing the ecosystems as a whole, and stressing the relevant geographical scales (Lee, 1993, p. 47).

A second European Directive followed on the assessment and management of flooding risks (2007/60/EC). Both directives require policy and plans to be based on water basins, and therefore require cooperation and coordination between regions. Cooperation between countries in the case of border crossing water basins is required. In both directives measures are prescribed to involve public and organized interests more strongly. The programmed measures aim to optimize river basins in the perspective of ecosystems and relevant scales and involved interests. Although such an overview considerably oversimplifies history, Table 1.1 summarizes the three eras of water management and their characteristics. This overview completes the historical perspective and we now position ourselves in the transition period between the second and third era.

With the exception of the rare untouched water basins, water managers hardly encounter a *tabula rasa* when they plan water programmes and water projects. Society changed drastically during the second era as industrialization, economic development and social development reduced space and interwove sector interests. At the same time the awareness of problem pressure has strongly risen. Knowledge about climate change, for instance, forces water managers to prepare for more frequent severe periods of droughts interspersed by periods of heavy precipitation. This touches upon the capacity to retain water locally as well as upon the discharge capacity. In low lying deltas the prospects are even more alarming because rising sea levels imply decreasing downstream discharge capacities at the mouth of water courses. Also large-scale scarcity of drinking water and irrigation water is expected to emerge.

The resources for water management have not increased to the same extent as the increased problem pressure and water challenges to be addressed. Meeting the challenges is demanding substantial interference in society and claims on society's resources. And that immediately implies requiring other actors' resources, bearing in mind that problem-solving capacity is now dispersed over many actors that hold ownership rights, user rights and management rights in society. Especially management rights are dispersed over policy sectors, governmental levels and actors. Many actors can allocate resources such as land, finances, technology, personnel, procedures, authority and legitimacy to water ambitions and water projects or refuse to do so. Water managers have to handle this new reality and built 'social capital' in order to be able to move forward. And they did realize this during the past decades, taking into consideration innovative water management approaches.

1.3 INNOVATIONS IN WATER MANAGEMENT

During the short period of overlap at the end of the second and the start of the third era of water management (Table 1.1), the signs of the time did not

Table 1.1 Three eras of water management characterized

<1900	**1900–2000**	**>2000**
Characteristics of (European) societies		
Developed next to seas, lakes, rivers and (later dug) channels. Depending on water but also threatened by water	Developed into a complex and vulnerable system, water taken for granted, capable dikes, drainage systems, water treatment etc.	(Over)developed into climate change, will take 100 years or more to reverse, meanwhile water-related threats that are interwoven with societal processes
Dominance in relation to water and societies' economic and social processes		
Water	Society	Interdependency
Ordering and facilitating principles in society		
Water 'planning' important ordering principle	Physical planning ordering, water planning facilitating	Water and physical planning, ordering and facilitating.
Typical water problems		
Floods, droughts, infectious diseases	Groundwater level, groundwater and surface water quality	Floods, droughts, water quality, ecological quality of waters
Characterization of water problems		
Unstable, untamed problems	Stable, tamed problems	Manageable problems
Role of water manager		
High profile but not very capable	Low profile but meanwhile very capable technically	High profile, very capable technically, complexity limits realization

stay unnoticed. In the dawn of the second era, starting around 1980, some new approaches developed within water management that are of relevance for the period thereafter. Three successive recent approaches will be introduced briefly in Section 1.3.1, followed by an assessment of the core model assumptions in Section 1.3.2.

1.3.1 Three Innovative Approaches

The three approaches are Integrated Water Management (IWM), Integrated Water Resource Management (IWRM) and Adaptive Water Management (AWM).

Integrated Water Management (IWM)

A few decades ago the concept of IWM was introduced and partially implemented. What in practice happened was that water managers started to link and coordinate between previously hardly connected fragmented water management tasks. These sub-sectors include, for instance, the management of groundwater, surface water, storm water, wastewater and drinking water. Substantial efforts were made on coordination between water managers in charge of the sewage system and those in charge of water treatment infrastructure to realize the best conditions.

The innovation was, as the examples illustrate, primarily an effort to make a bureaucracy work more effectively and efficiently; an effort towards a more optimal achievement of pre-established water policy goals and preferable actions that contribute to water goals as defined in more than one sub-sector of water management. This is sometimes also referred to as internal integration.

Integrated Water Resource Management (IWRM)

Water managers then realized that dependencies on other sectors of society and opportunities emerging in those sectors might also be of importance; either because such sector activities and policies might contribute to the existence of water problems, or because these sectors might contribute to their solution. This implies opening up to the idea of cooperating not only with water managers in other water sub-sectors but also with actors in other sectors in society. It is sometimes referred to as the external integration of water management. The external integration can cover linkages to and cooperation with fields such as agriculture, tourism, nature, economy, housing and transport. The most eye-catching difference between IWM and IWRM is restricted to the difference as depicted by the terms internal integration and external integration. In software language IWRM is often referred to as a 2.0 version of IWM.

The essence of IWRM is taking into consideration potential causes for water problems and potential solutions for water problems that are embedded in other policy sectors and their sub-sectors. The surface water quality, for instance, depends not only on installed public water treatment technology but also on the behaviour of businesses and households that emit into the sewage system and the behaviour of actors that produce diffuse sources of pollution, such as rinse off from agricultural land. The latter is determined by the nature and intensity of farming and the use of fertilizers, herbicides and pesticides.

Although for some observers IWM and IWRM might already reflect old school approaches, such observations do not appreciate the potential of these innovations to their full extent. IWM calls for restriction to the core tasks while IWRM requires opening up to other sectors and thus complexity. Raising the issue of how to deal with that complexity led to new ideas. Often the water systems or water resources are nowadays conceptually distinguished from the water chain. This is done in order to simplify and group the huge complexity that water managers have to address when they want to apply IWRM to the analysis of their water problems and possible solutions. The water system consists of groundwater and surface water and their hydrological, hydro-morphological and biological and chemical interrelations including man-made interferences. The water chain consists of withdrawals of water from the water system, for instance, for domestic, agricultural and industrial use, the production of domestic, agricultural and industrial waste water, the collection and treatment of waste water, and the disposal of (waste) water effluents into the water system. These concepts and innovations link IWM and IWRM and try to integrate respective strengths and inspire practitioners. Still a third approach developed over time.

Adaptive Water Management (AWM)

Gradually water managers realized that in the complex world of IWRM purely rational goal-oriented behaviour is difficult, if not impossible. Dispersed tasks, ambitions and resources imply that coordination and cooperation with other policy domains is complex and not without difficulties. Processes and dynamics of other policy domains might, for instance, be out of phase, problem definitions of actors might differ and also prove hard to influence. Water managers thus found out that they are not in control and could only influence others to a limited extent.

The flourishing perspective of AWM implies that water ambitions should be formulated and achieved in interaction with long-term and short-term opportunities that emerge from dynamics within the water sector and other sectors in society. So the whole perspective of more or less rational water managers that have at their disposal perfect information and choose the best rational solution is watered down. That comes close to a perspective of water managers that struggle for satisfying outcomes in the context of imperfect information and actor-related dynamics. From an engineering domain perspective, water managers realized more and more that they were working in a policy and politics domain. The science of mud particles had to be partially replaced by the science of muddling through (Lindblom, 1959). AWM assumes that revealed preferences do not necessarily cover actual preferences of actors. It is also assumed that preferences and priorities of actors are subject to change at any time.

An emphasis on AWM implies a greater emphasis on learning through experimentation on tasks and cooperation than on more conventional forms of water management. It therefore implies a smaller emphasis on short-term fixed water goals and efforts for achieving those short-term goals, effectively and cost-effectively. Thinking just in terms of short-term effectiveness and cost-effectiveness is considered to be the enemy of long-term, potentially large improvements that come with broad temporal and geographical scale perspectives. Kingdon describes these in terms of policy windows that emerge due to temporary links between social systems' perceived problems, perceived solutions and emerging political support (Kingdon, 1984). AWM thus might be described as skilfully using such opportunities for achieving more or less outlined water ambitions. March and Olsen (1976) had already enlightened the very essence of this by claiming that the complexity and inability to define precisely and recognize clearly the relations between problems, policy and outcomes are caused by actors that participate in decision making with diverging preference systems, especially while actors change their preferences during the process. Therefore even assuming recognizable and comprehensible rationality might often be proven wrong.

Westley (2002) is one of the few authors who did address the work of individual water managers in this paradigm. She suggests that reflective ecosystem management implies juggling four balls that need to be managed, the political ball (managing up), the bureaucratic ball (managing in), the community ball (managing out) and the scientific ball (managing through). The manager needs to interact with others, build up social capital and use it wisely. Wise use of social capital implies looking at the cycles that occur in each of these domains and seeks to use the chances that might occur. 'The experience of managing in complex adaptive systems is more similar to catching waves or looking for emergent corridors for action than pulling strings or working levers' (Westley, 2002, p. 354).

Adaptive management implies a shift in thinking about appropriate time horizons and strategies for the resource manager:

> The overall goal of adaptive management is not to maintain an optimal condition of the resource but to develop an optimal management capacity. This is accomplished by maintaining ecological resilience that allows the system to react to inevitable stresses, and generating flexibility in institutions and stakeholders that allows managers to react when conditions change. The result is that, rather than managing for a single, optimal state, we manage within a range of acceptable outcomes while avoiding catastrophes and irreversible negative outcomes. (Johnson, 1999, p. 1)

1.3.2 Embracing Both Parsimony and Redundancy

While IWM and IWRM largely stick to the idea of rationality, AWM stresses unpredictability, observes redundancy and preaches flexibility. The three models cover a spectrum that, at one extreme, emphasizes water management as the art of solving one-dimensional problems by perfect solutions, striving for clarity and parsimony, and, at the other extreme, the art of juggling multiple actors, multiple preferences, multiple problem perceptions and multiple options in a societal system that is characterized by uncertainty and redundancy. Adaptive managers accept the inevitable goal-seeking nature of policy processes in which intra-policy and inter-policy tuning and coordination is required or wished for to solve 'wicked' problems, implying that others' perceptions of water problems are accepted and active efforts are made in incorporating them into water management.

There are some fundamental diacritical assumptions with regard to the policy process that come with the rivalry assumptions. If we take the adaptive management approach and compare this with the more traditional IWM and IWRM models, the landscape of rival assumptions is as follows: the policy process is not believed to manifest itself as a series of consecutive phases such as preparation, decision, implementation and evaluation interlinked by feedback loops. The dominant pattern can be best characterized by unpredictable and dynamic rounds of decisions and the phases are mixed and interlinked in any order, as Chapter 9 by Evers in this volume especially illustrates. Decisions are not considered to be the outcome of a process of selecting among perceived and globally evaluated options in order to reduce the problem. Decisions now are perceived as the outcome of a process of selecting alternatives that are supported and can be linked to an ostensible problem. The goals and belief systems of actors are no longer believed to be clear and one-dimensional but are considered to be conflicting, sometimes redundant and are changing any moment. Power, knowledge and information are no longer considered as centralized. These now are considered to be dispersed over actors, to be of an ambiguous nature and used strategically by actors to serve their own interests (Klijn, 2006).

Replacing the short-term indicators of success by other goals such as reflexivity, redundancy, variability and memory thus might open up new playing fields with new chances (Gunderson and Holling, 2002, p. 61). Reflexivity implies a continuous process of reconsideration of frames and goals. Redundancy implies the maintenance of relations (social capital) that are not immediately useful but could serve as a backup or silent reserve for the future. Variability refers to the idea of trying out different approaches to a certain problem so that not all stakes are invested in one strategy (Berkes and Folke, 2002).

A strategy of redundancy is not in itself always better than a strategy of parsimony. The straightforward discussion about which framework to embrace as the best is not productive. As often when the empirical domain or claim is not yet well described in operational terms, the magic words are: it depends. The one size fits all approach might not be beneficial.

Each approach and model has its benefits and disadvantages. For instance, if well-known routine tasks are at stake and there is no debate on beliefs and goals and the way to do it is known, for instance monitoring surface water quality in small streams, why should the water manager then not consider themself as a rational single actor? Why make things more complicated than necessary? However, as described above, many of the recent water challenges are rather complex and the necessary dispersed resources in terms of management rights, ownership rights and user rights have to be assembled and attached to the challenges. This requires opening up in order to plan and realize a more comprehensive innovation in the system of water governance. This is another mode of rationality to which the water manager can shift whenever they learn and acknowledge its dependency on others and experience the lack of certainty and limited predictability.

The craftsmanship of twenty-first century water managers is likely to benefit from a role and task model that:

- uses one-dimensional approaches for simple routine tasks;
- uses strategies to integrate multiple dimensions for complex tasks in order to manage dependency;
- sometimes uses for this integration strategies based on a perspective of parsimony (less often than before);
- sometimes uses for this integration strategies based on a perspective of adaptive management (more often than before), implying boundary spanning between the domains as experienced by the various actors involved;
- acknowledges that true craftsmanship will often be in using both perspectives according to the situation in a flexible complementary approach.

1.4 BOUNDARY SPANNING

Boundary spanning of water managers is defined in this book as adaptive governance activities of water managers that encounter complex water challenges by linking their sector, scales and timeframes to previously independent other sectors, scales and timeframes.

We see boundaries here as inter-subjective constructed demarcations between different social worlds. Boundary spanning implies, therefore, influencing those demarcations, and efforts to create converging domain interpretations among several actors involved or potentially involved in a certain water management action. Not necessarily every established linkage between domains changes the relevant domains. The perceptions of what is ours, theirs and shared will most likely change only slowly. It is not unlikely that the number, stability and intensity of the spans is influential. Of course the strategies used and the characteristics of the occasion might also be of influence. Now a more detailed conceptual perspective of sectors, scales and the time perspective will be introduced.

1.4.1 Domain Dimensions

Water managers and others are thought of as acting from a specific domain that is determined by the perceptions of the boundaries of that domain. There are several dimensions in which such domain interpretations can differ. Taken together, these can be used to describe the domains as they are seen by those involved in water management.

The first dimension is relatively basic. This is the dimension of the policy sectors and the inter-subjective demarcations between sectors and sub-sectors. These are often the result of history and especially the institutional and cultural sediment of the past, but challenged by modern water projects. Boundary spanning over the sector dimension of the water managers' domain is preached by the innovations of IWM and IWRM. If spanning succeeds, relations between sectors will be created by linking aspects of sectors, such as actors, resources and policies. The word span refers to space, broadness and periods, duration, time and length, the word linkage refers to a social connection, alliance and liaisons (in practice they will be used as synonyms). Subcategories of actors can be governors as political actors, civil servants and organizations that represent institutional interests. Subcategories of resources are authority, knowledge and budgets. Subcategories of policies can be the problem definitions, the solution strategies and the process management. In Table 1.2 the dimensions and examples of various aspects connected to these dimensions are summarized.

Table 1.2 The three dimensions of a water manager's domain, including some aspects and sub-aspects

Dimensions	Aspects	Sub-aspects
Sector dimension	Actors	Organizations
		Staff
	Resources	Authority
		Knowledge
		Budgets
	Policies	Problem definitions
		Solution strategies
		Process management
Scale dimension	Geographical (water basin) scales	
	Administrative levels	Global
		Supranational
		National
		Regional
		Local
Temporal dimension	Time	Timing
		Time horizon
	Change	Speed
		Time pressure

With regard to the second scale dimension both administrative levels and geographical scales are relevant. The more or less arbitrary subcategories are global, supranational, national, regional and local. With regard to administrative levels we assume that a water manager is active at a certain administrative level and at a certain geographical scale, for example, a tributary river basin.

There is a third dimension distinguished, that of temporal scales. This longitudinal perspective, including time and change aspects, is of crucial importance. Previously in this chapter we roughly outlined some eras of water management and some innovative approaches that occurred during the last decades. For both storylines the depicted dynamics did not emerge from out of the blue. Changes are realized by change agents that perhaps by trial and error, however seen in retrospective perspective accurately and vigorously, coupled perceived problems and perceived solutions and found support for that. Often this kind of entrepreneurship will be based on opening up to longer time horizons and purposeful connecting to forces that strive for mid-term or long-term change. Not all actors will attach the same relevance to different time horizons. Creating linkages therefore often implies achieving a common time horizon for the water management issues (see Chapter 4 in this volume).

The threesome of sectors, scales and time represent the more long-term learning and change perspective of AWM. The observation has to be that this stands next to the more short-term oriented perspective of just spanning sector boundaries and perhaps scale boundaries that was highlighted by the IWRM perspective. The vast majority of day to day boundary spanning is devoted to relatively short-term water projects (3–10 years) and not to long-term water challenges. This is reflected in several empirical chapters of this book. Only after radical change has occurred, can the pattern be reconstructed on how day to day boundary spanning and linkages in the end add up and lead to more revolutionary innovations. Still, from the analytical perspective, it is clear that linkages always include some elements of the time perspective. The timing of procedural steps, time pressures resulting from subsidy rules, the speed of change in water management paradigms and so on are time aspects that have to be accommodated in many water projects. Again, the true craftsmanship of spanning the three domain dimensions will be in a flexible and complementary approach. In Chapter 2 a theoretical framework will be introduced on how perceptions of domain dimensions and dynamics in underlying boundary judgements and their impacts can be analyzed and explained.

1.4.2 Boundary Spanning Strategies

In its most abstract meaning, strategy, in this context, implies finding new ways and building bridges in order to resolve conflicts between well-organized interests and competing authorities (Scholz and Stiftel, 2005, p. 5). Within the conceptual framework it is clear that linking can be done horizontally over sectors and their aspects, vertically over scales and their aspects and diagonally, linking the domains in terms of both sector and scale. Furthermore all combinations with regard to the time dimension are thinkable.

As referred to above, in most cases the short-term strategy will be to span to another policy sector and link to resources or policies or both via actors at a certain geographical scale and at a certain administrative level. Therefore this section on strategies and linkages will be presented from this perspective. The linkage can be made for long-term intensive cooperation or be more fluid. This relates to the difference between building social capital and realizing projects pragmatically. In terms of strategies, building social capital will be created by redundant strategies of interaction that do not only focus on a concrete issue, project or crisis but are meant to exchange information, issues, knowledge and visions in order to build common grounds of understanding and trust and prepare for future, more purposeful cooperation. These kinds of strategies include, for instance, frequent meetings between governors or civil servants from water management organizations with local organizations such as municipalities. They might even include some joint development of agendas and programmes. The purposeful, short-term and mid-term boundary spanning efforts often have the character of fishing for needed land, expertise, finances and management rights and thus political support. There is a coarse distinction between direct and indirect strategies. Direct strategies aim for influencing actors that can offer what is needed themselves. Indirect strategies imply activating intermediaries that can influence the actor that decides what is needed; indirect strategies can also be used to influence intermediaries in networks that might try to frustrate the process.

What to use when?

For relative parsimonious boundary issues water managers can use directive, facilitative and advocacy strategies separately or combined (Bardach, 1998; Williams, 2002). At first sight the use of legal power bases do not make a lot of sense in boundary spanning. However various add-on coordination instruments to sector laws and regulations are created as the institutional sediment of previous boundary spanning. For instance, in spatial planning procedures the obligatory involvement of water managers in several forms is observed, reaching from expert-advisor up to an approval procedure (Lulofs and Coenen, 2007). Directive strategies are thus sometimes used for accommodating boundary spanning, however more likely they are used for attempts to emphasize boundaries. Emphasizing boundaries is done by actors that do not acknowledge the added value of spanning. Boundaries are sometimes interpreted as perimeters that protect a system from disturbances due to outside disruptions, and frontiers to keep resources critical for survival in (Yan and Louis, 1999). Since boundary spanning can be undertaken by actors that are active in other sectors, such defensive strategies should also interest water managers. In case of a power battle in an administrative system, ultimately it counts most who has the authority to force others to engage in cross-boundary cooperation or to refuse to do so.

Facilitative strategies are well known. They range from offering subsidies, contributions and grants; offering expertise, analysis, research and advice; indicative studies; offering organizational facilities such as exchange of staff; initiating study groups; advisory panels; participation facilities for interest organizations and individuals; process coordination and guidance and so on. Also the smoothing of processes by external project leadership and project management, exchange procedures, and buy and sell facilities sometimes do make a difference.

Advocacy strategies are strategies that often aim at peoples' and organizations' beliefs and views. However advocacy strategies can also play a role on a very pragmatic level. For instance, this is the case when politicians are used to influence other politicians across a boundary in order to build a link.

Linkages will differ accordingly with the setting up of strategies and their use when it comes to intensity and stability. This also relates to the fundamental question: what brings actors together in boundary crossing cooperation? When cross-boundary cooperation is based on shared ideas and beliefs among actors, then this will probably result in relatively stable linkages comparable to those that bind actors in policy communities. While strictly resources-driven cooperation can also take place in resource dependency networks that are relatively unstable (Lulofs and Hoppe, 2006), this might suggest that pragmatic boundary activities might be undertaken best in the context of established long-term relationships that create social capital. In Chapter 2 boundary spanning will be discussed further as attempts to integrate boundary judgements rather than just creating linkages while domain perceptions of actors remain unaltered.

Sometimes multiple strategies are used; for instance, when a boundary has to be emphasized while an unwelcome actor tries to link across a domain boundary by applying a directive strategy. Such an action can and often is countered by an advocacy strategy towards a third party government, most likely at a higher geographical scale or administrative level, to make use of the veto power they may possess.

Given the distinguished dimensions of domains, the multiple motives and strategies, many different situations might occur with regard to linkages. Taken together it does not come as a surprise that linkages can differ with regard to the number of characteristics that might change over time under the influence of mentioned factors (Whetten, 1982). In Table 1.3 an overview of relevant characteristics of single spans established is given.

1.5 SUMMARY

This chapter started with a concise historical outline of the role of water management in society. It was concluded that recently new challenges have emerged that cannot be dealt with by traditional approaches. Innovative approaches in water management have developed during the last decades. In Section 1.3 three of these innovations were dealt with in brief. This was followed by an analysis that concluded that the underlying assumptions of parsimony (try to be as simple as possible) and redundancy (try not to leave out any relevant issue) do make these models really different. A

Table 1.3 Characteristics of linkages

Characteristic	
Redundancy	Extent to which the purpose of the action is specific or generic, such as investing in social capital
Reciprocity	Extent to which the linkages are symmetrical
Multiplicity	Number of different types of linkages
Stability	Extent to which the linkages stay the same over time or not
Intensity	Extent of resources committed to exchange
Standardization	Fixedness of units/terms of exchange
Formalization	Extent to which exchange is formally organized

Source: Based on Whetten (1982).

central observation was that assumptions and resulting models all make sense in certain contexts. This led at the end of Section 1.3 to a role and task model for craftsmanship of twenty-first century water managers. Among others, it was concluded that since contexts vary, true craftsmanship will often be in using both perspectives according to the situations in a flexible complementary approach.

Boundary spanning by water managers is defined in Section 1.4 as adaptive governance activities of water managers by linking their sector, scales and timeframes to previously independent other sectors, scales and timeframes. Boundaries are perceived as inter-subjective constructed demarcations between different social worlds. Boundary spanning refers to passing dividing lines between domains. Domains are defined by the socially constructed dimensions, sectors, scales and time perspectives. Important subcategories or aspects of sectors are actors, resources and policies; important subcategories of scales are geographical and administrative scales; and important subcategories of time perspectives are timing and time horizon. Finally, redundant strategies for building social capital and direct and indirect strategies aiming for concrete linking of results were introduced. Directing, facilitating and advocating strategies were discussed as to their relative pros and cons. Lastly, some characteristics of linkages were mentioned.

2. Analysis of boundary judgements in complex interaction processes

Hans Bressers and Kris Lulofs

2.1 INTRODUCTION

In this chapter a model for the analysis of boundaries in actor interaction processes is unfolded. This model tries to be as parsimonious as possible, while also trying not to shut out relevant factors too easily (cf. Quade, 1980). Therefore we come up with a middle ground between reductionist and deductive theories of reality, such as those supported by linear quantitative modelling, and more interpretative and social constructivist studies. Both extremes have their virtues and limitations. There is no one-size-fits-all in social science. The structure of this chapter reflects this standing in two ways.

In Section 2.2 we describe how boundary judgements as part of actors' cognitive system play an essential role in complex interaction processes between persons, groups and organizations, such as those in water management. The adaptiveness of boundary judgements can also be labelled as the receptivity of the actors. In Section 2.3 we broaden the analysis to all basic actors' characteristics and all contextual factors that through them may also influence interaction processes, and in turn may influence the actors' boundary judgements and receptivity. In Section 2.4 we elaborate somewhat further on the dimensions of boundary judgements and how these might change over time. Finally, in Section 2.5 we present a summary and a synthesis in the form of a set of questions for case analysis of boundary judgements in complex interaction processes.

2.2 BOUNDARY JUDGEMENTS WITHIN THE COGNITIVE SYSTEM

Adaptive water management suggests water managers interact and interlink with others, their understandings of reality, ambitions and resources crossing boundaries. We see, as explained in Chapter 1, boundaries as inter-subjective constructed demarcations between different social worlds. Cognitive interpretations of these domain boundaries can differ a great deal. The question is: what are we talking about? What belongs to, for instance, integral water management and what not? This is a matter of boundary judgements, definitions of systems and problems, which underpin the conceptual models with which the situation is understood. Boundary judgements are socially constructed definitions of the domain of policy innovations in terms of relevant scales, sectors and temporal dimensions (cf. Bressers, 2007). The concept of boundary judgements stems from systems theory. While all of reality can be considered a system, when we think and speak about a certain subject we aim at parts of reality, subsystems. But where does the subsystem end? Explicitly or implicitly we have ideas about what belongs to it and what not, or is at least less relevant. Ulrich (1996, 2000) developed boundary critique as a method to disclose this inevitable partiality (see also Bausch, 2001, p. 126).

2.2.1 Cognitive System

An essential assumption of our analytical framework is that we assume that people interpret their observations of reality and categorize them as belonging to the set of issues they deal with within their sector or alternatively as belonging to the outside world. Furthermore it is assumed that more general boundary judgements play a crucial role in this process, as part of people's cognitive filters. Both aspects relate strongly to the actors' cognitive structure and especially to the frames of reference in use within the cognitive system. The structure and functioning of the cognitive system are studied extensively by cognitive psychologists. More precisely, cognitive psychology studies how human beings organize and structure the process of observation of facts, attribution of significance to observations and – if found relevant – the process of throughput into their readiness to act. This structuring is done on the basis of, among others, existing systems knowledge, memory, logical thinking and intuition. Such methods and filters are often referred to as the actors' frames of references. We assume that boundary judgements represent a fraction of the frames of reference in the cognitive system. This contains mental frames that facilitate the interpretation of what is within and what is outside their policy sector or sub-domain.

2.2.2 Frames of Reference

The supply of information is enormous. The overload of stimuli has to be reduced to manageable proportions, often for a large part without a deliberate choice to do so. Filtering this overload is necessary in order to review and attribute significance to observations. The same holds for the selection of information that impacts on the readiness to act. Cognitions present the world to the actors as a whole of opportunities and threats. Boundary judgements play a role in both steps. They are a part of the frames of reference and, as such, help in filtering out what observations of social phenomena are relevant and what are not. For groups or organizations we assume that alongside to individual boundary definitions collective boundary definitions are also constructed on the basis of interaction between persons in the group and their boundary definitions. In the case of organizations all kinds of informal rules will apply on how this process of pooled boundary judgements is organized. In every organization members have to at least adapt to its structure and culture, including boundary judgements, as part of the socialization process.

2.2.3 Convergence of Boundary Judgements

Adaptive water management can be considered an innovative concept, one that is not yet settled in its meaning and scope for many people. To enable such an innovative concept to be integrated in coherent governance and ultimately to be fully used or complied with, the boundary judgements of the actors involved should be both sufficiently similar and sufficiently flexible and open. There is an optimum here. Too much consensus on the boundaries of the traditional domain of water management might shut out new challenges, such as those put forward by adaptive management that involve attention for new subjects, for example, the protection of landscape and so on. Too much flexibility and openness could lead to so much variability and flux that it frustrates joint action and in this way also decreases the capacity to fully respond to the (policy) innovation (Winder, 2007).

Given an issue or policy problem, from the outset already existing rather than convergent boundary judgements between actors from two different policy sectors will enhance the likelihood that further boundary spanning activities of one towards the other will produce successful cooperation. However a second variable will play a role and specifies our expectations about what might happen. Next, but in interaction with boundary judgements, the receptivity of actors – people, groups or organizations – influences the expected reaction.

2.2.4 Receptivity

The receptivity of an actor is not only dependent on the degree of exposure to new knowledge, but also more specifically on the way the actor can

Table 2.1 Expected boundary activities and expected scores on created linkages

Boundary judgements	Receptivity of actors	Expected boundary activities by (some) actors	Expected degree of created linkages
Convergent	High	Boundary spanning	High
	Low	Reinforcing boundaries	Opportunistic/ coincidental
Divergent	High	Boundary spanning	Moderate
	Low	Bringing up new boundaries	Low

associate and exploit new knowledge around existing knowledge, activities and objectives. This requires that the actor lets the outside come in, opening and regrouping understandings in order to include reckoning with new knowledge (Jeffrey and Seaton, 2003/4). Identical boundary spanning efforts might lead to different outcomes on the basis of differences in receptivity of the actors involved.

Receptivity tends to play a major role in recognizing the opportunities that an enlarged domain perception might have to create synergies with the activities of other actors. If potential synergy is perceived by both parties, meaning that they see joint chances in cooperation, boundary spanning is more likely to create productive linkages (Bressers and Kuks, 2004, pp. 259–62). Thereby, it in turn reinforces the degree of openness towards enlarged domain boundaries. If one or both parties consider the situation purely as rivalry or even mutually exclusive, one might even observe attempts to reinforce existing boundaries or bring up new boundaries in order to keep domains apart or separate them. Jeffrey and Seaton (2003/4) discern four aspects of receptivity: awareness, association, acquisition and application. In the cognitive system these can be linked to, respectively, the observations, the filtering through frames of reference (including boundary judgements), the interpretations of reality and the impacts of the cognitive system on motivation, capacity and the process itself. We will revisit these when discussing this model in Section 2.3.

Table 2.1 outlines the expected relations between the dichotomized variables boundary judgements and receptivity and expected boundary activities and expected scores on the Whetten (1982) criteria which were introduced in Section 1.4. This framework is at such a high level of abstraction that it might be considered unrealistic by some. We acknowledge that in real life boundary spanning activities, boundary reinforcement activities and bringing up boundaries are in fact part of interaction processes of persons, groups and organizations. Furthermore, such interaction processes take place in a context that is much wider than just boundary judgements or the cognitive systems of the actors involved. So in the next section we will explore these considerations.

2.3 PROCESS ANALYSIS IN BOUNDARY WORK RESEARCH: CONTEXTUAL INTERACTION THEORY

In this section we will approach boundary activities as taking place in interaction processes in which persons, groups and organizations convert inputs, the arguments to act and interact, into outputs. Such outputs are often inputs for further processes, enabling us to see reality as a web of interrelated processes, but for simplicity we will concentrate on one here. Causal impact schemes of reality might be very illuminating in many cases. However they tend to make the reader forget that it is human beings and their organizations that in fact process causes into effects. Consequently we choose a process model for our relations.

The concept of process is not used here in one of its two common meanings: change over time, but in the meaning of conversion process, such as, for instance, in the famous early political science model by David Easton (1966). A conversion process is not a change of a phenomenon, but something that forms the relationship between phenomena. Several inputs in such a process are transformed into something new and different. In policy fields such as water management most of these processes are not natural, but social. Since in social reality this conversion is not produced by, for example, production lines, but by activities and interactions of actors (people, representing themselves and/or organizations), they are specified as interaction processes.

Figure 2.1 shows a basic input – interaction process – output scheme.

The interactions are visualized here as based on two actors. Of course in many interaction processes there are more active actors. So to some extent this representation is only symbolic. On the other hand, while in many water management processes multiple issues are at stake, in many cases per issue there will be two sides, only two groups of actors, often a realistic situation where boundary activities in water management are analyzed (Owens, 2008).

Apart from the fact that many actors can be involved in the process,

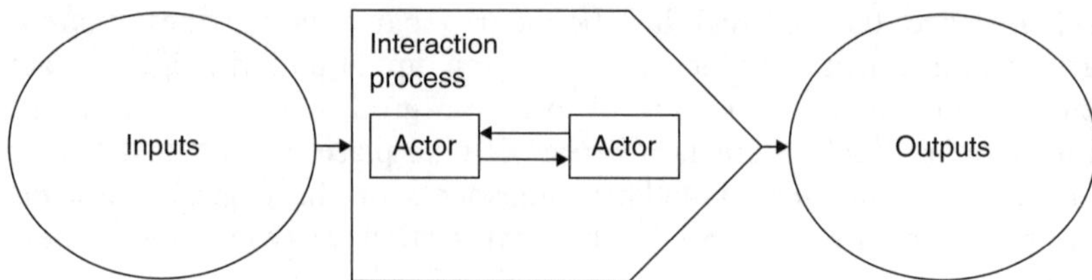

Figure 2.1 Interaction process as conversion of inputs into outputs

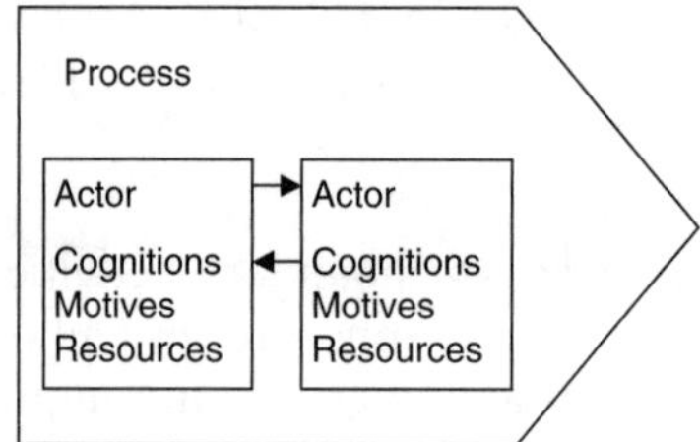

Figure 2.2 Process model with the actor characteristics used in the Contextual Interaction Theory

even when they can often be grouped per issue into two coalitions, there is another source of complexity. There are zillions of factors conceivable that might influence the course and outputs of an interaction process. Fifteen factors, each with only two values, define nevertheless more than 30 000 different combinations of circumstances. But since all influences flow via the actors involved it is possible to set an inner core of factors that is far more parsimonious, at least to begin with. In Figure 2.2 these factors are represented.

The actor characteristics are taken from the Contextual Interaction Theory, a framework that provides a layered explanation of social processes (Bressers, 2004, 2009). The basic assumptions of Contextual Interaction Theory are quite simple and straightforward. There is a dynamic interaction between the key actor characteristics that drive social interaction processes and, in turn, are reshaped by the process. The theory's main assumptions are: policy processes are actor interaction processes. Many factors have an influence but only because and in as far as they change the relevant characteristics of the involved actors. These characteristics are: their motivation, their cognitions (information held to be true) and their capacity and power. From these three characteristics hypotheses can be derived that predict the course and outcomes of, for example, policy implementation processes (see Bressers, 2004; Owens, 2008).

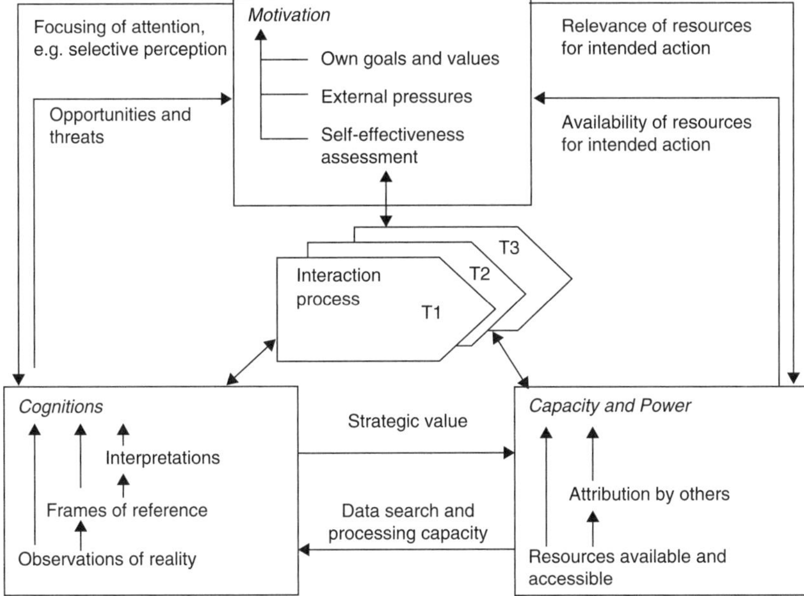

Figure 2.3 Dynamic interaction between the key actor characteristics that drive social interaction processes and in turn are reshaped by the process (Contextual Interaction Theory)

A first layer of factors influencing these characteristics is specified in the boxes of Figure 2.3. Of course these factors can in turn be influenced by numerous other factors from within or outside the process. The three core characteristics are influencing each other, but cannot be restricted to two or one without losing much insight. The characteristics of the actors shape the process, but are in turn also influenced by the course and experiences in the process and can therefore gradually change during the process. The characteristics of the actors are also influenced from an external context of the governance regime (that is, institutions and more or less stable network relationships, but also property and use rights) (represented in Figure 2.4). In this context there is yet another more encompassing circle of political, socio-cultural, economic, technological and problem contexts (see also Figure 2.4). Their influence on the actor characteristics may be both direct and indirect through the governance regime.

In Figure 2.3 many theorems and other ideas are employed that are not elaborated upon in this text. Nevertheless many relations will be understandable. Compared to Figure 2.1 this figure also shows process

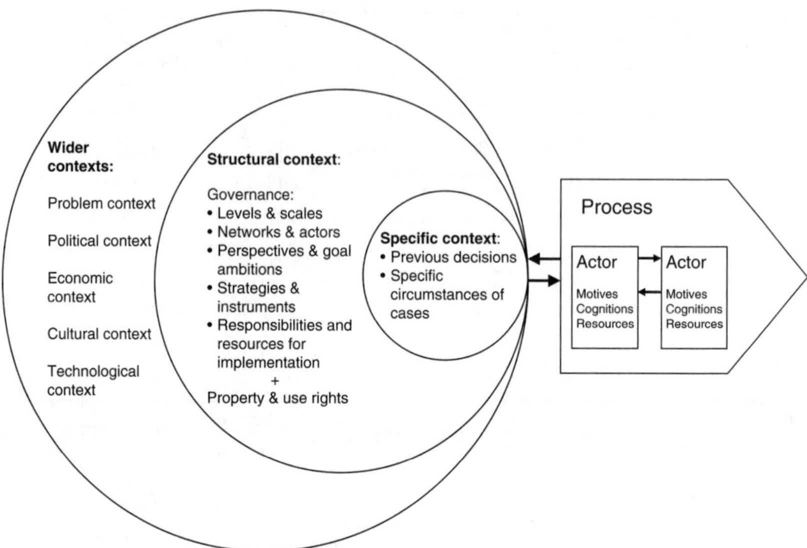

Figure 2.4 Layers of contextual factors for actor characteristics (Contextual Interaction Theory)

development (change processes – in the form of the processes over time). The actor characteristics are much more detailed here, not visualized as linked to specific actors, and for simplicity reasons are placed outside the process box. This enables us to also show the mutual influences between these factors and the process itself.

The characteristics of the actors shape the process, but are in turn also influenced by the course and experiences in the process and can therefore gradually change during the process. These three characteristics are influencing each other, but cannot be restricted to one or two without losing much insight.

In the box showing actor characteristic cognitions in Figure 2.2 we specified the boundary judgements and receptivity as elements of cognitions that are of special relevance for boundary work. In Figure 2.3 boundary judgements are part of the frames of reference. To some extent such judgements can be regarded as having direct effects on the process, for instance, when matters arise such as when one determines whether a person, group or organization is an actor of relevance, thereby recognising such an actor as a legitimate player.

The receptivity of actors consists of awareness in observation of (new) realities, association in the frames of reference, acquisition in new interpretations and application in their use to present new opportunities and threats, new strategic values and direct impacts on behaviour in the process. Of course the three actor characteristics and slices of them, such as boundary judgements and receptiveness, can in turn be influenced by numerous other factors from within or outside the process.

The dynamics in the development of cooperation between actors in the process are also related to the three actor characteristics of cognitions, motivations and resources. There is a set of mechanisms that increase the bonds in a well-functioning partnership as time goes by as an influence from the activities and interactions that happen in the process on each of the characteristics. The first mechanism is that mutual adjustment arises from the tendency of actors to act from a set of consistent values, avoiding cognitive dissonance after accepting compromises. The second mechanism is that mutual adjustment arises from the tendency of actors to use a common reference frame to interpret cognition. The third mechanism is that mutual adjustment (increased dependence of actors on each other's resources) arises from the tendency of actors to concentrate on their relative strength. Of course external change drivers can disrupt such tendencies. But these 'natural tendencies' will then provide a degree of resistance preventing disturbances, because together they build up a collective resource: trust. Furthermore, standard operation procedures and sunk costs prevent deterioration of cohesion. The opposite might also happen. Failed attempts can disrupt motivation, let the actors perceive the possibilities in a more negative way (cognitions), and can lead to a retreat to solitary (non) action and accompanying raised or emphasized boundary judgements.

The characteristics of the actors are also influenced from the external context of the governance regime (that is, institutions and more or less stable network relationships) and within this context there is yet another more encompassing circle of political, socio-cultural, economic, technological and problem contexts (Bressers and Kuks, 2003, 2004). All social processes simultaneously convert specific inputs into outputs, but are also both influenced by more encompassing contexts such as input and might change these to some extent at the same time. In this way the process is not only influenced by the layers of context that are specified, but it also influences the contexts (Figure 2.4).

2.4 DIMENSIONS OF BOUNDARY JUDGEMENTS AND HOW TO CHANGE THEM

Section 1.4 specified three main dimensions that can be used to delineate the boundaries of the domain:

1. A domain can be regarded as fitting one geographical scale and subsequently often also one level of relevant actors, or alternatively more than one scale.
2. A domain can be regarded as a relatively narrow bundle of relevant purposes or wider, encompassing several (policy) sectors that are often viewed as domains in their own right.
3. A domain can be regarded as stretching over a rather limited short time period or alternatively as a permanent evolution far into the future.

The example of a water management project might illustrate these dimensions further:

1. A local project to raise the water level of a bog, creating relatively wet meadowland between this bog and the next one, can be regarded as purely local, but also as part of a national policy to create an ecological infrastructure of vital and linked nature areas, or as the implementation of European habitat protection policies. Actors and procedures that are regarded as relevant will differ accordingly.
2. The same project can be seen as a purely water management affair but also to include nature policy (quite obvious here, but still not always accepted), recreational and tourism policy, revitalization of the rural economy, land use planning and so on. Actors and procedures that are regarded as relevant will differ accordingly.
3. The same project can be seen in project terms with clear beginning and completion dates, or as an ongoing and permanent effort to improve the quality of the natural resource. Actors and procedures that are regarded as relevant will differ accordingly.

The three dimensions might not be unrelated. The time dimension may, for instance, behave differently at various scale levels, with different speeds. Natural resource regime developments at the national level could, for instance, best be described in long periods of decennia, covering a hundred years or more for the national level, while practical cases could be described in periods of a decennium or even shorter periods. Convergence of boundary judgements is not the better kind of criterion. While clarity and stability is often a prerequisite for action, redundancy and flexibility can be helpful under challenging or changing circumstances. This indicates a degree of acceptance of uncertainty and ambiguity (cf. Smith and Stirling, 2006). The optimum can change over time. The optimum will likely move more towards convergence as time and maturity of the innovation develops, unless extreme volatile circumstances make redundancy and flexibility as important as ever for the robustness of the system.

2.4.1 Changing Boundary Judgements

When the boundary judgements of the active actors are very divergent, attaining convergence in governance will be often be difficult. The domain becomes unstable and diffuse and in that sense there is a boundary problem. Policy innovations tend to require such new boundary judgements and so introduce some promising instability (Deutsch, 1966, p. 147) to the system. To build bridges between the divergent domain perceptions that are the consequence of new and unevenly spread boundary judgements, direct inputs into the cognitions of the actors involved could serve, but these are by no means the only possible mechanism. The 'intervention points' (there need not be a conscious intervention by one of the actors) could be the actors at the scene, the arenas where actors meet and the cognitions, motivation resources and power of the actors involved (Figure 2.2). Each intervention that enters at one of these five points could in principle cause others to follow suit (Figure 2.3). The best way to influence one of them could even be indirectly through one of the others.

Below are ideas on at what points of action in the model the convergence of boundary judgements could be stimulated. They are presented as new because they express possible additions to the status quo that could help developments towards convergence. Again, their labelling as interventions is not necessarily because someone intervenes, but because they are new developments – be it deliberate or spontaneous – that create dynamics in the system.

1. New actors

There can be new actors introduced that have no contents, but rather process-oriented – in this case convergence-oriented – goals. A strong pressure of policy brokers (Sabatier and Jenkins-Smith, 1999) could increase the likelihood that actors in the process absorb new knowledge and that they are able to adapt boundary judgements to new circumstances. Policy brokers are actors (individuals or organizations, such as intermediaries) that have process-oriented goals rather than contents-oriented goals, and for that reason are more concerned with, for instance, the speed and consensus of decision making than with the precise contents of the decision. These are often ideal boundary spanners. Also some other actors can enter the scene leaving a considerable impact, for instance when a newspaper, radio or TV channel exposes the issue to a wider public or non-governmental organizations (NGOs) take up the issue.

2. New arenas

While part of the challenge is to bridge between networks that were previously not seen as connected, some authors discern alternative adaptive networks to the usual power networks. Here – freed from short-term gain-oriented debate – innovative ideas could develop that can be brought back into the power networks once they proved sufficiently attractive for creating win-win opportunities or breaking stalemates (Nooteboom, 2006). More generally, there can be a variety of new meeting points that serve the purpose of convergence of boundary judgements, such as occasional meetings, regular meetings, a platform, association or communication means, such as a professional journal and websites. These can be realized as individual or joint stakeholder initiatives. Also, installing committees can serve to explore new venues, though sometimes they serve more as a strategy to place the issue outside the discussion, window dressing for legitimacy or even to encapsulate potential opponents. The use of committees to explore a subject among representatives of various organizations and agencies and/or among so-called experts has been ubiquitous for a long time. It is said that Churchill once remarked on committees: 'We're overrun by them, like the Australians were by rabbits!'

3. New cognitions

In a sense, this is what it is all about. No doubt boundary judgements belong to the category of cognitions themselves. This does not preclude that they can also be modified by other cognitions. On the contrary, exposure to other cognitions might even be the first and foremost option to get boundary judgements to become more flexible and possibly change.

A first possibility is to introduce new information into the system. This often takes the form of reports, which contain new information from recent studies or even existing information brought together and applied to show its relevance. Such information could reveal joint problems or joint chances to the actors. The diffusion of the information is dependent not only on its reporting to the actors, but also on the form in which this is done, by whom it is done and by the receptivity of the actors themselves. Media attention can amplify the exposure to such new information manifold. Apart from 'direct' information, messages that could impact the frames of reference of the actors involved could also be important here (Figure 2.3). Schematic overviews, one-liners, wordings, stories, analogies and so on could even in this indirect way have a bigger impact on the boundary judgements of actors because they can help in opening up their minds to enable new ideas to come in (of course the opposite is also possible). Alongside external new information, own learning processes (interpretations of own experiences) can contribute to the new information that forms the judgements of the actors. Challenging or conflict situations, with stalemates will sometimes stimulate attempts to find a way out. To enhance the likelihood of such own learning, exposure to new experiences counts. New actors entering the scene and new arenas can be important here, but so also can job rotation schemes, job qualification accreditation schemes, joint training programmes and policy planning processes.

4. New motivation

Alongside cognitions, motivation and resources (see below) can also be intervention points to influence boundary judgements. Motivation to accept changes in domain perceptions is not only a matter of position, but also of saliency. When motivation is positive and there is enough saliency, it will create selective attention towards new boundary specifications. It will, in other words, increase receptiveness, in line with how the interaction between cognition and motivation was described earlier. In contrast, when motivation is negative and there is enough saliency, it can create barriers to accept new specifications (for example, the island mentality of upstream water managers towards downstream problems). Low saliency will tend to make an actor passive in this respect and even implicit shifts in domain specifications by others can go unnoticed. While the importance of motivation is not difficult to understand, ways to influence it are harder to elaborate.

In Figure 2.3 three sources of (de)motivation are specified: own goals and values, external pressures and self-effectiveness assessment, influenced by cognitions, resources and by experiences during the interaction process. Deeper values are especially hard to change, even by friendly and informal contacts during the interaction processes. Apart from external factors also internal reflection on the situation can change someone's values or goals, but cannot be regarded as a way in which other people can try to achieve such changes. Motivation to open up towards extended or changed boundary judgements can be changed via cognitions when new chances to attain existing goals are presented that rely on the acceptance of such extended domain specification. This is, for instance, the case when restoration of wetlands in nature policy could contribute to the target of creating more water buffering capacity. Through resources and power such motivation can be evoked when there is a resource dependency or an alternative threat that makes continuation of the present conceptualization of the domain uncertain; for instance, when obligatory tasks in the European Water Framework Directive are far beyond the capacity of the water management, but combining recreational developments with water projects make these water projects affordable by providing access to large additional subsidy schemes. In practice, a lot of boundary spanning is done by luring other parties with resources that are needed, thereby gradually creating a great joint resource: the social capital of trust. In a sense, such opportunities and restrictions of resource exchange also impact motivation through their impact on self-effectiveness expectations.

5. New resources and power

Boundary judgements are a small, but important part of cognitions. Resources and power can influence cognitions both directly and indirectly, via motivation. It is important to keep in mind that changing resources is here a way to get these specific cognitions (boundary judgements) to change; and that this will also occur even more indirectly via motivations change. At this point this is not dealt with as a way to get changes directly in the governance structure (or even in the acceptance by actors of such changes). Only in so far as boundary judgements are what stand in the way is the latter the case. Now how could resources and power change boundary judgements of actors, change what they perceive as the extent of the right domain?

When resources and power are used to influence boundary judgements, this presupposes a user, an actor, that is motivated to do so. One could say that such an actor uses and exerts coordination power. A source of such power could be their centrality in relevant networks (cf. social network theory). An important asset (or resource) is the degree of respect and trust by others of such an actor. This also helps in the acceptation of information messages. For the rest, power is not only an objective, resource-based, strength, but primarily a matter of attribution by others. As long as this attribution is not falsified, assumed power is real power. When people are forced to open up an enlarged extent of the domain because a powerful actor makes this unavoidable, they will often gradually accept this. In principle this can be done by direct hierarchy forcing openness to new boundaries. More often a softer approach will be taken, for example, via the conditional provision of money (golden cords, budgeting), standardization requirements (procedures, instructions, forms) or plans – all creating forms of resource dependency. Resources can also be employed to enhance the learning capacity of other actors to increase the chance of more openness towards an extension of what is regarded as the relevant domain.

2.5 SUMMARY: QUESTIONS FOR EMPIRICAL STUDIES

In this chapter we unfolded a model for the analysis of boundary judgements in interaction processes. This is not to be considered as a fixed format that should be and is followed in all the cases studied in this book. As explained at the end of Chapter 1, they all have different emphases. Chapters 5 and 6, however, do follow this approach and Chapters 7, 8 and 9 to some extent. Since we have already presented the model in a very condensed form we do not attempt a further summary here.

As a summary, we specify some issues that could be relevant for case studies using the approach explained in this chapter (see also Dente et al., 1998).

What is the initial issue the researcher wants to focus on?
This is a pre-choice question that is a necessary starting point that cannot be derived from empirical observations.

What processes developed around this focus? Were there any linkages with other issues during these processes and, if so, when and with what?
Coupling with other issues requires that the boundary judgements of the actors involved move along with these linkages. This is not necessarily the case.

What were the relevant motivations, cognitions and resources of the actors involved? To what extent and how do these factors explain the course and results of the process?
Here Contextual Interaction Theory can provide analyses of the processes.

What is the role of boundary judgements in these factors and the process?
Boundary judgements that differ among actors can cause incoherence and can even be a source of conflict. Boundary judgements that are too narrow for the adequate use of adaptive water management or so wide that complexity becomes unmanageable can also cause all progress to stagnate.

What is the role of the receptivity of actors involved in these factors and the process?
The role of receptivity in the process as a whole also refers to the receptivity of the set of actors as a network. Often though, a central actor will get most attention here.

What was the interaction with the specific context, the structural context (elements of governance and property and use rights) and/or the wider contexts, like the cultural context?
Here the impact of the various contexts enters the picture.

To what extent did one or more actors use specific strategies to manage the boundary judgements of themselves or other actors and/or to cope with differences and perceived too narrow or too wide scopes in order to enhance the degree of coherence of the process and its structural context? To what effect? What lessons could be drawn from this for other situations and with what specifications of conditions?

This final question leads to the lessons to be learned on boundary spanning.

3. A boundary perspective on flood management in the Netherlands

Wim van Leussen

3.1 INTRODUCTION

In this chapter we assess boundary spanning in flood defence policies in the Netherlands. We use Luhmann's work on social systems. The complementary perspective in this chapter is a long-term analysis of flood management developments, in which the level of analysis is not actors, such as in Chapter 2, but systems. By this, the analysis is not restricted to the parsimonious lenses of the three dimensions scales, sectors and time as described in Chapters 1 and 2.

Our analysis of flood management practice concentrates on recent developments, but will be viewed within the history of many centuries. In Section 3.2 we describe our approach which is semi-structured, and concentrates on the viewpoint from the social sciences. In section 3.3 we give a concise outline of the developments of flood management in the Netherlands. Section 3.4 deals with the management of boundaries, starting from a systems approach. We discriminate between physical, biological and social systems. Special attention is given to social systems, applying the social systems theory of Luhmann. In Section 3.5 we finally reflect upon our findings. Similarities between the contextual interaction theory from Chapter 2 and the application of the social systems theory of Luhmann are exemplified.

3.2 THE BOUNDARY APPROACH TOWARDS FLOOD MANAGEMENT

From a governance point of view, the trend in water management includes increasing levels of complexity and increasing numbers of interdependencies. The complexity comes from connecting with a number of other policy fields, through which a problem does not stand by itself, but is part of a collection of problems. Through connections to policy fields, such as agriculture, recreation and spatial planning, the number of stakeholders, positions and involved interests increases significantly. Thus many actors are participating in the decision-making process. Within the European context an important role is played by the so-called catchment approach, through which water and land are strongly connected to each other. In Article 2 of the Water Framework Directive (2000/60/EC) it is specified as the area of land from which all surface run-off flows through a sequence of streams, rivers and, possibly, lakes into the sea at a single river mouth, estuary or delta. Generally, within the catchment a number of sub-catchments can be distinguished and from an overall view a hierarchical system with subsystems appears. Through the connection of land and water, the complexity of this system increases significantly.

The question is how to govern such a complex socio-physical system with respect to the issue of flood management. For a long time the physical system was concentrated upon the hydrological and hydraulic aspects with special attention on precipitation, river discharge and water levels. However, during the past decades the focus also shifted to the social system and actors' cognitions, motivations and resources. Both systems behave quite differently and need different scientific approaches. Integration, however, is needed to arrive at an overall flood management perspective.

For social systems the focus is on communications, and governance is the activity to coordinate actors and actions for achieving the collective goals. This is in line with the social system theory of Luhmann (1984), where communications represent the basic elements. Luhmann suggested that the overall system should be characterized by its primary mode of internal differentiation. Internal differentiation means the way in which a system builds subsystems. Modern society has evolved into a functionally differentiated system with subsystems such as the political system, the economic system, the institutional system and the cultural system. Due to this differentiation the important question of how to handle the boundaries between these self-referential subsystems emerges, and also the question of how to handle this in relation to the physical environment with its specific dynamics in time and place.

The primary spatial scale is the catchment or river basin, within which smaller subscales are nested. These sub-basins are the basins of the tributaries, within which also again smaller sub sub-basins can be distinguished. Finally a nested collection of hydrological units results through which the water flows from the smaller to the larger streams. Also other spatial scales are relevant such as eco-regions. An eco-region is a relatively large unit of land or water, containing a geographically distinct assemblage of natural communities and species. The biodiversity of such an area tends to be distinct from that of other eco-regions. Within such eco-regions again smaller areas can be distinguished, such as natural communities and ecotopes. In both cases, a hierarchy of levels calls for attention.

Such a multi-level approach is reflected in how social processes appear at different social scales and in subsystems. Both social scales at which people are living, as well as political scales, at which decisions are taken, are relevant. Often the political scales do not coincide with those of the catchments, which makes the decision-making process extremely complex for water management in accordance with the catchment approach.

This brings us in the centre of the present-day governance problems of modern water management. From a governance perspective, the main challenge in complex social systems is collective action, and then reaching a specified goal. Bressers and Kuks (2003, 2004) and Kuks (2004) use the term water governance for collective action to address water issues. Their governance model consists of five elements that represent the features of modern governance systems: multi-level, multi-actor, multi-faceted, multi-instrumental and multi-resource based (included in Figure 2.4 in this volume). This model helps to understand the complexity of governance structures and shifts in governance systems. The multi-level element of governance systems reflects the history of boundary judgements with regard to geographical and administrative scales as described in Chapters 1 and 2. The other four elements reflect the pre-existing views with regard to boundary judgements on sectors and special aspects within sectors. Finally, shifts in governance systems can be perceived as institutional change due to boundary judgements on the time and change dimension as described in Chapters 1 and 2. Applying the five elements of the governance model helps to understand how modern water management in practice is struggling with a variety of spatial, social and political scales. The question is how to handle the boundaries between these units of scale in a sensible manner.

We aim to obtain more insight into the development of the flood defence policy in a period where boundaries became blurred. Progress then can be obtained only through partnerships, interdisciplinary studies and complex institutional arrangements, within which flood defence measures are embedded to nature and landscape and to social systems. The work on social systems by Luhmann (1984) describes social contacts through a system of bodies of thought, ideas and critique, which are separated from each other and from the environment by boundaries. Such boundaries have the double function of separating and connecting. Boundaries separate elements but not necessarily relations. Boundaries can facilitate or block communication. Therefore, the so-called boundary organizations play an important role in the functioning of these boundaries (see also

Table 3.1 *Catchment areas of the major rivers flowing through the Netherlands*

River	Total catchment area of the river basin (km²)	Catchment area within the Netherlands (km²)	Percentage in the Netherlands
Rhine	185920	28275	15
Meuse	36000	7700	21
Scheldt	21860	1860*	8
Ems	17500	2700	15

Note: *Without the Eastern Scheldt.

Chapter 7). The boundary concept as used in studies of anthropology helps to clarify cultural differences. Now we extend these concepts in social science to the science of physical geography. An example of such applications and the multi-dimensional nature of such boundaries is presented by Pellow et al. (1996). They showed how boundaries might be physical, social, temporal, conceptual and/or symbolic.

3.3 FLOOD MANAGEMENT IN THE NETHERLANDS

The Netherlands is situated in the delta of four major rivers, the Rhine, Meuse, Scheldt and Ems. More than 50 per cent of the country is situated below sea level. The larger part of the catchments of these rivers is located in the surrounding countries. The sizes of the catchment areas and their relative percentages within the Netherlands are given in Table 3.1.

It will not surprise that the history of the Netherlands, as representative of low-lying delta nations, is characterized by a continuous struggle with water, particularly with extreme floods. Since 1200, about 140 flood disasters were recorded with casualties and severe damage. An extreme flood in the Middle Ages was the St Elisabeth's Flood, which occurred on 18 and 19 November 1421, through which about 70 villages were destroyed. The most important cause was the neglect of the maintenance of the dikes at that time. As a result of a political quarrel at the local level concerning dike repair, the St Felix's Flood followed on Saturday 5 November 1530 with severe inundations in the south-western part of the Netherlands. The most severe flood was the All Saints' Flood on 1 November 1570. A long period of storm pushed the water to unprecedented heights, which broke at a number of places through the coastline.

Almost all lower parts in the Netherlands (below sea level) were inundated, including areas in Belgium. The total number of casualties must have been far above 25 000, but exact data are not available. The last river flood with breaching of dikes was on 29 December 1926, where the rivers had their highest discharges ever measured: 12 000 m^3/s for the river Rhine and 3000 m^3/s for the river Meuse. The storm surge of 1 February 1953 caused one of the biggest natural disasters of recent times in the Netherlands: 1836 people died and the economic damage was in the order of 1 billion euros.

Generally, after such an extreme disaster an updated or new flood defence policy appears. Three weeks after the storm surge of 1953 a Delta Commission was installed, advising the national government on how to prevent such disasters in the future. Their final report in 1960 proposed advanced safety levels for the coast and estuaries. Also safety levels for the major rivers were presented. However, the safety levels for the major rivers resulted in many discussions in society. Commissions (Becht; Boertien I; Boertien II) were installed to advise the national government. In addition to the advice of the Delta Commission, the Dutch government proposed in 1956 a safety standard of 1:3000 along the major rivers. However, much opposition arose because of a fear of the destruction of the idyllic river landscape and doubts about the necessity of the strengthening programme. The Commission Becht, installed in 1975, proposed in 1977 a safety level of 1:1250. Continuing resistance against the dike reinforcements resulted in the Commission Boertien I (1992). This commission advised in 1993 a safety level of 1:1250. For the river Meuse, the Commission Boertien II was installed in 1993, and advised in 1994 a safety level of 1:250. More downstream along the river Meuse the safety levels of the dikes were also 1:1250.

The extreme high waters of 1993 and 1995, during which about 250 000 inhabitants were evacuated within two days, started again discussions on the safety levels along the major rivers. The government decided to establish a Delta Plan Large Rivers, speeding up the process of dike reinforcements and the implementation of the recommendations of the Commission Boertien II. In 1996 the policy 'Space for the River' was introduced, through which the Dutch government initiated a shift from traditional flood protection policies (that is, raising the dikes) towards creating increased water discharge capacity as well as storage of surplus water in large retention areas. The safety levels along the rivers represent a flooding chance of once in 1250 years for river discharges of 16 000 m^3/s for the Rhine and 3650 m^3/s for the Meuse.

Because a number of floods and periods of intense precipitation threatened the Netherlands in the 1990s, and particularly some high water inconvenience in 1998 due to intense precipitation, the national government installed a committee to investigate whether the whole water system is still prepared for the twenty-first century. This Committee Water Management for the 21st Century (WB21) delivered their report in August 2000. They made a plea for adaptations of the water management, giving more space to water, improvement of the water governance and proposed an integrated policy for water and the physical environment. A special water test was introduced, which is now required by law and widely applied, to test possible effects of great infrastructural projects on the water conditions. The WB21 report stimulated a number of activities, both at the national and regional level, and is nowadays one of the cornerstones of the Dutch water policy. Among the group of low-lying delta nations, the Dutch level of ambition is rather high.

Because ideas and circumstances change in time, it is important to evaluate regularly the effectiveness of the flood management policy. In the Netherlands such evaluations occur once every five years. A recent evaluation showed that the strength of the dikes is higher than ever before and the probability of floods from the rivers or the sea has been reduced significantly. Yet the risks of casualties and economic damage have become much larger in the last 50 years. It seems like the public no longer considers flooding in the Netherlands to be a natural hazard. Flooding seems to be regarded as a risk similar to external risks, such as industrial hazards and plane crashes. Through intensive economic developments the vulnerability of the areas behind the dikes has increased significantly, and thus the damage in the case of a flooding. A further increase in flooding risks is expected due to the effects of climate change: a rising sea level and larger peak values of river discharge.

These developments and new insights resulted in discussions and research on an updated flood policy for the twenty-first century. This new approach includes not only an actualization of the prevention of floods, but also the reduction of damage in the case of extreme flooding, and more societal awareness of the possibility of threats by floods in the future. The trend is a transition from probabilities of maximum water level rise to probabilities of real flooding, in which all possible mechanisms of failing of the flood defence structures are taken into account. Furthermore, their consequences are also taken into account and studies are performed on differentiation of the safety levels. Cost–benefit analyses are part of these studies and do include economic damage. Special attention is given to flood management in relation to, among others, spatial planning, including risk zoning and evacuation strategies. The challenge is to create a flexible and robust physical structure of the environment with low levels of damage in the case of an unfortunate flooding.

3.3.1 Boundary Spanning

The subsequent new flood defence policies, generally drawn up shortly after a disaster and then modified under the influence of discussions in society, show elements of crossing boundaries. In the fifteenth century, after several times of breaching of the dikes, large inundation areas were planned to keep the maximum water level in the rivers below the height of the dikes. This approach resulted in a significant reduction of the maximum water level at critical river discharges and had an important function during a number of centuries. However, it was not always sufficient in extreme situations. An example of such an inundation area is the Beerse Overlaat along the river Meuse, which had been closed in 1942, but was since 2002 again a serious emergency option for controlled flooding. Under political pressure it was decided by the Dutch Parliament in 2008 to close it definitely. The Delta Works after the disaster of 1953 also started considering ecology as a relevant issue in flood engineering works.

The most recent and proactive programme is called Water Safety 21st Century (WV21). It addresses the paradox of being well protected, the chances of floods being smaller than ever before, but at the same time it is realized that when such a disaster would occur, the damages would also be larger than ever before. As a result of climate change, the sea level is rising and the peak discharges of the rivers will increase. Also the soil subsidence is important, for which up to 2050 a downward movement of between 2 and 60 centimetres is predicted for the western part of the Netherlands. At present, policy makers believe that heightening the dikes is not the solution. A robust solution can only be achieved by combining the flood protection measures with adequate spatial planning. This means the cooperation of more policy fields, through which also the number of stakeholders will increase substantially. At the same time it is felt that the classical approach of prevention should be extended by limiting the consequences of a possible flood disaster and an increase of the awareness within society of the possibility of flooding. Due to the taken for granted high level of protection, citizens often are not aware of this threat of water, even where they are living in a polder more than 6.00 m below sea level.

It is becoming usual now to take the whole safety chain into account, related to safety approaches for disasters in other policy fields in the Netherlands. This safety chain consists of five elements:

- pro-action (protecting vital infrastructure and so on);
- prevention (heightening of the dikes and so on; in the past almost all attention has been given to prevention by technical measures);
- preparedness (early warning systems and so on);

- response (alarming and coordination and so on);
- after-care (insurance, restoration, psycho-social help and so on).

In looking for sustainable solutions, more and more the catchment approach is a starting point in modern flood defence policies. For the Netherlands this means cooperation with other countries, and deliberating on the so-called upstream-downstream problems. This will be strengthened by the *European Directive on the Assessment and Management of Flood Risks (2007/60/EC)* (EC, 2007). This new directive asks for a preliminary flood risk assessment, flood mapping in all areas with a significant flood risk, coordination within shared river basins and production of flood risk management plans through a broad participatory process. Strong emphasis is placed on the role of flood plains and sustainable land use practices. Climate change adaptation will be considered in the first implementation cycle, for which the European Union (EU) member states take a planning approach in three stages:

- preliminary flood risk assessment of their river basins and associated coastal zones (2011);
- flood hazard maps and flood risk maps (2013);
- flood risk management plans (2015).

In the case of international river basins, EU member states must coordinate so that problems are not passed on from one area to another (2007/60/EC).

From a boundary perspective these developments indicate that several boundaries have been crossed, blurred or dismantled, and particularly the present developments in the twenty-first century seem to show a number of new boundary crossings. These will be elaborated on in more detail in the next section.

3.4 THE MANAGEMENT OF BOUNDARIES

Boundaries discriminate between systems, which according to the General Systems Theory (Von Bertalanffy, 1968) are defined as a set of elements standing in interaction. These include any grouping with any sort of relationship, such as a group of people, a forest, a catchment, a river basin or anything else. Therefore, systems can be, among others, physical systems, biological systems and institutional systems. There can also be a hierarchy in systems, when smaller systems (subsystems) are situated within other, larger systems, for example a sub-catchment within a larger catchment.

There are essential differences between physical systems, such as rivers, biological systems, such as living organisms and social systems, such as groups of people or organizations. The physical systems are generally characterized by causal relations, although much uncertainty can be present. The biological or living systems are self-referential, which means they have their own autonomy and interact with their environment. This yields also the social systems, but they have additionally the particular characteristics that their actions are driven by a subjective intention or meaning (Luhmann, 1984).

We will now concentrate on the boundaries, which determine what is inside or outside flood management. The analysis will be made from a governance perspective, where governance is defined as the capacity of government to develop flood defence policies and to implement them (cf. Van Leussen and Lulofs, 2009).

Boundaries are at the heart of the social systems theory of Luhmann. In his theory of social systems (Luhmann, 1984), Luhmann defines systems as the difference between system and environment. It seems to be a paradox, but it shows how he made a step from the general systems theory to a system/environment theory. Such a theory of system/environment differentiation could lead to a more accurate understanding of the whole by simultaneously using varying viewpoints within subsystem differentiation. The basic elements in this theory for social systems are communications: the transfer of information and the processing and understanding of this information. Social systems by definition are observing systems, which form an impression of the environment, including the other systems. The systems themselves are self-referential. Each system reacts to external stimuli through an internal organization. In this way the systems are operationally closed systems, but open for signals from the environment, processing them by their internal organization. Handling the complexity of the whole system is the challenge of systems management. The theory of Luhmann is searching for complexity reduction, which can be obtained through well-considered selection and intervention. Through selection the complexity of the systems is always lower than that of the environment. The governance of such complex social systems occurs by continuously making selections out of the arising communications. Criteria for the selections are given by meaning, through which potentials of the present situation are indicated in relation to the actual situation. So meaning is a strategy of selective behaviour, through which the complexity can be reduced. It is at the basis of the theory of social systems. In the systems/environment theory the boundaries are situated between the systems and their environment. It must be remarked that from the viewpoint of a system, all other systems belong to the environment. It should be realized that system boundaries are distinctions brought into life by an observer. Boundaries are in fact the result of decisions or judgements, made by a decision maker, analyst, scientist or practitioner. This is in line with the ideas put forward in Chapters 1 and 2.

In the following we will make a subdivision in three categories of boundaries. The enclosing boundaries bind a specific area of interest, a relevant time period or other quality set, which are relevant for flood management. It will be shown that such boundaries are not static. The intermediary boundaries are important distinctions but also connections between different systems. The dynamics in sense-making boundaries refer to possible changes in the ideas and concepts, through which meaning is given for actions in the social systems.

3.4.1 Enclosing Boundaries

Geographic boundaries

In the specific location of the Netherlands in the low-lying delta of four major rivers, originally the flood management was directed by local conditions. The water levels at local level and their variations mark the dominant boundary conditions for the struggle against the floods. In earlier times, people started to live on dwellings and then within areas, surrounded by dikes. Through the lowering effect on the water level, flooding of some areas could help neighbouring areas. The centralized governing system at the end of the eighteenth century supplied the badly needed national coordination and resulted in a higher level of protection. First, the focus was on the river channel, and more recently on the whole river basin. Through the recent European Floods Directive it can be expected that ultimately a harmonized approach will arise in the EU and adjacent countries. Effective and efficient flood risk management is most feasible at this level.

At the regional scale already comparable boundary shifts occurred. Across the Dutch-German border, agreement has been reached to develop a joint flood strategy, to take measures for flood defence, to inform the public and to make maps of expected developments of river discharges as a consequence of climate change.

Temporal boundaries

The temporal scale, at which flood risk management receives attention, develops into a wider perspective through boundary spanning. For many centuries the flood risk policy responded to disasters. Measures were taken, or only intended to be taken, to avoid reoccurrence of a critical situation in the future. The low-tech solutions were setting maximum water levels, as measured during the flood, and raised the dikes to at least this level.

Since the storm surge of 1953 a system of safety levels was agreed upon, which connects to the predicted maximum river discharges. These river discharges were analyzed statistically, and after each period of five years, new hydraulic boundary conditions were agreed by the Dutch parliament. This was reinforced by the discussion on climate change. Nowadays the policy no longer waits until a new disaster strikes, but looks forward on the basis of developed scenarios for the future. These include periods of 50 years or up to some centuries (Klijn et al., 2007; MNP, 2007). Chapter 4 in this volume deepens the analysis of the temporal dimension.

Boundaries of the river

For a long time flood risk management focused on the river within the dikes. When it became clear that only raising the dikes was not sufficient or even worsened flood effects by damming the water flow, boundaries shifted. Inundation areas behind the dikes were activated during extreme floods. This had been done successfully since the fourteenth century, although it was not always sufficient under extreme conditions. After great improvements of the major rivers after the extreme river flood of 1926, the overall feeling was that the rivers were under control by the engineering works. The inundation areas were closed. The extreme river floods of 1993 and 1995 started a process of reorientation with regard to flood risk management and new policies arose. 'Space for the River' became the new philosophy: allocating more space to the river through moving dikes further away from the river and giving areas of reclaimed land back to the river, for instance, by constructing side and/or flood channels parallel to the river over some distances and deepening or widening of the flood plains (Van Leussen et al., 2000; Van Stokkom and Smits, 2002). This started in 2006 and costed more than 2.1 billion euros. Raising the dikes is not foreseen, but remains available as, in this era, a final possibility.

Boundaries of policy fields

Climate change and the rise of climate change policy intensified the discussions on the spatial dimension of flood risk management. It was the starting point to perceive flood risk management in the Netherlands as a challenge for spatial planning (Pols et al., 2007). The central question is how spatial planning can contribute to a higher safety level during periods of extreme floods, especially by limiting the damage risk. The national government started a National Programme for Spatial Adaptation to Climate Change. In July 2007 50 million euros was allocated to innovative research in the period 2007–12 to keep the country liveable under the effects of climate change. Flood protection and mitigation are only some of the aspects. All relevant stakeholders, that is, government bodies, business community, scientists and civil society organizations, will share in the responsibility for developing and implementing the programme activities.

3.4.2 Intermediary Boundaries

Boundaries between scientific disciplines

Crossing boundaries, as described in the previous paragraphs, and resulting in a higher complexity of problems, require an interdisciplinary approach. Soon after the catastrophic 1953 flood ecologists found their jobs in areas where previously only hydrologists and civil engineers were working. This in the context of the Delta Plan. A balance is found between hydraulic and ecological knowledge and expertise. All national flood defence projects have two targets: the reduction of the flood risk and the improvement of the spatial quality. In an overview of the period of 20 years it was concluded that large ecological improvements have been achieved but that also many points need further attention (Reeze et al., 2005).

Interdisciplinary research programmes are financed by the Dutch government, within which interdisciplinary projects must contribute to innovations in the Dutch water sector. An example is the programme 'Living with Water' (Leven met Water, 2007). In this six-year programme collaboration is stimulated between the domains of water management and spatial planning, science and practice, economy and sociology. Practical experiments are carried out in the form of so-called Communities of Practice. In this volume several chapters are based on research in this programme.

Boundaries between science and policy

Boundary-work indicates the activities at the demarcation of science and non-science. This term was introduced by the sociologist Gieryn (1983), who showed that these boundaries often have an ideological nature. No uniform or undisputed notion of science exists, particularly because science may be both pure and applied and also theoretical and empirical. Since politicians tend to expect that research will offer unambiguous answers to complex and contested environmental policy problems, the pursuit of certainty is a central task in science for policy. Already the effects of climate change on flood management represent an example. In such situations politicians, policy makers, stakeholders, citizens and scientists often do not agree on how the problem really should be defined, and of course not on the measures to be taken, let alone their expected effects. Therefore the number of boundary organizations is increasing, facilitating the transfer of usable knowledge between science and policy. An example in the Netherlands is the Netherlands Environmental Assessment Agency (MNP – Milieu en Natuur Planbureau), which translated the outcomes of the IPCC reports (Intergovernmental Panel on Climate Change, 2007) and made *Summaries for Policymakers*. Due to the rising sea level they concluded that in the Dutch situation the major rivers are more critical in the coming centuries than the coast. In particular some locations along these rivers near the cities of Rotterdam and Dordrecht are vulnerable.

Boundaries between relevant stakeholders

The Netherlands is a decentralized unitary state, combining centralized, hierarchical control by the central government with delegation of authority to regional and local governments: provinces, water boards and municipalities (Andeweg and Irwin, 2005). The national water policy generally results from intensive deliberations between the responsible ministry, related ministries and representative organizations of the subnational authorities. The decision-making process is strongly consensus based, which means that decisions are negotiated between the leaders of each of the authorities. The real implementation of the water policy occurs at the regional and local level (water boards and municipalities) and by the State Department for Infrastructure and Water Management (*Rijkswaterstaat*) for the major national rivers, estuaries, coastal waters and seas.

The aforementioned developments illustrate that the areas of (potential) flooding no longer belong to the jurisdiction of one political authority, but that a number of authorities are always dependent and joint decision making is required. Political boundaries in flood risk management have been changed, resulting in an adapted distribution of responsibilities between the national, regional and local authorities and concerned citizens (Roth et al., 2006).

Multi-level governance boundaries

Water policy is developed at the national level. As mentioned before, the discussion is open and national representatives of governments at lower levels are given the possibility to contribute to the final texts of the policy documents. Nevertheless, the final decisions are at national level. Subsequently, these policies are implemented at the regional and local level. Generally these policies are rather ambitious, and only a portion will be realized during a certain period of time. Politicians at the regional and local level normally agree to specify measures on the basis of local knowledge and information. Of course, the national government has the legislative authority to give formal instructions to the regional and/or local democracies but this resource is not often used in the Dutch political culture.

However, now the influence of European legislature is increasing, and agreements have to be made on objectives to be achieved within agreed periods, which is quite different from agreements on ambitions. Now the national government is responsible for the progress on agreed measures at the regional and local levels. This means strict agreements must be made between the national and regional/local authorities concerning the implementation of agreed policies. In this case agreements of the national government with the representatives in the public umbrella associations for provinces, water boards and municipalities are no longer sufficient, but direct agreements should be made with the responsible authorities at the regional and local level. It implies a drastic change in the vertical institutional boundaries. This had already happened for the implementation of the Water Framework Directive. For the European Floods Directive a comparable shift is expected for flood risk management.

Also the horizontal boundaries show essential changes. Agreements on the flood risk policy need the agreement of all relevant sector ministries, which implies that the boundaries must be much more permeable than in the past, and transparent communication is a prerequisite for effective implementation at the regional and local level. The changing horizontal boundaries at the regional and local level find their base in the catchment approach of modern water management. Regional and local actors are working together intensively in sub-catchments and smaller areas to make agreements on the objectives, measures and the sharing of costs.

Boundaries of phase

From a governance point of view a number of phases can be discerned around extreme floods: pro-action, prevention, preparedness, response and after-care. In the past centuries most attention has been given to prevention, and the safety levels were increasing continuously in the rhythm of the flood disasters. This resulted in the so-called safety paradox: an extremely high level of protection, but at the same time extremely high consequences in the case of such a disaster. The last point results from the fact that while high investments have been made in the lowlands, a 100 per cent guarantee for protection can never be given. Therefore the Dutch strategy for flood risk management now covers all phases. This also corresponds to the lessons learned from Hurricane Katrina in 2005 in the USA (White House, 2006). Nevertheless, modern governance of reducing the flood risks also involves blurring the boundaries of phase, although prevention remains the cornerstone in the flood defence policy.

3.4.3 Cognitively Constructed Boundaries

Mental boundaries

The change in mental boundaries is important. In accordance with Berger and Luckmann (1967), one could say these are socially constructed based on experienced derived knowledge of river systems and (harmful) situations. Actors who share such social constructs and interact are called discourse coalitions by Hajer (1995). He defines discourse as an ensemble of ideas, concepts and categories through which meaning is given to phenomena. The previous analysis shows how these boundaries are widening more and more, including larger areas (whole catchments), longer periods of time (climate change), other policy fields (spatial planning), other disciplines (ecology), and a dramatic increase of stakeholders and authorities in the decision-making process. These shifting mental boundaries gave a completely new view of the river.

3.5 DISCUSSION AND CONCLUSIONS

The list of boundaries is not exhaustive. More forms of spanning boundaries occur, such as for example the public–private boundaries. The design of flood defence structures nowadays involves public and private organizations. An example is the moveable flood defence structure (Maeslant Barrier) in the Rotterdam Waterway, which has been designed (1997) by a public–private partnership.

Remarkable in the set of enclosing boundaries are the shifts in all of these boundaries, which result in an impressive widening of the respective fields of interest. The geographic areas developed from river sections to whole river basins, of which the catchments often cross national borders. The temporal boundaries showed comparable shifts from ad hoc time scales, looking backwards to the previous flood, to periods ahead of 50 to 200 years, particularly in the perspective of the expected effects of climate change. The same was the case with the boundaries of the river. Through this spanning of boundaries the scope of the problems increased dramatically, as exemplified by the increased spatial dimension of flood risk management. Not only the boundaries of the policy fields blurred, but also the number of relevant stakeholders increased significantly. Together these observations gave an adequate impression of the almost revolutionary developments in flood risk management. The boundary approach was shown to be a valuable concept for clarifying the underlying processes.

The set of intermediary boundaries showed how boundaries between scientific disciplines were spanned, resulting in interdisciplinary research. Also the boundaries between science and policy blurred more or less, resulting in a joint work of science and non-science, where particularly the local knowledge and experience was shown to be of increasing value. Chapter 8 of this volume also addresses this issue.

The boundaries between groups of relevant stakeholders showed that decisions on flood management are no longer the jurisdiction of one political authority, but require joint decision making. An adapted distribution of responsibilities occurred between the national, regional and local authorities and concerned citizens. These changes were also exemplified by handling the multi-level governance boundaries.

Crossing and blurring all these boundaries illustrates a modern holistic view on flood risk management. It requires an overall view or vision, with which all the parts are connected. It means a highly relational system where the smaller elements (regional and local areas) are connected to the total system (catchment or river basin). It means a system full of interactions that increases the complexity of effective governance. It also indicates that problems are not solvable from the viewpoint of one discipline, but it is also not the sum of hydraulics, chemistry, ecology, economics, politics and public administration. Particularly the blurred boundaries and the corresponding holistic approach require new competencies of present-day water managers. In fact it requires the skills of handling the whole system, including a large number of self-referential subsystems, of high complexity. It corresponds with the statement of Luhmann of increased functional differentiation, which could only be managed effectively by a justified complexity reduction.

It should be realized that the real implementation is at the regional and local scale, where specific local conditions are to be taken into account, both physical, social and political. This means an essential boundary must remain to be respected between both areas of scale: the national level, at which an overall policy is developed, possibly with the input of actors at the regional and local level, and the regional/local level, where this policy is further elaborated and implemented.

Most impressive are the changes in mental or conceptual boundaries. The vision on sustainable flood risk management has been changed so intensively that a turn back is impossible. These recent developments correspond with Adaptive Water Management in Chapter 1, with an increasing number of stakeholders and broad geographic and temporal scale perspectives. Notwithstanding the need for thinking on longer time scales, real implementation should also occur in the short term with strict deadlines. The respective time boundaries should be spanned by the adaptive approach with learning through experimentation. The whole of communications between the systems, in accordance with the social system theory of Luhmann as used in this chapter, is comparable with the social interaction processes in Chapter 2. The meaning, or subjective intention, which was shown to be at the basis of actions in the social systems, has an analogy with the role of motivation in the social interaction processes in Chapter 2. The choices for the boundaries at the edge of the self-referential social systems and their environment illustrate the perception of the total system with its subsystems. The differences in system/environment represent the backgrounds of the interaction between the groups of actors with the various layers of contextual factors in Chapter 2. They are key factors for an effective governance approach.

So a number of parallels are demonstrated between the contextual interaction approach and boundary judgements in Chapters 1 and 2, and the approach in this chapter on the basis of the social system theory of Niklas Luhmann. One could say that the analysis with the theory of Luhmann starts at a higher level of abstraction, but its application in real situations, and its plea for justified complexity reduction, supports the use of the toolbox of boundary work as given in the first chapters of this book. Although the social system theory of Luhmann proved to be a rich framework for longitudinal analysis over long periods, the enclosing boundaries found show similarities with the parsimonious dimensions of scales, sectors and time as described in Chapters 1 and 2. The intermediary boundaries are sometimes subcategories of these dimensions, for example, with regard to science versus non-science (see Chapter 8), phase (see Chapter 9), scale (see Chapter 10) and boundaries between stakeholders and scales (see Chapters 5, 6 and 10).

It may be concluded that the boundary perspective on flood management clarified the backgrounds of the recent developments with its increasing complexity, both concerning its broadening geographic and temporal scales, its increasing connections between scientific disciplines, science and policy, institutions and relevant stakeholders, but most impressively by its shifting conceptual boundaries, which made boundary work a suitable tool for a better understanding of the major processes for effective water governance.

4. The temporal dimensions of boundary judgements

Aysun Özen Tacer

4.1 INTRODUCTION

'We do not want *plan*, we want *plav*.'[1] Quote from the primary opposition party in Turkey responding to the five-year development plan in discussion.

Most policy decisions and actions within the domain of water resource management have delayed consequences, which introduces temporal dimensions at which boundary spanners might focus. Delay may not be perceived identically by all actors, the delay may lower the perceived magnitude and impact of future outcomes by some actors and delay may also be beyond the time horizon of some actors. And of course stemming from the above issues, delay may be a cause of conflict or dilemma. This touches upon time as one of the three dimensions of boundary judgements alongside sectors and scales. In this chapter the time dimension will be elaborated in a cognitive approach, also addressing implications for boundary spanning and boundary spanners. The time dimension itself will be assessed as a multi-dimensional phenomenon.

A case of water depletion threat is analyzed in order to illustrate the arguments. As we will refer to in the case study in the following sections, farmers who overdraw groundwater for irrigation act rationally from an individual and short-term point of view, as this behaviour means more water is available for irrigation and hence more crops, while, on the other hand, in the long term this means less water is available to all farmers who draw water from the same underground resource.

The structure of this chapter is as follows. In Section 4.2 some related concepts, such as time horizon, temporal perception, temporal orientation and temporal discounting will be introduced and described, among which is a powerful, yet parsimonious palette of multiple time frames, with proven reliability (Zimbardo and Boyd, 1999). In Section 4.3 the impact of aspects of the distinguished temporal boundary judgement dimensions are assessed. In section 4.4 the consequences for boundary spanning and boundary spanning strategies are assessed. In Section 4.5 conclusions can be found.

4.2 CONCEPTS

As referred to in the vast literature accumulated in the past 40 years, cognitions, or more precisely cognitive structures, are in effect concerned with forming judgements and to some extent in taking action. In essence, cognitions of actors are built on frames of references, which also include the temporal ones. The mental frames of actors are effective when processing and interpreting the data to produce an action. Recalling previous chapters, frames of reference serve as filters that reduce the amount of vast and unmanageable size input data, and affect the way people attribute significance to available action options. Temporal frames present a filter that enables people to take the input that is compatible with their temporal frames. It should be noted that while cognitions pave the way to actions, readiness to take action is not solely dependent on cognitions, but is influenced by some other factors, which are beyond the scope of this chapter. Here we will suffice to say that cognitions, in our case specifically the temporal frames, are effective in defining the domain of the input data and in assessment of the available options.

Referring to Ainslie's (2005) definition, among many similar others, a choice between options whose consequences occur at different points in time is an inter-temporal decision, and regarding the delay inherent in their consequences water-related decisions can be considered as inter-temporal. Therefore, decision makers must make tradeoffs between outcomes occurring at different points in time (Loewenstein, 1998): immediate loss versus future gain and so on. Further, most conflict and resource dilemma cases have a temporal component, as short-term individual interests versus long-term collective interests (Messick and McClelland, 1983; Hendrickx et al., 2001). Essentially, a delay of consequences inherent in water-related decisions has a reducing impact on motivation for action, as people typically find it hard to judge the future consequences. Yet the tendency to perceive future consequences is closely related to some cultural, contextual or personal variables, such as temporal orientation, time horizon and discount rate. These variables all belong to the temporal boundary judgements.

The impact of temporal factors (labelled temporal boundary judgements in this book) on resource management, or more specifically water resources management cases, is still an under-researched topic (Hendrickx et al., 2001). A quick search of academic research topics using keywords such as time horizon, temporal discounting or temporal orientation yield hundreds of articles that combine these concepts with dominantly financial decisions, while the number of research papers that combine these concepts with natural resource management or with the environmental behaviour of stakeholders is limited, yet has increased in recent years. Works by, for example, Kortenkamp and Moore (2006) on time as an individual difference in the decisions related to resource dilemmas; Milfont and Gouveia (2006) on time perspective and values in relation to environmental attitudes; Joireman et al. (2004) on future orientation and car use or generally commuting preferences; and Hendrickx et al. (2001) on temporal factors in resource dilemmas illustrate this. Throughout the chapter we will refer to the temporal factors and try to explore their effects as forms of boundary judgements. The temporal perspective covers the time horizon and temporal orientation of people, which in turn have an effect on the level of temporal discounting that people use while assessing the preferability of options with delayed consequences.

The time perspective has been considered as a determinant of human decision making; numerous psychological researches have been conducted on this topic since the 1950s. Referring to Lewin's (1951, p. 75) definition of time perspective as the 'totality of the individual's views of his psychological future and psychological past existing at a given perspective', we can well say that future and past events have an impact on present behaviour to the extent that they are actually present on the cognitive level of behavioural functioning (Nuttin, 1985, p. 54). Bandura (1997) relates time perspective to contemporary social-cognitive thinking with referral to self efficacy beliefs. Accordingly, self-efficacy beliefs are grounded in past experiences, current appraisals and reflections of future options, which altogether are reflections of temporal influence on behavioural self-regulation, forming the temporal profile of the individual in the final analysis.

In order to get an analytical view of temporal perspectives, it is instructive to start with the concept of temporal discounting, which is actually the definition of the process that occurs when making inter-temporal choices, and then to continue with the factors that are in effect during this process.

4.2.1 The Process: Temporal Discounting

Is discounting or discount rate a purely financial concept? Actually, rather implicitly, discount rates are always in effect in our non-financial decisions. When decisions whose consequences are delayed or are in question, discounting is in the scene. In economic theory, when evaluating future outcomes, future outcomes are brought to present value by some predefined discount rate, which is generally the interest rate. This discounted utility (cf. Samuelson, 1937) is generally lower than the future outcome in absolute terms. While the logic behind this normative theory holds true, in reality evaluation of temporally distant outcomes is more complicated and contains some inconsistencies and anomalies. The temporal discounting phenomenon that is mentioned here thus means more than just the normative discounted utility, but also acknowledges these anomalies. From a normative perspective it is sometimes said that the use of temporal discounting is in essence contradictory with sustainable development, although many generations later natural resources should be available also, and thus may not be considered virtually worthless. However we do not present temporal discounting as a normative concept here but as a description of how decisions are factually made.

The essence of temporal discounting is that people regard more remote outcomes as less important or less severe in magnitude than more immediate outcomes. In other words, people tend to lower the subjective value of events that would happen in the future. This discounting is affected by a variety of factors, such as the person's time horizon or temporal orientation, which together form the person-specific discount rate.

Anomalies in inter-temporal decisions can be defined by using discount rates as a variable. The discount rate indicates the relative weight one assigns to current versus future outcomes. To the degree that delayed outcomes are regarded as less important to a person, then the person's discount rate is higher. Likewise, if delay does not lower the value one assigns to future outcomes, then the person has a very low discount rate.

As well as the future outcomes, delay itself may be discounted. This means that people may not perceive the identical time intervals in the near future and far future. Just like seeing closer objects as larger than the similar sized objects that are located further away, people typically perceive the identical time periods close to the present as longer than the identical time periods that are in the far future. An example is that if you are 30 years old, the two-year period between 30 and 32 looks longer, and is expected to be more eventful than the two-year period between the ages of 55 and 57. It is possible to summarize the consequences simply by: a smaller-sooner is preferred to a larger-later gain.

It should be noted that not every person discounts with the same rate. The tendency for preferring smaller-sooner rewards for larger-later ones is regarded as an anomaly in decision making and does not apply to everyone. Even for those for whom this tendency applies, there are limits that determine how appealing the smaller-sooner option is. The person-specific discount rate is thus one variable that must be used for demonstrating the variations in temporal discounting. Discount rates differ for each individual, depending on characteristics such as temporal orientation and time horizon, among other factors. Discount rate is thus of both a situational and dispositional nature (Chapman, 1998). Conclusively, numerous studies converge in demonstrating that there is a systematic difference in the relative importance that individuals attach to temporally distant events (Svenson and Karlsson, 1989; Hendrickx et al., 1993; Strathman et al., 1994). Typically, in resource dilemma situations, individuals with low discount rates, as they consider future consequences more, are more willing to cooperate (Mannix, 1991; Hendrickx et al., 2001). Likewise, a high discount rate is an indicator of less future consideration and less inclination to cooperate.

4.2.2 The Factors

The relevant factors and variables are discussed below.

Time horizon and awareness of future consequences

While it is relatively easy to be aware of the immediate consequences in resource management decision making, this may not be the case for the delayed ones. Awareness of delayed consequences is in the first place related to one's time horizon. Defining time horizon as the most distant point in time that is considered when making a decision (Svenson and Karlsson, 1989), the time horizon is the boundary of outcomes to be considered relevant. Therefore, options available are within the limits of the horizon. The time horizon thus provides the domain of discounting. An individual with a short (or close) time horizon considers typically the near-immediate consequences and fewer options, while a further time horizon would enable the person to consider and be aware of future consequences and consider more options. Similar to mental frames, time horizon is unique to individuals, and each individual builds judgements relying on what is available within the subjective time horizon.

The concept of time horizon can be found in studies that incorporate the Consideration of Future Consequences (CFC) scale of Strathman et al. (1994), which proposes an individual difference variable that differentiates people who consider the long-term future consequences of their actions from those that are more likely to consider short-term immediate consequences. Accordingly, evidence of pro-environmental political behaviour is related with higher scores on the CFC scale.

Shorter time horizons are associated with a low tendency to cooperate in resource dilemma cases (Hendrickx et al., 2001; Kortenkamp and

Moore, 2006). The person-specific time horizon is to some extent affected by the temporal orientation of people.

Temporal orientation

Consciously or unconsciously, all individuals have a temporal frame in their mind while making decisions which have a delayed component. The frame may be the future, present or past, in its very simplistic form. When one develops a tendency towards overemphasizing a temporal frame in making decisions, or in other words, frequently presents a time perspective of the same frame, this tendency becomes a temporal bias. This can be towards a past, present or future orientation. This orientation becomes a dispositional component when chronically elicited (Zimbardo, 1997).

In Zimbardo's definition, temporal orientation is a 'unique cognitive style of processing information and acting based on a learned, preferred focus on one or another dimension of the temporal environment as past, present or future' (Zimbardo et al., 1997, p. 1020). Accordingly, when one of these preferences becomes the dominating and chronic one, the person uses only a narrow and biased temporal frame in making judgements. Temporal orientation as a disposition is predictive of individuals' daily life choices. At this point, it should be noted that, despite the subtle effect of this orientation, people are often unaware of it and its consequences and live with the enduring bias (Zimbardo et al., 1997). Zimbardo further suggests that the invisible temporal construct provides a foundation for other more visible constructs such as risk taking, sensation seeking and achievement motivation.

The most easily distinguished frames of temporal perception are present and future ones, which are often associated with achievement motivation and anticipated action consequences (as can be seen in the works of Nuttin, 1985; Strathman et al., 1994; Zaleski, 1994). In most studies western societies are associated with future orientation while oriental ones are coupled with the present. However, in reality, orientation schemes are not as simple as present and future, but include past frames and the filter through which the frames are seen, such as hedonistic and fatalistic. On top of numerous scales that aim to explain variations in time perception, Zimbardo and Boyd's (1999) Time Perception Inventory presents a powerful, yet parsimonious palette of multiple time frames, with proven reliability.

As one would expect, present-oriented people tend to rely on the immediate, salient aspects of the stimulus and social setting for their judgements and actions, while future-oriented individuals tend to build on anticipated consequences of the possible future. Past-oriented individuals tend to rely on recall of reconstructed past scenarios. The five categories of the

Zimbardo Time Perspective Inventory (ZTPI) can be summarized as follows:

1. Future: emphasis is on the future, resulting in planning and striving for the achievement of future goals. As one may expect, a future frame is associated with a high consideration of consequences, and controlled risk taking. As far as sustainability is concerned, a future frame is the most favourable orientation.
2. Present-hedonistic: emphasis is on the here and now, hence on present pleasure. This reflects a hedonistic orientation attitude toward time and life. This frame discards sacrifices today for rewards tomorrow. It involves less consideration of consequences, and is typically associated with a tendency to take risks. High levels of consumption without caring about sustainability are closely related with this view.
3. Present-fatalistic: emphasis is on the here and now but with a fatalistic, helpless and hopeless attitude toward the future and life. Individuals who hold this frame think that they have no control over the world, and they cannot make any changes in whatever is going on. Rather they believe that events are controlled by some other greater forces. Therefore a present-fatalistic frame is typically associated with low responsibility and adaptability. Holders of this frame, although they may have a consideration of future consequences, would not choose to take corrective or preventive action.
4. Past-negative: a pessimistic, negative or aversive attitude toward the past. Thinking about the negative events that happened in the past is dominant, including a deeply rooted regret. Recalling that past (memories) is of reconstructive nature rather that absolute, and that people are typically inclined to remember the dramatic or traumatic events more than the others, it can be concluded that holders of a past-negative temporal frame may be subject to substantial biases. Within the domain of natural resource use, a manifestation of past negative frame would be: measures for drought should have been taken 20 years ago, now it is too late to take action.
5. Past-positive: a warm, sentimental, nostalgic and positive construction of the past, with the motto: good old days. In the good old days: all the land was covered with trees and rivers were full of fish. Holders of this frame demonstrate the rosy retrospection bias, meaning that a realistic evaluation of past events is hindered, which weakens the ability to make causal analysis of the past actions and events. Low ability to link past actions to present or future outcomes imposes hardship on problem definition and adaptive action.

4.3 TEMPORAL DIMENSIONS OF BOUNDARY JUDGEMENTS

Many basic psychological processes, including habituation, conditioning, memory, reinforcement contingencies, self-efficacy, anticipation, violations of expectation, evolutionary adaptiveness, guilt, depression and anxiety, co-rely on some temporal aspects (Zimbardo and Boyd, 1999). Referring to the definition of boundary judgements as cognitive perceptions of actors on the relevancy of specific issues for a domain, it may be concluded that time dimensions are associated with many aspects of that domain in question. Actually, the time perspective is a general psychological construct, dominant in much human motivation and decision making (Gonzales and Zimbardo, 1985), functioning like a filter on any element of a decision: from available alternatives to with whom to cooperate. Indeed, perception of time is a fundamental determinant of election and pursuit of social goals, with important implications for emotion, cognition and motivation (Carstensen et al., 1999). A point to note here is that, while immediate outcomes or responses are related with emotions, by evolution, cognitions are rather associated with later adaptations for planning and reflective responding (Zimbardo and Boyd, 1999).

In order to address the impact of temporal dimensions of this boundary judgement, we may identify the following points:

1. (Differing) Temporal perspectives may be a source of conflict.
2. (Differing) Temporal perspectives may be a source of rivalry.
3. Temporal perspectives have impact on problem definition.
4. Temporal orientations are related to the selection of adaptive action.

In the next subsections we will further elaborate these and illustrate the arguments with citations derived from a study on water management in Konya Closed Basin (Turkey). The case study is characterized by unsustainable water use by farmers who prefer to plant sugar beet, for which the government grants a buying guarantee. Unfortunately this requires very high levels of irrigation. Farmers typically drill for artesian wells in the fields and draw substantial amounts of water, which in turn causes constant and significant drops in the groundwater level, even leading to the formation of large sinkholes in the area. The World Wildlife Fund (WWF) has been working on a capacity building project in the Konya Closed Basin and tries to promote drip irrigation systems instead of the aggressive system.

4.3.1 (Differing) Temporal Perspective as a Source of Conflict

The availability and distribution of natural resources, in our case water, create social conflict between the collective interest of society and the individual interests of its members (Van Vugt, 1999). As mentioned in the opening paragraphs, resource-based dilemmas typically have a temporal component (Dawes, 1980; Messick and Brewer, 1983; Messick and McClelland, 1983; Vlek and Keren, 1992; Van Vugt, 1999; Joireman, 2005). Behaviour which is rational from a short-term and individual point of view may result in a suboptimal outcome for people as a whole and for the individual in the long term (Messick and Brewer, 1983). Short-term outcomes of the actions are usually regarded as positive, such as getting more from the common pool and thus enjoying the further benefits of getting more, while long-term outcomes are regarded as negative, as they are associated with depletion of the common pool and thus very little for each individual to benefit. Social conflict is linked to individual variations in social value orientation, whereas temporal conflict is analyzed through individual differences in the consideration of future consequences (Joireman et al., 2001; Joireman et al., 2004). Would people still act to enjoy the short-term benefits of overusing the common pool resources if they are fully aware of the long-term consequences? Some research (for example, Joireman et al., 2004 on car use versus public transport use) reveals that an eye on the future in the form of future orientation or a long time horizon does not guarantee cooperation, however significantly there are increases in the tendency to cooperate in resource use.

Within the domain of water resources varying time perspectives might make it hard to develop a common wisdom and a rational solution that would please all the stakeholders, or even in extreme cases, might be an impediment to reach an agreement. Especially, when different parties do not share the same time horizon, it is very hard to say that the domain of the problem and relevant options are common to the parties. Limited in number, yet effective research reveals that a shorter time horizon is typically associated with a low tendency to cooperate. Hendrickx et al. (2001) present evidence on the effect of varying time horizons on actors' behaviour in resource dilemma cases. Some citations now illustrate what was encountered in the case:

> These people do not need an authority to tell them how much water to use or when. They think they have to watch their children's share in the resource as well as their neighbours. They do not know what sustainability is, but they live by it by saying that they owe their children! (Project manager of Sivas-Erzincan Rural Development Project, UNDP, Central-East Anatolia, commenting on the effective water use system of one of the villages (well known for its good management) in the area)

The above quotation addresses a mindset that considers along with the values, *now* in the form of watching the right of their neighbours, and *future* in the form of watching their children's.

> They say that *God will handle about tomorrow.*[2] How can I expect them to reduce their water drawal by only saying that with the business as usual, they will not be able to get water from the wells after a few years. (Project manager, WWF Capacity Building Project, Towards Wise Use of Konya Closed Basin, commenting on the villagers' unsustainable drawals from the groundwater)

> I do not see any reason why we need that swamp. What we need is land to grow more crops. We want this swamp to be drained and turned into arable land. The birds dwelling here are just fantasy. (Villagers in Bafa Lake region, responding to the WWF project manager while he tries to explain that a nearby swamp is a valuable wetland and has to be preserved with all its flora and fauna, including flamingos that dwell on it)

In the last quote it is possible to track how, among other differing frames of reference, temporal reference affects the assessment. In the long term, there is a clear linkage between the equilibrium of nature and the resources available to the farmers, for example, birds dwelling on the area feed on the insects that otherwise would multiply to damage the crops nearby, and thus reduce the need for chemical insecticides. Nevertheless it is possible to conclude that the time horizon of villagers of the above quote is confined to the present, which makes them only consider the short-term gains in the form of more crop rather than the equilibrium of nature, which is a long-term phenomenon.

4.3.2 (Differing) Temporal Perspective as a Source of Rivalry

While elaborating temporal rivalries some issues require attention. Actually, immediate outcomes and delayed outcomes are often rivals of each other. Put another way, there is a rivalry between today's needs, pleasures or deprivations and future needs, pleasures or deprivations. Further, as stated above, differences in stakeholders' time perspectives may be reflected in rivalries just like in the conflicts. Regarding the use of a river basin, some (future-oriented) water users may be in favour of using the water in a sustainable way (for example, drip irrigation instead of aggressive irrigation) and investing in it (infrastructure), while present-fatalistic oriented users would be against the initial cost of investment for sustainable use, and may be in favour of saving the day. The illustrations derived from the case:

> The land is valuable and fertile. We advise the farmers to plant pistachio trees, as it means good profit and requires little irrigation. However they do not prefer

> it, on the grounds that it takes years before the tree yields crop. Despite the huge irrigation requirement, cotton is what they prefer to plant, as they get the crop in just one season. (Project coordinator of Diyarbakır-Batman-Siirt Rural Development Project, UNDP, South-east Anatolia)

The above quotation refers to such a rivalry, as immediate gains from cotton and long-term and sustained gains from pistachio compete for the same resource: land. A more dramatic example of present and future as rivals for manpower is from the villagers in eastern-central Anatolia:

> When we first started our project here, I thought villagers were having the problem of funding the pesticides, or finding the market to sell their crops, and we were here to solve their problems. I am much surprised to see that they are not even interested in farming, as they say: *we cannot wait for a year or a season to get our money. It is much too late.* Instead of being patient for a season, even for very profitable industrial crops, they prefer working as foremen in small construction works around. (Project coordinator of Sivas-Erzincan Rural Development Project, UNDP, Central-East Anatolia)

4.3.3 Temporal Perspective Effects on Problem Definition

Problem perception is obviously related with one's framing and an important contributor to this framing is the temporal perspective (Loewenstein, 1998). Time horizon and temporal orientation have implications for problem definitions. As referred to above, people evaluate outcomes only within their time horizon. Likewise, people can only see the problems within their time horizon. Therefore, it is not rational to expect an actor who has a short horizon to perceive future problems which are beyond the limits of their horizon. This point matters when answering both is there a problem? and what is the problem? As for the temporal orientation, people can only perceive problems which are compatible with their orientation. An example is the problem of drought: people with a present time orientation cannot easily recognize the long-term impacts of water scarcity problems, while future-oriented people would be inclined to foresee the future consequences of a drought and recognize it as an important problem in the present too.

In order to illustrate this proposition, we may refer to the situation in Konya Closed Basin, where farmers typically plant high irrigation demanding sugar beet and continuously drill for groundwater to irrigate their field. This subsequently causes substantial drops in the groundwater level, seriously threatening the sustainability of water resources in the basin. When asked about what has been going on in the basin and what the problems are, farmers, professionals who carry out capacity building projects for sustainable water use and regional water management authorities reveal different problem definitions and it is possible to observe the temporal component in their views:

> Groundwater level drops nearly 100 cm a year. It is not being replenished enough. This means that the business as usual is not sustainable. It is mainly due to the irrigation habits and crop preferences of farmers, they consume far too much water. We need to change the pattern of water use before it is too late. (Project manager, WWF Capacity Building Project, Towards Wise Use of Konya Closed Basin)

Villager farmers in Konya Closed Basin, who get their irrigation water from the artesian wells, have to dig deeper each year in order to access water. They are aware that there is a water scarcity problem. However, they do not link the decrease in water resources with their irrigation habits. The slowly accumulated and delayed consequence of present water use habits, which in the end leads to substantial decrease in the water level, does not fit in their time horizon, as their time horizon is not that long. Rather, they tend to think that the availability of water resources is dependent on seasonal snow or rainfall, which, in turn, is believed to be an act of God. This serves to illustrate the present-fatalistic time frame.

4.3.4 Temporal Orientation has an Effect on the Selection of an Adaptive Action

Problem definition and selection of adaptive action, though closely related, are not actually predictors of each other. Yet, the impact of the temporal perspective is somewhat similar on both: present-hedonistics and present-fatalistics are less willing to take adaptive action while future-oriented are more open to adaptation.

However, at times, the temporal orientation may hinder an adaptive action even though the problem is defined correctly. Especially present-fatalistic frames cause deviations. An example is that even though an individual with a present-fatalistic orientation recognizes the drought problem, the person may not bother to take action as this represents fate and is meant to happen.

There are consistent, yet few, studies which reveal that the temporal perspective is closely associated with risk taking behaviour (e.g. Zimbardo, 1997; Zimbardo and Boyd, 1999; Milfont and Gouveia, 2006 and so on). Accordingly, future-oriented people are typically less inclined to take risks, while present-hedonistics have a higher tendency to take risks. In Zimbardo and Boyd (1999) a strong linkage between risky (fast, ignoring rules and regulations and so on) driving habits and a present-temporal orientation is proven. We may well regard risk taking behaviour as related to adaptive action. As adaptive action involves exploring the options available for the case and acting in line with the best interest of the whole, risk is by definition inherent to all options. In the pursuit of sustainability, doing nothing or choosing the business as usual option might well be some of the riskiest options. This does not, however, imply that all forms of adaptive action are benefiting long-term sustainability.

Given the decrease in groundwater problem in Konya Closed Basin, the municipal authorities have also been working on the problem. From their perspective, all available options to provide irrigation water should be considered, including the water transfer from the neighbouring Göksu Basin. Authorities who have to work to get the citizens' vote are hardly in a position to consider the long-term drawbacks of inter-basin water transfer that are emphasized in, for example, the European Water Framework Directive:

> As well as building capacity for farmers, we have to build capacity for the local authorities. It is very hard to communicate the danger of transferring water from another basin. This is definitely not the solution. This basin (Konya Closed Basin) has to be self-sufficient for the sake of natural equilibrium. (Project manager, WWF Capacity Building Project, Towards Wise Use of Konya Closed Basin)

4.4 IMPLICATIONS FOR BOUNDARY SPANNERS

Up to this point, a view has been presented of how preferences are affected by variations in the temporal dimensions of boundary judgements. In this section we will try to refer to the implications of the temporal dimensions from the point of view of the boundary spanner, presenting some hints for productive boundary spanning activities.

Convergent boundary judgements were in the introductory chapters referred to as a factor that enhances the likelihood of success in boundary spanning activities. Hence, convergent temporal perspectives – which might actually be rare, given the heterogeneity of the parties involved – would increase the chance of success. Our position is that understanding other people's time frames, be they convergent or divergent, and adjustment of a frame to span other people's frames would be a key attribute for the boundary spanner. In this respect, we have identified three attributes for the boundary spanner (see Section 4.1) and tried to present an analysis of how a boundary spanner might manage across varying temporal frames in Section 4.2.

4.4.1 What Time Should it be for the Boundary Spanner?

The boundary spanner should be aware of the variations in people's time

Referring to adaptive water management as being about opening up to strategic solution opportunities rather than focusing on the effectiveness and cost-effectiveness of short-term actions, and on focusing more on the long-term, large impact improvements, we may well argue that the boundary spanner has to have a wide time perspective in order to have a wide domain perception of problems, options and consequences.

Reflexivity, variability and redundancy are to be mentioned among the features of boundary spanning activities. Among these, reflexivity, which implies a continuous process of reconsideration of frames and goals, is also related to the wide spectrum of temporal perspectives that the boundary spanner should be aware of. Accordingly, reflexivity should cover the consideration of various temporal orientation schemes and time horizons of varying lengths. By acknowledging the variations in temporal perspective, the boundary spanner gains insight on how conflicts are formed, what kind of different problem definitions are at stake and what the options for adaptive actions are.

Not all the time can the boundary spanner get an understanding of the other parties, for example, why the others are not able to see the problems or possible actions in a similar and converging manner. One of the many reasons for this might be differences in temporal perspective. Hence, a boundary spanner might be expected to be aware of the existence of shorter time horizons which may limit other people in their understanding. As referred to in Chapter 1, adaptive management implies a shift in thinking about appropriate time horizons and strategies for the resource manager. The consequence has to be that boundary spanners should be able to recognize the variations in the time horizons of different parties involved.

The boundary spanner's own time perspective should be flexible and unbiased

Can we speak of an ideal time perspective for a boundary spanner? Putting all the concepts that are mentioned above together, it is possible to sketch such an ideal temporal perspective. First, as a boundary spanner should always keep their focus on sustainability, the approach to inter-temporal decisions should be as unbiased by the discounting tendency as possible. In other words, a boundary spanner should be aware of the temporal discounting phenomenon, and should try not to devalue future outcomes in comparison to outcomes of present time.

In inter-temporal choice cases, just like the other decisions, people typically base their decisions upon a reference point, a psychologically relevant point which determines what is gain or what is loss (Loewenstein, 1998). An illustrative example may be whether people evaluate the abundance of water resources by comparing with that of the previous year or with reference to what they expect to have next irrigation season? A boundary spanner thus should construct a rational and carefully selected reference point to base evaluations upon, and pay attention to the reference times of actors. A point to keep in mind is that, rather than integrating delayed consumption plans, people often represent future consumption options as gains or losses or as deviations from some standard such as a past level of consumption (Loewenstein, 1998).

Recalling that the time horizon sets the boundaries for the available options or the foreseeable problems, the boundary spanner should preferably have a wide time horizon which would enable consideration of more options and more problems. Alongside, a boundary spanner, while seeing as far as possible, should be able to cut the time line at the same point as the other actors (Svenson, 1979) in order to attain empathy.

In the above sections, we emphasized that the ZTPI frame is associated with planning for the future. Recalling that individuals without a well-developed future frame may not have the cognitive scaffolding on which to hang mental scenarios of the negative future consequences of their present behaviour (Frederick et al., 2002), it is essential that the boundary spanner should have a firm frame to base future related plans upon within the domain of water management. Further, it is essential to understand that actors may have different temporal orientations and these differences should be taken into consideration in any boundary spanning activities. This implies that a successful communication strategy for actors with present-hedonistic orientations may not work for those with, for instance, present-fatalistic orientations. Zimbardo and Boyd (1999) refer to balanced time orientation, which is an idealized mental framework that allows individuals to flexibly switch temporal frames among past, future and present, depending on situational demands, resource assessments, or personal and social appraisals. Thus a balanced time orientation is foremost a multiple time orientation, enabling an understanding of and ability to speak with people of various singular orientations. Accordingly, holders of such a balanced time orientation on average can make compromises, or balance among the representations of past experiences, present desires and future consequences. Therefore, for a boundary spanner, rather than just a strict future orientation which would allow them to focus on sustainability and make future plans, a balanced time orientation would enable them to develop empathy and be more integrative.

The boundary spanner should understand what time is for others
Success of boundary spanning activities to some extent may depend on the spanner's ability to understand the drivers beneath the actions of the other parties. Being aware of why people do the things that they do may well lead to solutions as presenting the key to: how can this action be changed? At this point, the ability to understand and speak the same language with others is an important asset. The temporal perspective, along with the other frames, defines the language and, conclusively, a boundary spanner should understand the characteristics of the temporal perspective of the other parties, for example, which temporal orientation schemes are prevalent and the length of the time horizons.

4.4.2 Managing Across Time

Boundary spanning people of different temporal frames calls for the attribute receptivity. The boundary spanner should seek for opportunities where people see a benefit in cooperating and seek for opportunities to create synergy. Keeping in mind that unmatching temporal perspectives might be a factor in people's failure to cooperate, a boundary spanner might be bound to change the case to match the temporal frames of people.

Essentially people with different temporal perspectives often also have different motivations that fit to their temporal perspectives. These can be based on their understanding of the reality or on the basis of their own values and interests. The boundary spanner thus should recognize these variations and be able to approach them accordingly. With regard to concrete actions required of people, these might involve using measures that make required action compatible with their own values and interests. These values and interests previously shaped their negative motivation. Often such measures adapt reality to their boundary judgements, for instance, temporal boundary judgements. Consider the following quote:

> There was an enormous resistance to shifting from traditional irrigation to drip irrigation. It was very difficult to persuade them that this was in their best interest in the long run, as the initial cost of installing the pipes were high. We provided them with extremely cheap loans to buy the equipment and pay for the installment. They still are not much interested in sustainability, but they understood that their water costs will be lower and they still will get the same crop yield. (Business development expert, Agricultural Bank of Turkey, trying to create a market for drip irrigation system loans in the Central Anatolia)

The business development expert recognized the short time horizon of the farmers. Instead of presenting them with the option of shifting to drip irrigation from a long-term perspective, the expert engaged in speaking with the same language, mentioning the decreased costs of water, which represents purely a short-term motivation.

In some cases, where people's time perspective reference points are the determinants of their likelihood to cooperate, boundary spanners need to understand the reference point on which people base their assessments and seek ways for ensuring cooperation either by presenting the cooperative option in a way compatible with their reference point, or by completely changing that reference.

4.5 CONCLUSION

Most policy decisions and actions within the domain of water resource management have delayed consequences, which introduces temporal dimensions. It may be concluded that the time dimension in itself is multi-dimensional. It is useful to refer to some related concepts, such as time horizon, temporal perception, temporal orientation and temporal discounting.

Throughout the chapter, we have presented a knowledge base on how delay itself and varying conceptions of delay affect decisions within the domain of water resources management. We addressed the variability of actors' temporal perspectives and tried to derive implications for boundary spanners.

In a nutshell, typically people who discount future outcomes too much are less willing to cooperate, and those who discount less are more inclined to cooperate (Mannix, 1991; Hendrickx et al., 2001). Discount rate might be due to the temporal orientation of people, for example, past, present or future, or due to the length of their time horizon. While not in absolute terms, people with a wider time horizon might be considered as more likely to cooperate for adaptive action (Hendrickx et al., 2001). The opposite also holds true: people with a short time horizon might find less reason and incentive to cooperate. Regarding the consideration of future consequences, people who are more future oriented typically show more inclination to cooperate. ZTIP was discussed as a framework that specifies the views: people who have a present-fatalistic and present-hedonistic frame show less intention to cooperate while future frame holders are much more willing to cooperate.

For productive boundary spanning activities, it is crucial to be proactive, which requires a great deal of understanding of the boundary judgements and an ability to make integrated plans. A boundary spanner, while avoiding the temporal discounting bias as much as possible, should have a flexible temporal frame, which would enable them to see the future as realisticly as possible and enable them to empathize with the temporal frames of other people in order to ensure productive boundary spanning activities. In that respect, it was concluded that a boundary spanner should seek for opportunities to present cooperation options in a way that is compatible with the frames of the other people or seek ways to change their frames where possible.

NOTES

1. Plav: pronunciation of *pilav*, Turkish word for rice, which is a major food like bread.
2. In Turkish: '*Seneye Allah Kerim*', a very commonly used phrase for the cases where one does not need to think of what would happen in the coming days or years, as God would take care of the future developments.

5. Space for water and boundary spanning governance

Hans Bressers, Simone Hanegraaff and Kris Lulofs

5.1 INTRODUCTION

Contemporary climate change leads to irregularities in rainfall and river levels. Protection against river floods has become more and more difficult. In order to prevent the excessive costs – and sometimes even impossibilities – of continuously strengthening dikes for very rare peak levels, a new policy has been developed. This policy lowers top peak river levels by enabling controlled inundation of areas that are physically prepared for that function. This includes means to protect inhabitants, their houses and cattle if inundation is effectuated. The case analyzed in this chapter concerns an area that represents one of the first Dutch official and inhabited retention areas of contemporary water management. The initial case description originated from an extensive evaluation study on this case, commissioned by the involved water authority (Lulofs, 2003).

The tributary river that is relevant in this case study flows from its German origins into the IJssel Lake in the centre of the Netherlands, just after being merely connected to – not even flowing into – the river IJssel, one of the branches of the Rhine. The location is in the east of the Netherlands, part of the sub-catchment area of Rhine-east, as defined for the implementation of the EU Water Framework Directive. The river is called the Vecht.

This chapter follows the issues of attention as stipulated in Chapter 2. In Section 5.2 the case history will be told and the various linkages between the initial water management purpose and other purposes will be illuminated. In Section 5.3 we will explain the perspective of various phases of the process from the characteristics of the actors involved. In Section 5.4 the boundary issues will be identified and the degree to which the governance context was helpful for productive boundary spanning. In Section 5.5 the influence of the structural context of the process is assessed. In Section 5.6 the strategies used for managing complexity by boundary spanning are reviewed. In Section 5.7 some observations and conclusions are presented.

5.2 PROCESSES AND COUPLING

The story starts when in October 1998 the river Vecht, coming from Germany, was rising to such an extent that four towns were seriously threatened, also because the rising water eroded the stability of protective works. On the basis of emergency authorities given by law and a semi-official, and for the public an unknown manual on what to do in these kinds of situations (even suggesting this particular area) the decision was taken to prepare the case study area for evacuation and deliberate flooding. The area was closed and controlled by the police and a crane was installed on top of the dike to take action. Ultimately, and by a narrow margin, the action could be cancelled. The flood crisis and its immediate aftermath can be seen as the first of the three processes that make up this story. We will briefly describe these processes and discuss which spatio-temporal or sectoral linkages were established that result from some form of boundary spanning.

5.2.1 Crisis and Aftermath

Directly after the flood crisis the inhabitants of the area, mostly farmers, were shocked. While before World War II flooding was not an unusual phenomenon, protective works had been greatly improved afterwards. The well kept dikes around the area proved to be no guarantee at all that their properties were safe. It was completely unknown to the public that in a crisis manual the area was designated to be sacrificed if necessary. Although during the development of the policy plan Vechtvisie (Outlook for river Vecht) (1997) there had been some deliberation on the possibility to equip the area to be a designated retention area, the decision was then made not to do so in the immediate future and only to reassess this issue after 2002 (Vechtvisie, 1997, pp. 55, 60, 78, 84–5).

After the crisis, the water authority and the agricultural association (GTLO) took the initiative for a public meeting with the inhabitants for consultation about future prospects. The inhabitants demanded that such unprepared crisis situations would not occur again and that measures needed to be taken. The water authority agreed and made an unconditional promise that they would equip the area as a retention area with all the facilities needed to prevent damage to buildings and people. Though as a process the crisis and the meeting form a brief episode, it is dealt with here because of its crucial importance for the central decision-making process to follow. It shows that the next and central process did not start at a *tabula rasa*. It was probably more using a window of opportunity (Kingdon, 1995; Zahariadis, 1999).

In this process the following linkage was established:

1. The linkage that takes place here is that the crisis awareness and safety concerns of the citizens were linked with the perspective on the possible future creation of a retention area, that previously was as much inspired by the purpose of nature development as it was by the water safety issue and was part of the space for water policy innovation. Both temporal and sectoral boundaries were thus spanned.

5.2.2 Challenges to Integrated Decision Making

In the subsequent planning and decision-making process (the main process in this case), the central arena became the Sub-area Committee Gramsbergen that was to elaborate the integrated area-oriented policy on this area as a designated precious cultural landscape. This committee was already working on this task before the flood crisis. What is new is that the development of the retention area became a prioritized and major subject, while previously it was postponed to be reconsidered after 2002. In this committee the municipality, the water authority, the province and the agricultural association were represented, the last one providing the chair and two members, of which one actually lived in the area. The setting of the integrated area-oriented policy scheme deliberately strives for a lot of sectoral policy integration. It also requires that all concrete steps will be taken voluntarily by the partners involved, thereby restricting the acceptability of using formal powers to a large extent. We concentrate on some of the main issues of this decision-making process.

In the committee the discussion initially concentrated to a large extent on nature development, arousing the member from the agricultural association that was also an inhabitant, who felt that the quality of the agricultural infrastructure in the area should be a main concern. He was accused of mixing personal scale interests with the general scale area planning discussion and eventually left the committee. This was, however, for the agricultural association a signal to take the inhabitant's interests seriously and it started to make an inventory of the wishes of the inhabitants. This proved important to channel the raised commotion from the citizens and to mediate between them and the water authority. The gathered wishes concentrated on the facilities (impact on living conditions, guaranteed dry access) and financial damage compensation (both property value and inundation compensation).

Meanwhile the purpose of substantial nature development (which would have brought subsidies for the project as a whole) proved unfeasible, at least in the voluntary context of the area-oriented policy. When the province decided not to accept already fallow grounds as part of the newly to be developed nature, it effectively de-coupled this sectoral purpose. (Salient detail: in the implementation phase, the third of our processes, a farmer offered his area to be sold for nature development after all, making a re-coupling of the purpose feasible at the very end of the process!)

From the European Interreg programme IRMA (Interreg Rhine Meuse Activities), meanwhile, a very substantial subsidy had been obtained, together with the matching funds from the environment ministry ultimately covering approximately half of the expenditure. The programme sponsors projects with an integrated approach: 'A permanent improvement in high water policies and protection can only be achieved through integrated action in the fields of water management, spatial planning, economy, nature protection and agriculture as well as with physical planning' (IRMA programme, 2007). So, it fitted very well with the integrated approach of the area-oriented policy scheme. The principal requirement that caused a lot of pressure and trouble was that all subsidized activities had to be realized before the end of 2001. This was transposed in the process into an extra effort to keep all relationships in the network, both inside and outside of the committee, as pleasant as possible. This implies urging the water authority to achieve consensus with the inhabitants with regard to their wishes and with regard to the necessary land acquisition. Expropriation was furthermore not an option since area-oriented policy is based on voluntariness.

A big issue that popped up, unexpectedly and late in the process, was the necessity to change the municipal zoning plan. This was a clear misjudgement of the water authority and its advisors (both their own judicial advisor and the consultancy firm that was hired to speed up the process). The representative of the municipality had spoken before about this issue but was not taken very seriously, until in the beginning of 2000 he actually threatened to effectively halt all preparatory activities that had started by then. The enormous time pressure created overlap with the in principle following process of implementation. The water authority found itself at an awkward moment (remember the high time pressure) in a very dependent position. Lobbied by (representatives of) local inhabitants, the municipal council acted as a defender of the area's inhabitants' interests (even while also other parts of their towns would be threatened by flooding). The province refused to step in and use its influence and powers to speed up the process. Some inhabitants submitted objections that in principle could cause lengthy procedures, likely partly under the guidance of the agricultural association. Retreating fully and continuing the old situation of a non-prepared, but still designated area to be flooded when necessary to protect towns would, however, not only not satisfy the water authority's own purposes, but also break the unconditional promise made to the inhabitants at the meeting directly after the crisis. The water authority had no alternative than to agree to all demands from the municipality, including some that referred to individual farms and a guarantee to compensate all damages. Only then the municipality cooperated with special regulations that enabled the start of the activities pending the formal approval of the zoning plan. However, there were considerable differences between the cooperative civil servants, the mayor and aldermen that were especially weary of possible plan damage claims, and the members of the council. This differentiation explains why the municipality could change so quickly to active cooperation once the barriers were removed. The necessary permits were issued in October 2001, only months before the deadline of the IRMA subsidy. Ultimately the last remaining formal objections were withdrawn, again likely under the influence of the agricultural association that had the procedures used to exert maximum pressure, but also was aware of the fact that stubborn objections by individual inhabitants/farmers could endanger the whole project, which by now was adapted to the wishes of many.

In this process the following additional linkages were established:

2. Inserting the planning of the retention area in the area-oriented policy implied a broad sectoral linking of flood protection with outlook on physical planning (strangely enough without attention for formal physical planning), nature, landscape and in principle also the infrastructure for agriculture.
3. Later efforts by the agricultural association to channel the wishes of the inhabitants led to the issue of living conditions for inhabitants (dikes too close around houses), and financial compensation to enter the scene.
4. The problems with land acquisition for nature development led to boundaries being brought up towards this previously very important aspect (only to be realized coincidentally in the third, implementation, process).
5. A large European subsidy (from Interreg) provided much finance but also a huge time pressure. So linking temporal scales became an overwhelming issue, for the planning, for the next issue for linkage and physical zoning planning, but also for the building activities (see the following description of the implementation process).

6. While physical planning was already included as a perspective in the area-oriented policy scheme, the formal physical planning requirements were overlooked until they were forced upon the process, making linking with those under high pressure unavoidable.

5.2.3 Working Under Pressure: No Time To Lose

Under the given time pressure it was no surprise that the actual implementation (specifying and construction) had to start while the planning process was still unfinished. The inhabitants and the agricultural association representing them claimed that valuation of property to be sold to the water authority was impossible, as long as the physical measures taken and the resulting living and working conditions were not yet fixed. In practice, the water authority faced a lousy negotiation position. Everybody knew it was under time pressure, expropriation was not feasible, the inhabitants/landowners communicated among each other proudly displaying their negotiation successes – and sometimes exaggerating them – effectively creating a race to the top (for them) and confronting the water authority with ever new demands. In addition – after some confusion about to what extent the agricultural association would also provide advice in individual cases (a branch of the national association does, but for pay) several external advisors were hired by the inhabitants that did not ease the negotiations, but boosted the results.

Even when the necessary permissions and land was obtained, the activities were not an easy job, on the contrary. Even though, ultimately, a six months extension was obtained from the IRMA administrators, time pressure was intense, since only from October onwards could the real work start. This severely overstressed the supervising of building capacity, caused several irritations and led to inefficiencies, such as working large scale under very adverse weather conditions. At some point almost all parties involved had the inclination to stop this madness: the inhabitants, the building contractors, the supervising consultancy. However, the guillotine of the subsidy deadline made this impossible. As a matter of fact, though the budget was indeed exceeded as one would expect under these circumstances (half a million on a 12 million Euro budget), this does not really represent an unusual degree.

Mid 2002, less than four years after the flood crisis, the retention area was realized.[1] Now, in hindsight, the retention area North and South Meene case is presented at many fora as a successful example and is favourably compared with other projects that got really stuck somewhere in their trajectory.

While in this third process no new linkages were made, apart from the

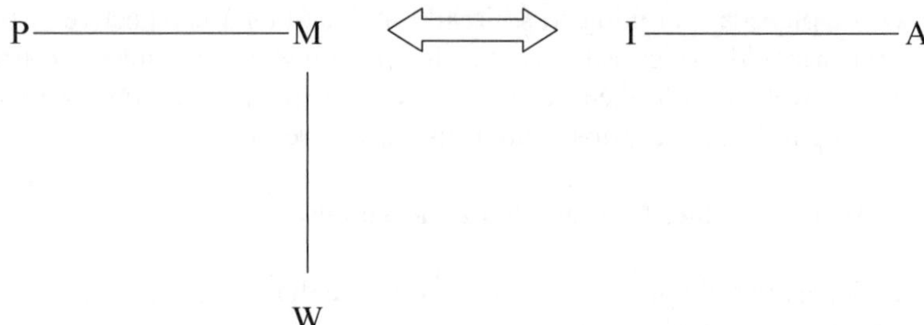

Notes: W water authority, I inhabitants, P province, M municipality, A agricultural association, ⇔ central interaction.

Figure 5.1 Actor constellation flood crisis

lucky re-coupling of nature development to the project that we mentioned before, it should be noted that especially the linking of temporal scales that stemmed from the Interreg subsidy was a menacing challenge to the process.

5.3 ACTORS AND THEIR MOTIVATION, COGNITIONS AND RESOURCES AFFECTING THE PROCESS

Each process had some sub-processes of interaction between actors on specific issues. In this section an overview is given of these actor constellations and the interaction that took place is explained from the actor characteristics: the motivation, cognitions and resources of the actors involved (see Chapter 2, and for more details Bressers, 2004).

5.3.1 The Flood Crisis

The actor constellation during the flood crisis consists of the water authority, the inhabitants, the province, the municipality and the agricultural association (Figure 5.1). The central interaction was between the latter two actors. During the thrilling days of the flood crisis the inhabitants were negatively motivated for the inundation and evacuation that was suggested by the crisis manual. In fact, they were as shocked as they were ignorant before that this could happen (cognitions). However there was nothing they could have done to prevent it when it would be decided (power). The municipality did have enough knowledge (cognitions) and resources (capacity and power) to do so (the police have been actually on stage with orders for evacuation). However their motivation to follow the manual in this was only positive when it would become unavoidable. Luckily this did not happen. If put through, forced cooperation would have generally been the case (Bressers, 2004, p. 298).

While in the first sub-process the arena was partially the site itself, the next story was confined in space and time to a crucial meeting in the back-room of a pub, organized by the agricultural association and the water authority. Here the inhabitants were still shocked by threat of deliberate inundation (and its secret policy basis in a manual) and urged measures to protect them and their property when flooded, also fearing for the value of their property now that the status of their area had been revealed. This point was well taken by the water authority that regarded protection as their core business (motivation). The concept of what to do was already there in the form of the policy innovation of a well-prepared retention area (cognitions) and the only resource needed at this stage was decisiveness, which it displayed. While the motivations of the actors involved had different roots, they were pointing in the same direction. Not hampered by false cognitions nor lacking resources, consequently measures were announced to enable controlled inundation and the protection of people and buildings. So there was agreement by the evening.

5.3.2 Planning and Decision Making

The main stage (arena) for the next process was not so confined in time and place, the so-called Sub-area Committee Gramsbergen, making the Area perspective WCL Vecht Regge. This committee was already active but the preparation of the retention area was now made part of its task. As the sub-processes are rather integrated, we will show the actor constellation in just one figure (Figure 5.2).

Because it fitted better in this overview, in the actor constellation above also the interaction on agreeing measures with individual inhabitants is included, even though this ran through both the planning and the implementation phase. While the main interaction on the design of the plan took place in the slipstream of the developments in the relationship with the inhabitants and later also in the physical planning process, it is not separately analyzed.

Though not directly in the sub-area committee, in fact the inhabitants of the area were central stage most of the time. Only in the beginning were their wishes more or less ignored, a fact that later still had some impact on the degree of trust in the interactions with the water authority. Their main motivation was initially mainly concentrated on the necessity of measures to protect themselves and their property, but when the fear of the flood had

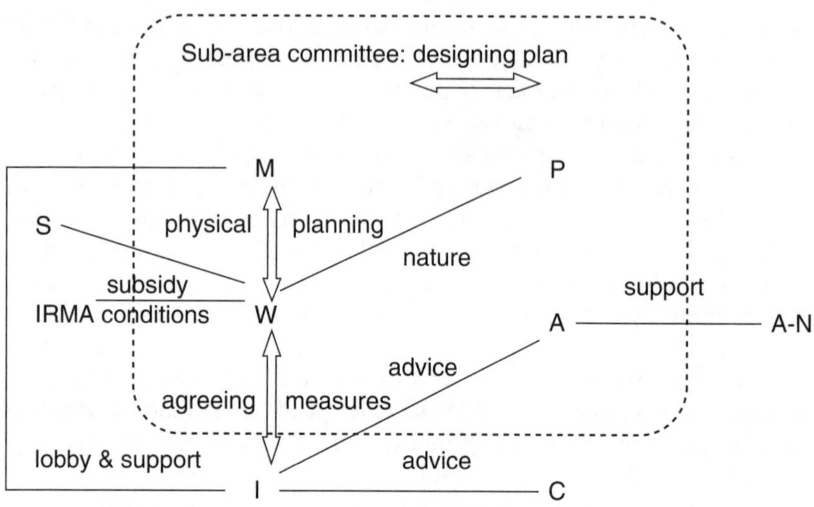

Note: New acronyms: A-N national agricultural association, C private consultants, IRMA Interreg programme, S construction supervising consultancy.

Figure 5.2 Actor constellation planning and decision-making process

faded, the impact of the measures on living conditions and the compensation for damages became more important. When issues of land acquisition arose later in the process, many were very eager to get the most out of it, even with the help of advisors. So in many issues their motivation went quickly from supporting to opposing the proposals of the water authority, in the sense that they wanted more and more adaptations to their wishes. For them, and thus inevitably for the water authority too, it became a negotiation game. Their cognitions of the situation and its opportunities and threats evolved, as well as their awareness of the resources at their disposal to influence the process. For instance, these were the rules of the area-oriented policy process in which framework the committee worked, urging that all action would be based on voluntary agreement, strengthening the position of the inhabitants considerably.

Supporting their positions, not only the individual consultants that several inhabitants hired later in the process, and the agricultural association that inventoried their wishes and brought them into the process – which was helpful – but also the municipal council acted, and even went as far as demanding solutions that were satisfactory for the inhabitants in individual cases. The municipality in general displayed a motivation that was more representative of the wishes of the inhabitants of the area than the need to quickly realize the project to protect the towns that needed this retention area in case of threatening water levels. With this municipalities' stance, the physical zoning plan process thus became a hard nut to crack for the water authority. Especially since the powers in the zoning process are on the side of the municipality, with, in addition, ample options for consultation and objection for the inhabitants.

The province took a deliberate back stage position, at crucial moments not supporting the water authority. It kept a strict interpretation of rules on nature development which made the inclusion of this objective in the plans virtually impossible. It also initially denied the inclusion of the retention area in the indicative regional physical plan, since it preferred to follow and facilitate agreements of other actors rather than acting itself towards the municipalities' zoning plan changes (displaying process objectives rather than contents objectives as a source of motivation). The retention area indeed was included in the provincial water plan, although not in the region plan. Of course, the province is not always a single actor, and in this case this shows. The region plan counts for the issue of getting through the zoning plan requirements.

This left the water authority in a rather isolated position, with its motivation to realize the retention area to protect people and property, but also to improve the robustness of this part of their territory to more varying water levels, and – if possible – to realize more nature development. Despite their public–private partnership with a construction supervising consultancy, enabling them to issue some contracts before the IRMA deadline, they did not get proper advice on the necessity of a change in the municipal zoning plan, making them work under false cognitions. As for their resources, their formal powers were not applicable under the integrated area-oriented policy scheme and due to the Interreg subsidy there was a serious lack of the resource, time. Money was available but still only a restricted amount. There was also the fall back option to retreat fully and continue the old situation of a non-prepared, but still designated area to be flooded when necessary to protect towns: an option that was worse for the inhabitants and in fact an all lose option. A further problem with this option was the unconditional promise made during the initial meeting with the inhabitants just after the crisis. Nevertheless this lingering option might very well have been a hidden and unacknowledged source of power of the water authority, for instance, to let the municipality realize after a while that, being a co-government, they should be more cooperative, or to let the agricultural association guiding the inhabitants with remaining formal objections to withdraw these.

But in the last phase of decision making there was (often already while the construction had started) also an actor that had a double role. On the one hand, the agricultural association acted as an interest group that promoted the interests of the inhabitants (all farmers) and stimulated them to make good use of their legal rights to object and appeal. This could have been very disruptive and could have easily caused the failure of the whole process in light of the rather individualistic attitude that by then many inhabitants held. However, when a majority of the inhabitants had reached an agreement with the water authority, it became a threat to them and the association alike that a very small number of more stubborn farmers would block any progress and could even provide an excuse for the water authority to call the whole project off. At this stage, on the other hand, the association became a broker and stimulated the last remaining appeals to be withdrawn.

All in all this resulted in a rather turbulent process with conflicts between the water authority and the inhabitants and high time pressure. With power not clearly on its side the water authority had no other option than to ensure a positive motivation with the inhabitants and municipality by making many concessions. In the first year the stalemates often emerged as predicted by theory in such instances; the flexible line of the water authority, gradually satisfying the demands of the inhabitants, resulted after 2000 in more constructive processes.

5.3.3 Construction

The construction process moved the arena back to the site where it all began. The central interaction was between three contractors and the area itself while also the water authority, the constructing supervising consultancy and the inhabitants played roles in the actor constellation. The main interactions took place in the field.

The high time pressure caused the process to speed up, but at the price of a lot of irritation and inefficiencies. These accumulated even to the extent that the motivation of the actors involved almost completely faded away. Contractors that did not want to continue their work and had to be forced and inhabitants that denied contractors entrance to their property were signs of such tensions. While at the end the realization of the project did prove not to be beyond the capacity of the constructors – though at the expense of some extra money resources – they were not convinced of the feasibility during part of the process.

5.4 BOUNDARY JUDGEMENTS AND THEIR IMPACTS

Boundary judgements are definitions of systems and problems, which underpin conceptual models. For the purpose of our case study, they can be defined as socially constructed definitions of the domain of relevance (in terms of relevant scales, sectors and temporal dimensions – see Chapters 1 and 2). Boundary judgements that differ among actors can cause incoherence and can even be a source of conflict. Boundary judgements that are too narrow for the adequate use of the innovation or so wide that complexity becomes unmanageable can also stagnate all progress.

In this section we will contemplate what kind of boundary judgements of the actors involved can be observed and how they could have influenced the actor characteristics and the resulting processes. Some relevant boundary spanning was already mentioned as instances of linking. Some of these linkages did not really have the character of boundary disputes over the relevant domain while there actually was no disagreement about the linkage. But there are more boundary judgements that are recognizable and had an impact on the process.

5.4.1 Spatial Dimensions of the Domain

A first issue is the location of the retention capacity to be created. The location was taken as granted right from the start. While this may be self-evident at the confined level of the municipality(-ies) nearby or even the water authority, it could have been different within the larger Vecht basin, including the German part.

Neighbouring water authorities and German authorities were, however, reluctant to integrate their areas in a more encompassing review of flood lowering possibilities. Nowadays such an approach is required by several policies, among which, the European Water Framework Directive. The water authority of Velt and Vecht also had problems with enlarging the domain in the sense that they feared the situation in which they would not be in control of the operational handling of the inundation process. Being dependent on a German governor when the safety of Dutch downstream towns requires action (implying the flooding of German areas) was not perceived as an appealing situation.

On the other hand, many inhabitants have a quite understandable not in my back yard (NIMBY) attitude, by which the initial support for the realization of the retention area waned. Their considerations were often confined to the direct surroundings of their own dwellings.

Another spatial boundary judgement became obvious when the province did not see it as its task to play an active role in helping to fulfil the physical planning procedure requirements to enable the retention area and wanted to follow and accommodate rather than guide the local level authorities. Of course the water authority disagreed with that emphasis on the very local scale by a government that was able to overview the regional scale.

5.4.2 Sectoral Dimensions of the Domain

Several stakeholders emphasized their own sectoral interest, sometimes even while fully ignoring the others. The water authority concentrated on flood lowering capacity and nature development. The agricultural association assessed the project on its role to improve the agricultural structure. Also recreation and tourism are often part of integrated area-oriented programmes. Many inhabitants felt they and their interests were excluded from initial planning under this policy scheme. The inhabitants, and also the city council in support of them, assessed the plans on the basis of value of property, consequences for living conditions and/or financial compensation.

The too narrow initial sectoral boundary judgements also led to the late recognition of the relevance of the official municipal physical zoning plan and confusion over the legal basis for planning damage compensations.

5.4.3 Temporal Dimensions of the Domain

A relevant background here is that the area policy committee initially postponed decision making on peak level protection by a retention area to 2002. Initially this was before the 1998 crisis and thus beyond the immediate time horizon that aroused any actor to take action.

The time perspective also played a role while many inhabitants proved to have a short time perspective, losing their support for measures rather quickly after the almost-disaster. So during the course of time of the case period the motivation to cooperate was for a while wrongly assessed by the water authority. They did not reckon with such swift erosion of the motivation to cooperate that existed shortly after the crises.

By far the most compelling time issue was the European Interreg IRMA subsidy regulations that fixed very short temporal requirements – even though these were ultimately relaxed by half a year – conflicting with other procedures' (and related actors') time perspectives.

The boundary judgement issues described above can be related to the five (excluding the almost de-coupling of nature issue) linkages that are listed in Section 5.2.

1. When the idea of the retention area was linked to the safety concerns of the inhabitants after the flood crisis, the previous time perspective to be considered after 2002 gave way to a perspective of immediate action. This also reinforced the taken for granted location of the spatial area to be considered for retention.
2. When the idea of the retention area was inserted in the ongoing area-based policy, it was linked with issues concerning landscape, nature,

recreation and infrastructure for agriculture. Even this broad collection of actors did explicitly regard the concerns of individual inhabitants out of scope, eventually leading to:

3. Later efforts by the agricultural association to channel the demands of the inhabitants. This included issues of living conditions for inhabitants (dikes too close around houses), and financial compensation to enter the scene. But by then the domain specification of many inhabitants had already shrunk in terms of time, place and subject to their immediate individual circumstances (leaving the agricultural association wrestling between its collective action and member support roles).
4. The large European subsidy provided much finance but also a huge time pressure conflicting with other time perspectives.
5. The formal physical planning requirements were overlooked until they were forced upon the process. Clearly they were out of focus in the domain specifications of almost all actors involved.

5.5 COHERENCE AND FRAGMENTATION IN THE GOVERNANCE CONTEXT

The structural context of the process consists of the elements of public governance and the property and use rights that are not specifically developed for the processes studied (see Chapter 2). Innovations often require new combinations of scales, actors, perspectives, strategies and resources compared to the ones that have developed in the past for more conventional purposes (Bressers and Kuks, 2003, 2004). This implies that the extent of relevant elements of governance has to be widened. The real boundary spanning challenge, however, is not the widening of the extent, but the protection or regaining of the coherence within and between these elements. The issues to be assessed can be addressed in a couple of questions: is there any development towards more coherence – or restoring coherence – of these elements of governance during the process? Or is the opposite true and was fragmentation the result of the widened domain? And if so, to what degree was this a troublesome context for the process that required boundary spanning efforts?

The levels and scales context shows the kind of spatial boundary issues that were mentioned in the section above. From the very local (dwellings and their surroundings) to the European level (be it in the form of a programme for Rhine and Meuse only) all levels of government were involved, maybe the national level least. It is hard to find any form of coherence here, while even the province did not really take up a guiding role. The river basin approach that is demanded by the European Water Framework Directive (WFD) is clearly not fully operational in an integrated fashion.

There was not really a ready networks and actors context that was the obvious setting for the processes of this case. For the main process the actor setting of the integrated area-oriented policy scheme was chosen. However, this setting was not really attuned to the realities of the development of an inhabited retention area. The representation of the inhabitants was disputed since a number of issues were regarded as out of scope by the other actors. As a result, the only inhabitant in the committee left and there was a small riot when the first plans were presented. The province was represented at a rather low level, not really committing the province to the negotiated results. In so far as this network setting was insufficient, for example, for the zoning planning and the nature development issues, the enlarged collection of actors was definitively in need of establishing productive relationships over these subjects. Later policy developments include the National Administrative Agreement on Water (Dutch acronym: NBW) (of representatives) of all ministries, provinces, water authorities and municipalities involved. In this agreement and its implementation some progress has been made with structural cooperation between these actors.

The problem perspectives and goal ambitions context reflected this. While the collection of actors was not really coherent around this issue of planning a retention area, their perspectives were neither, each actor emphasizing other stakes. While the policy scheme WB21 (Committee Water management for the 21st century) has specified problems and tasks, it did so with a perspective mainly on water quantity management. In the reality of water projects such as the one in our case study, this extent of integration is, however, still not enough.

The strategies and instruments context also shows a lack of coherence. The choice for the integrated area-oriented policy even implied that the use of some of the instruments available to promote the realization of the retention area became hampered. For instance, the way in which in physical planning the link with property and use rights is made – through the restricted and highly regulated use of expropriation in the general interest – became almost not done. All coherence rested upon the cooperation of the actors involved, and we have seen this was far from obvious. Later some instruments are developed that should strengthen the role of water management instruments compared to those of other sectors. The so-called 'Water test' gives the water managers the right to test new plans of other governments against the necessities of the water management in the region. However, this instrument is still more a means to be heard at all than a device that stimulates all involved into coherent activities (Lulofs et al., 2004).

Last, but not least, there is the context of the responsibilities and resources for implementation. Again a lack of coherence can be concluded here. The responsibility of realizing retention areas that protect towns against flooding is taken up by the water authorities, but this – together with many more projects that stem from the WB21 and EU WFD – is beyond what is regarded as their normal or even acceptable regional financial capacity. Other national financial resources were only found to match the European Interreg subsidy. This, however, had complications of its own, since it was not attuned at all with the procedural requirements of the zoning planning legal rights of municipalities and citizens. Even though partly their own towns were to be protected by the retention area, the municipality for a while did not seem to make itself co-responsible for the realization of the project.

All in all, we conclude that there was no ready structural context for the realization of this innovation. It had to be extended, even beyond the, as such, also integrative area-oriented policy scheme. This resulted in a clear lack of coherence, which often hampered the process. While later policy developments can be read as attempts to organize some coherence of governance for this policy (space for water), our estimate is that these are still insufficient to create a new governance structure with both enough extent and coherence to lessen the demand for continuous boundary spanning efforts.

5.6 MANAGING COMPLEXITY BY BOUNDARY SPANNING

In many respects the North and South Meene case shows ailing boundary spanning efforts. In crucial situations boundary judgements of involved actors were misjudged by the water authority. The lack of stability in the preferences of involved civilians was a crucial event in this case. In the aftermath of the crises converging boundary judgements were more or less shared between the water authority, the farmers and their representatives. This was interpreted by the water authority as a license to operate. This license eroded quickly and efforts to broaden the domain in order to realize the water authorities' plan clashed with the actors. These actors emphasized pre-crisis boundaries that some time after the crisis were restored. In some cases boundary judgements really clashed with those of the province and the farmers and the farmers' association. With regard to the province, the water authority misjudged early in the process the possibilities to link to nature. Derelict domain land was unexpectedly excluded by the province from the area of nature to be created. Also with regard to the farmers' association the trio water, nature and agriculture were not linked. The cognitions of the farmers' association and the farmers about which issues should be dealt with while realizing retention areas differed from those of the water authority. Instead of initiating a mutual learning process with regard to these cognitions, the water authority tried to use its power base to force its ideas. These efforts boomeranged because civilians and their representatives mobilized their resources in order to delay and block. With regard to the time dimension, the different time frames of the various negotiation processes, the EU subsidies and physical planning procedures clashed.

The water authority compensated these unfortunate efforts, including the nosebleed from the confrontation with the municipality, by practical trial and error boundary spanning efforts in order to maintain the project. This case emphasizes two thinkable linking strategies. Efforts to link can focus specifically on the boundary judgements – as a precondition for fruitful cooperation – but also the wider and practical boundary spanning that is required to make a project run can be found in the toolbox of the boundary spanner. Often the division between the two is not very clear, while creating fruitful cooperation across boundaries can also be one of the best methods to gradually integrate the boundary judgements of the actors involved. The relationship between (restricted or divergent) boundary judgements and the cooperation in the process can also be reversed in so far as reasonably successful interaction and cooperation can help boundary judgements to open up. And despite the difficulties during the project, the water authority was successful in bringing the project to a successful end.

The water authority responded with a whole array of strategies (cf. Chapter 2, Section 2.4).

New actors and arenas were used, although not always successful:

- using the area-oriented policy committee;
- replacing within the water authority the project leader with the traditional hierarchical attitude for a project leader with a more egalitarian attitude;
- removing the GLTO member from the committee;
- making as much use as possible of access to actors within the municipality, sometimes aiming at the civil servants involved, sometimes aiming at the local aldermen, and efforts to activate the province in the battle with the city council;
- private consultants entered the scene as new actors, but with own commercial interests magnifying the interests of their clients.

Some can be labelled creating new cognitions and trust by open communication and exchange:

- quite close and restricted communication to the farmers in the first period of the project; quite open, very active and emphatic communication to the farmers in the later periods, including extensive home visits;
- once aware of the bottleneck, working with the farmers' association and farmers towards a shared cognition about what should be included in a retention area project, communicating a moral obligation to the initial unconditional commitment.

Others are a bit more manipulative, or should we say steering communication, that is directed somewhat closer to influencing motivation, be it still predominantly with communication:

- communicating that the start situation of the farmers in the provisionally emergency inundation area was the worst thinkable and that the water authority would help to realize a better situation, that of controlled inundation;
- in the final phase of the project communicating that the whole project could become at risk when the blocking behaviour of some individuals would remain;
- convincing the Interreg office that refusing some postponement of the deadline of the subsidy would involve destruction of capital and that such a decision would be considered incomprehensible in the region.

The last category consists of facilitating and compromising, where the water authority really transfers resources to make the project more attractive to (potential) critics:

- the list of requirements of the farmers and the farmers' association with regard to what should be included in the retention project in terms of accompanying measures;
- in individual negotiation a generous approach was used;
- expressing to the municipality that the water authority was willing to pay the damage if the necessary change of the municipal zoning plan resulted in depreciation of real estate that had to be compensated. In normal situations this has to be paid by the municipality;
- close to the end of the project the water authority succeeded in linking to nature and the province, an effort that failed in the early stages of the project;

- the Interreg subsidy attained was very helpful in terms of available resources.

In these ways gradually much of the opposition was overcome just in time, in fact already in extra time.

5.7 CONCLUSIONS

In this last section we present two lines of conclusions: first, observations and lessons with regard to the framework used for analysis and, second, observations and lessons that consider this specific case.

The framework we used for analysis was described in Chapter 2. It starts from the perspective that complexity can be managed by linking across sectors, scales and time perspectives. This linking can concern specifically boundary judgements – as a precondition for fruitful cooperation – but also the wider and practical boundary spanning that is required to make the project run. Often the division between the two is not very clear, while creating fruitful cooperation across boundaries can also be one of the best methods to gradually integrate the boundary judgements of the actors involved. The relationship between (restricted or divergent) boundary judgements of the actors involved affecting the cooperation in the process, thus can also be reversed in so far as reasonably successful interaction and cooperation can help boundary judgements to open up.

The process analyzed shows some lessons to be taken into account in similar complex water management projects. One is that alongside the hydrological water system aspects other issues are also crucial; legitimacy and support under the inhabitants and landowners, the possibilities to acquire land, and possible zoning planning barriers were issues that were not well previewed in this case.

The organization was initially not well prepared for this boundary spanning task. It urges other very different capabilities compared to a planning and producing mode. Very substantial promises were made early in the heat of the debate, without having consulted the organization's experts on their feasibility. This is not only a matter of preview, but also of capacity for learning while doing. A careful assessment of the wishes of actors that are too manifold to all be involved in the process proves important too. It was also illustrated by this case that strong representing organizations do not only transfer demands, but also mitigate and compromise on behalf of their members. So, do not leave out and frustrate actors that you will definitively need later. This adaptive approach also includes keeping the purposes that cannot be realized on the agenda. Circumstances develop, and what cannot be realized now might meet better conditions further in the process, such as the nature area in this case.

NOTE

1. For more information see http://projecten.nederlandleeftmetwater.nl/html/topic_6_100.htm (accessed 14 September 2007).

6. Building a new river and boundary spanning governance

Hans Bressers, Simone Hanegraaff and Kris Lulofs

6.1 INTRODUCTION

On 1 July 2004 the construction of a new stream, 13 km in length in the Dutch province of Overijssel commenced. This was a long-cherished dream of the regional water authority: the stream would help prevent flooding and droughts and would contribute to maintaining and even improving water quality in the system of streams in the countryside, which the new stream would separate from the urban system.

The land was originally agricultural or was in private hands, but project developers were active. Constructing the stream thus necessitated changes to the provincial and local authority plans, the operational plans of the railway management company (a railway had to be crossed) and the natural gas authority (pipelines involved), the project developers' plans and those of the landowners. Moreover, the water authority would be neither able nor willing to bear the 40 million euros cost of the project. Obviously, therefore, a lot of boundary spanning was involved before the water authority could build the Breakthrough, which is why the project is such an excellent case study in this volume.

Just as in Chapter 5, this chapter will follow quite closely the framework for analysis of boundary spanning and boundary judgements as stipulated in Chapter 2. In Section 6.2 the storyline of the Breakthrough is told. In Section 6.3 we will explain the course of various phases of the process from the characteristics of the actors involved. In Section 6.4 the boundary issues will be identified and the degree to which the governance context was helpful for productive boundary spanning. In Section 6.5 the influence of the structural context of the process is assessed. In Section 6.6 the strategies used for managing complexity by boundary spanning are reviewed. In Section 6.7 some observations and conclusions are presented.

6.2 PROCESSES AND COUPLING

As early as the 1980s the province and the water authority agreed that something should be done about the situation in which relatively clean countryside water was mixed with relatively polluted water in the urban system in the densely populated region. It measures 1350 square kilometres and has 600 000 inhabitants, more than half of them concentrated in three almost adjacent cities, also leaving room for quiet rural areas. A 1992 strategic document announced a number of projects of the water authority that would allow the concept to be implemented. The idea of separating countryside from urban water by constructing a new stream could be recognized in this document, but was not set out as a concrete project. In 1993 the water authority commissioned a number of students at Wageningen University to conduct a multidisciplinary, exploratory study of the construction of a stream, 13 km long and 25 m wide, in an area that the province allocated as an ecological corridor. At the time, a land use re-ordering process (see Chapter 7) was underway, in which landowners aimed at the more efficient re-ordering of land use functions and preventing droughts. Since these plans could be united with the construction of a new stream, and because both the ecological and hydrological conditions appeared favourable, the students concluded that the construction of the stream was not only technically feasible; it was also a viable policy option. The outcome of their study led to further research into options.

6.2.1 Sharing Ideas: Initial Plan Development

By 1997, the water authority was sufficiently well aware of the technical feasibility and decided to go public and mentioned the initiative to construct a new stream in a plan (WRD, 1997). This document named the conservation of relatively clean country water quality and handling drought as the most important reasons for digging the Breakthrough.

Simultaneously with this publication, the water authority initiated government links by inviting leading government figures – upon whom the water authority deemed itself dependent – to come together in a governmental steering committee for joint consideration of the plan for the Breakthrough. The invitation was accepted by aldermen from the various local authorities, and representatives of the province and the regional agricultural association. In the meetings that followed it turned out they all agreed that the Breakthrough was both necessary and useful. Thanks to the support for the abstract idea of separating country from urban water by means of a waterway, the steering committee was almost immediately able to go on to consider how the water authority could implement its plan. Before this how? question got on to the agenda, though, the province emphasized that any actions would be assessed within the overall context of their 1992 Nature and Countryside Policy Plan (in Dutch: *Beleidsplan Natuur en Landschap Overijssel*). This made it clear that the province's cooperation was conditional on the Breakthrough functioning as an ecological corridor. This condition had consequences for the design: if the Breakthrough were to function as an ecological corridor, the water authority would have to add 25 metres of greensward to both banks in country areas. As much as 75 metres extra would have to be reserved on both banks in areas where the stream bordered urban functions and infrastructure.

This involved a major expansion of the land area needed, well beyond the 25-metre wide stream that the water authority had been discussing up to then. It was obvious to the members of the steering committee that this would be necessary only if the Breakthrough could be useful for both purposes, both of which they supported. Subsequent negotiations on the route to be adopted (there were still four options under consideration) were thus all based on the wider, dual purpose version.

Some participants also had other ideas about the way the space in the area planned for the Breakthrough should be used. For example, the local authorities of the three major cities were toying with the idea of locating a regional business park in the sector of the planned Breakthrough area. The council member from a village introduced ideas from the Land Re-ordering Committee (which he chaired) projects aiming for fewer drought problems for agriculture in the area. The province proposed that the Breakthrough should be included in the land re-ordering project, which would mean that, when the time came, the province could use (legal) instruments and funding from the land re-ordering project for the construction of the Breakthrough. Under the Land Re-ordering Act in force at the time, funding from this source could only be used for strict land re-ordering objectives and not for such matters as the implementation of the ecological corridors or a new waterway. The province was aware, though, that the Ministry of Agriculture, Nature and Fishery was considering amendments to its land re-ordering policy, which, it was presumed, would relax restrictions on the use of funding from this source, in the sense that it would then be available for creating the ecological corridor within the so-called National Ecological Network. In order to be able to profit from this funding from the land re-ordering policy, the Land Re-ordering Committee could not present the land re-ordering project to the provincial government before the national government had passed its amendment to the Land Re-ordering Act. This implied that the land re-ordering project would be delayed; since it had been in preparation for years, it was now nearly complete, and would be ready for implementation in a far shorter time frame than central government needed for its amendments. Nevertheless, the governmental steering committee speedily agreed to link the Breakthrough to the land re-ordering project.

In this way, the steering committee gathered ideas about the area's development, which were not connected prior to that time. These exchanges clarified the criteria that each participant proposed for assessing the four alternative routes and especially the origins of the criteria. These were worked out by an external consultancy, leading in 1999 to the report *Country Water through the Urban Belt* (*Landelijk water door de Stedenband*). The multi-criteria analyses performed for this report showed a preference for a route that followed existing waterways as far as possible. Only the agricultural association was against this, since it objected to the extra crossing of the agricultural area that this plan involved.

Already in this first phase a number of linkages took place with extra objectives. While the initial goal was (1) to separate relatively clean rural water from more polluted urban water, (2) preventing droughts was quickly added by the water board itself. These were both still water policy goals (quality and quantity, respectively), but the province added a major goal from another policy field: nature protection, demanding that (3) the project area would serve as an ecological corridor, with great consequences for the contents of the project, especially its spatial characteristics. From – predominantly – agricultural policy (4) the contribution of the project to land re-ordering, improving, among others, the agricultural infrastructure was put forward, also shifting the temporal aspects of the project. Thus the project evolved very quickly into a complex multi-purpose enterprise. In the background another issue was already visible, though as yet only as a possible competitor for space: the plan for a regional business park.

6.2.2 Fear for Nature

Complaints were also voiced in a small village when others pressed for a link with the land re-ordering project under development there. They had no problem with a link between the waterway and the land use re-ordering project as such, but the link with the ecological highway was a cause for concern, since the rules for a nature reserve might then become applicable, which might hamper their agricultural practices. The forceful suggestion that the project should be presented only after the Land Re-ordering Act had been amended also encountered great resistance, since this would involve yet another delay. This being said, the Land Re-ordering Committee itself was convinced that the Breakthrough would be a valuable addition to the land re-ordering project. True, it would take longer, but the water budget would improve the situation for the landowners, while a beautiful nature reserve would also be created. This was why the committee members also took a great deal of trouble to convince their constituencies. Besides this, the chair also had to take pains to convince his own constituency, the Wierden local council, of which he was an alderman. He had to fight his corner a number of times, as several farmers expressed their displeasure directly to a number of individual councillors, who then, of course, started putting critical questions to the alderman.

As the amendment of the Land Re-ordering Act neared its completion, the Land Re-ordering Committee succeeded in recruiting support for the steering committee's preferred route. Finally, the Land Re-ordering Committee was able to offer its land re-ordering plan to the province, including the preferred route for the Breakthrough.

In this phase not a new project goal was added or removed, but in another way a necessary linkage was prepared: with the local physical planning of the municipality of Wierden. While an important part of the course of the stream was decided upon, the story on the physical planning of the municipality of Wierden does not end here. It will be resumed later, but first we will explain a more or less simultaneous developing part of the story.

6.2.3 Hot Land

The land re-ordering plan afforded clarity about the location, width, detailed planning and funding of the first part of the route in Wierden. There was, however, maximum uncertainty about the next part of the route that might border the mentioned regional business park, about which the local authorities of three cities were, as mentioned, in consultation. The only certainty the province could offer was that, if the business park were to border the Breakthrough, then the stream would have to be widened yet further at that location. To get some clarity about whether the business park would in fact be located there, the province initiated an Environmental Impact Statement (EIS). This involved obligatory publication of the initiating memorandum, which meant that the landowners in the province's and the local authority's preferred area for the business park realized they were sitting on 'hot land'. Land prices in the area thus rose considerably, including the land needed for the Breakthrough. Speculation about the business park thus resulted in greater estimated costs for the Breakthrough. Those landowners who might have to vacate their property or who would be imposed a view over a business park would benefit by clear information on the business park's location. The land area needed, including that needed for the Breakthrough, would increase if the business park were to lie adjacent to the Breakthrough, so land acquisition could not start soon enough.

It could have taken years to pass through all the stages needed for an EIS, but there was urgent need for a speedy resolution of the matter. The provincial government, which was involved in and benefited from both projects, therefore considered ways to accelerate the process. In 2000 the province divided the EIS procedure into two. This meant that an advisory committee would first work on a location impact statement. As soon as this process generated one likely location, this would be opened to public consultation, leading to greater clarity. Only then would the EIS be prepared for the actual detailed planning of the site.

Again, this story does not end here and will be resumed later. However, already in this phase the position of the province made clear that the project could be linked to an additional function, namely (5) creating a buffer zone for the business park separating it from residential and other zoning. Herewith, in fact, the spatial scale of the domain of the project was increased.

6.2.4 Detailing and Presenting the Plan

While the preparations and actual drafting of the EIS were in progress, another investigation of the Breakthrough started. After the route had been chosen, the next logical step was to look at possible detailed planning. In late 1999 the governmental steering committee once again formulated a number of objectives that the planned stream would have to fulfil. The objectives derived from a number of disciplines: water, ecology, agriculture, landscape, leisure and management. The detailed plan resulting from this investigation was presented to the public in November 2000 in three very crowded information evenings. Compared with the 1998 plans some striking changes were adopted. The stream was originally presented as being 25 metres wide, but had now been expanded to 75 metres, being also an ecological corridor, while it could even be as wide as 175 metres along the tentative boundary with the business park. The emphasis was no longer on improving water quality but on flooding. The water authority expected some marketing advantage from this changed accent since in 1998 it was found that the water system was inadequate to cope with heavy rainfall, which had led to serious problems. This was recalled by most residents, who would therefore more easily understand and subscribe to the need for the Breakthrough. Moreover, central government had launched a national campaign to persuade people that water needed more space because of climate change and similar issues, which could also help recruit support for the Breakthrough. This national campaign started in response to the new motto introduced by the Committee Water Management for the 21st Century (WB21) in its advisory note, which suggested that a policy of integrated water management should be replaced or supplemented by the concept of adaptive water management, meaning that water should be given more space, to include its dynamic aspects.

In this part of the process – on the more detailed planning and presentation of the project – some new objectives were added to the existing ones. In the assignment to develop the plan, (6) landscape and recreation were also mentioned. Next to that in the domain of water purposes, (7) flood prevention was now emphasized. Even though the means of creating retention areas was quickly removed from the plan, the river with its wide natural banks would create a lot of storage and discharge capacity. Interestingly, the water quality issue of separating rural and urban waters was now less emphasized, while of course it was still included and – given the EU Water Framework Directive – probably even more important than ever.

6.2.5 Gold Rush

The attention to new types of water management was also manifest at the European level, and the Breakthrough's project leader discovered to his delight that this attention also formed part of the European subsidy programme Interreg 3b, which is intended to encourage projects that lead to more space for water. The project leader was correct in his appraisal that the Breakthrough would be eligible for a subsidy under this programme. The most important requirement for participating in the programme was that the water authority should have at least two foreign partners. The project leader rapidly found Dutch partners. In search of foreign partners he visited an exhibition in Rotterdam in 2001, where he was successful. With them he submitted a funding request, which was granted, and so there came a decisive moment. Accepting this subsidy meant that the ground would actually have to be broken, and very soon, to start construction of the Breakthrough: the funds would only be paid out after concrete results had been achieved within a set period. This meant that the funding process had actually overtaken the legal and practical processes that the water authority was pursuing to make the Breakthrough a reality. This involved a public tendering process that itself depended upon completion of the legal procedures to make the Breakthrough possible. The legal aspects meant at least that the water authority had to acquire title to the land needed for the Breakthrough, while the local authorities and the provincial government would have to amend their planning, which involved long, drawn-out procedures. If the residents were to avail themselves of all avenues of appeal open to them, then the period within which concrete results could be achieved in order to gain the funding might be very short indeed.

In brief, accepting the subsidy would bring exciting times, which in the worst case would lead to immense costs, but to a vast financial injection if all turned out well. Another advantage could be that the construction of the first part of the Breakthrough might call forth such enthusiasm that other funding options would suddenly open up.

While the water authority was wrestling on the horns of this dilemma, the governmental steering committee was successful in reaching a cost allocation. The steering committee formalized these agreements in the form of a Declaration of Intent in December 2001, in which they also formally affirmed their support for the Breakthrough. Partly thanks to this government support, now set down in black and white in the Declaration of Intent, and because the subsidy appeared to be a real possibility, there was a general increase of confidence in the Breakthrough's feasibility. The water authority therefore resolved to take the risk associated with accepting the subsidy.

The subsidy demanded a great amount of administration and also meant that the project would have to get underway very soon, so the Breakthrough project leader was rechristened subsidy coordinator. The actual development of the Breakthrough was put in the hands of a new project leader, who until then had only been peripherally involved with research into the technical and substantive aspects. The water authority also asked someone from the National Countryside Service (Dienst Landelijk Gebied) to steer the process and to act as a neutral, independent party. By coincidence, one member of the National Countryside Service staff had acted as tutor to the students who had published the first report on the Breakthrough in 1994. This person thus seemed eminently suitable and rapidly joined as process manager. The new project leader, the process manager and a person from the province now made up the steering committee. Even though the Breakthrough's go-ahead could not yet be guaranteed, they nevertheless started to acquire the land in 2002. As agreed with the provincial government, they were able to access the funds available for land re-ordering and reconstruction. There was, however, a maximum price per hectare for the land that the National Countryside Service could buy with this money.

Speculation about the business park had led some land prices to climb above this maximum. In late June 2002 the water authority's management board extended a credit of 8 200 000 euros so that this land could be acquired. Additional funds were secured from the national programme to increase flood prevention and storage capacity in the perspective of climate change, re-emphasizing flood control as one of the purposes of the project.

This part of the process did not lead to extra purposes added to the project. Having typical EU demands such as recreational opportunities included in the no less than seven purposes we mentioned already, this was also hardly conceivable.

6.2.6 Bypassing the Physical Plan for the First Trajectory

We left the scene at the town of Wierden at the moment that the trajectory was proposed. However, that was not the end of this story. Between 2002 and 2005 a number of enquiries had been held by both internal and external experts to detail the main outlines of the plan and test their feasibility, both technical and substantive, and to answer the questions raised by interested parties and ultimately to gain their support.

While various enquiries were in progress into the substantive issues surrounding the Breakthrough, an external consultancy was asked to prepare a draft zoning plan for the area surrounding the stream. The water authority's intention here was to save time and expense for the four local authorities, which would have to amend their zoning plans to make the Breakthrough legally feasible, and to maintain the pace of the process, which the water authority itself needed as there was no time available to attend to all the zoning law procedures before starting work on the first part of the Breakthrough's route: the subsidy was time-limited. The water authority therefore asked the Wierden local authority, in whose area they wanted to start excavating, to use such legal options as were available to depart from the current zoning plan. Thanks to the council member's involvement and enthusiasm, the council agreed to this proposal in September 2003. The water authority's draft resolution, the draft zoning plan, and a petition of 25 September to 24 October 2003 to depart from the then current zoning plan in Wierden were opened to public inspection that same month. In the meantime, the water authority organized an information evening, attended by 150 interested actors. Their reactions were set down in a memorandum, which, with responses, was later distributed to the attendees. It was clear from the memorandum that the water authority was genuinely open to reactions: some of them had actually resulted in changes to the plans.

The reactions had other consequences too. Many of them revealed a real need to be involved in the process, which led to an intensification of the communication. The water authority had a logo designed for the Breakthrough, to be printed on all the illustrated newsletters. They also planned noticeboards, they launched a website, they visited the most directly involved landowners in their homes, and they held information evenings and published articles in the daily press and magazines. There was a risk that journalists would perceive minor irregularities in the process as major blunders, so the communication strategy also meant that every journalist would be referred to the same spokesperson.

Support for the Breakthrough increased steadily in the local council of Wierden where the first part of the Breakthrough was planned, especially when the water authority promised that all instances of possible planning blight would be compensated at the water authority's cost. When the time came for the council to pass the final resolution, however, the alderman who had always been closely involved with the Breakthrough actually had to confess that this agreement was not permitted by law. He was able to convince the council that central government was preparing to scrap the right to compensation for planning blight, so no risk was involved. This was accepted by the council and it was thanks to the subsequent resolution that the first part of the route could start. When, on 19 February 2004, the time came for the water authority's general council to decide on detailed planning and changes to water management, the most serious legal hurdles had in fact been crossed, and the spade went into the ground for the first part of the route in July 2004.

6.2.7 Nature Against Nature?

While the legal impediments to the first part of the route were history, many hurdles still had to be crossed for the parts of the route passing through some other local authorities. Especially the residents in the central part of the route voiced their concerns. It is also the area where the projected regional business park would be situated. The media lent extra force to their protest by inflating the negative picture that the landowners had sketched.

The entire population of the region, including politicians, were thus able to enjoy the conspiracy theories and tales of dishonest government dealing. The media were also invited when the farmers involved organized an information meeting in one of their farmyards when they presented their alternative to the Breakthrough to governors.

Where the stream passed through their area, the farmers' alternative reduced its width to the original 25 metres. The farmers did, in fact, support this original 25-m width. They agreed that water needed more space to carry off rainwater. What actually annoyed them were the nature reserves on both banks of the Breakthrough, which they planned to scrap over a 3-km length. Besides the extra area, on account of agricultural land, many farmers still feared that the nature reserves would impede their farming practices and any possible expansion, since they would be governed by environmental legislation. To meet the requirement for nature reserves shown in the Breakthrough plans, they had cooperated with a nature group in order to propose an exchange. The nature reserves alongside the Breakthrough would be substituted by a new nature reserve to be developed on land in the nature organizations' area. They realized that this would mean the disappearance of the ecological corridor function, but they assumed that the water authority had only incorporated that to gain access to EU funding. When the process manager told them that the extra width was also necessary for engineering and water management reasons, they merely voiced their disbelief, as they did when they were told that they would receive generous compensation.

Of course, while the process manager stoutly maintained that changes to the plans such as those proposed were impossible, other invitees did seem to appreciate the alternative. The agricultural association, residents' associations and even one of the political parties lent their support to the alternative plan. Some of the councillors and members of the provincial council stated they would study the alternative plan before deciding on amendments to the zoning plan that would make the Breakthrough with its ecological zones legally possible. The alternative plan thus posed a threat in that the necessary change in the zoning plan might not be realized, even though work on the first part of the route had already been going on for six months, and the ecological corridor function was demanded by the province right from the start of the development of the concept.

The alternative, coupled with the farmers' continuing protests voiced directly to local politicians, led to conflict in a city council and delayed the resolution on the Breakthrough within the council's territory.

Ultimately, in January 2005, they resolved to go ahead, after the water authority had agreed to a regulation wherein agricultural use would be allowed for seven years in areas ultimately destined to become nature reserves. This gave them seven years to reach an agreement with the landowners. Also, some of the residents gradually understood that the wide nature area would be an ideal buffer against the future extension towards their properties of a development that was even more threatening to them; the creation of a regional business park. Some farmers attempted to get their way through the courts, but without success.

6.2.8 From Planning to Implementation: Still Issues to be Resolved

Despite all the research, there were still surprises in store. Unexpectedly, the bulldozers had encountered glacial boulders. Further research, a search for suitable earth moving equipment and a new round of tendering involved a delay of several months. Another delay was caused by the absence of a permit from the Ministry of Public Works. Even though the contractor's clock was ticking, the ministry followed the time-consuming, formal permit procedure, to the immense annoyance of the Breakthrough steering committee. Later, however, the ministry performed a sterling service for the water authority. Part of the Breakthrough was to cross a motorway, which was not especially beneficial to nature, of course. It turned out, though, that the ministry still had some funding available for an ecological pass way and was prepared to spend it on the Breakthrough.

Negotiations proceeded on the subsequent parts of the route in 2006 and 2007. Almelo, for instance, had also planned a new housing estate near one part of the route, which meant that the gas and electricity providers would have to move existing underground supply lines. The parties with plans for the area through which the Breakthrough was to run collaborated, by agreeing on a shared timetable for their activities. The gas and electricity suppliers would do their work first, after which the ground would be excavated for the Breakthrough so that the local authority would be able to use the soil to raise the ground level for the new housing and industrial estates.

Those parts of the route that had already been dug attracted a lot of attention as nature increasingly became established there. This increased the support from more and more of the residents, who communicated their positive views to the water authority. This support was of a kind that is sorely needed in the years to follow as the Breakthrough is shaped to become a reality.

6.3 ACTORS AND THEIR MOTIVATION, COGNITIONS AND RESOURCES AFFECTING THE PROCESS

As the case description shows, in the interaction processes surrounding the Breakthrough a number of objectives from more policy programmes than water management alone became interlinked. This section presents an analysis of these interaction processes. Two of them are composed of two processes described in Section 6.2 above, these pairs follow each other but stretch chronologically over a longer period. The processes are first explained by considering the three characteristics of the parties involved: motivation, cognitions and resources. Thereafter the analysis goes on to deal with boundary judgements as part of the cognitions involved, in Section 6.4. Next, in Section 6.5 the influence of the layers of contexts is studied: both the structural context of the governance structure and the wider contexts.

6.3.1 Initial Plan Development

The interactions between the water authority and the provincial government that led to the Breakthrough being linked to the provincial planning and zoning policy, the National Ecological Network policy and the land re-ordering policy together form a first interaction process to be analyzed. The actor constellation during the initial plan development phase consists of the water authority and the province as the axis of interaction and furthermore the Land Use Re-ordering Committee (see also Chapter 7).

Linking the Breakthrough to the provincial zoning and planning policy can be understood in terms of the characteristics (motivation, cognitions, resources) of the water authority and the provincial government. There was a clear congruence between the objectives of the provincial zoning and planning policy and that of the water authority, which were both served by constructing the Breakthrough.

Provincial policy in fact aimed to maintain and improve nature by linking natural areas, while the water authority concentrated on linking relatively natural wet infrastructure. These objectives were very much in accord with one another. An objective is in accord – or 'congruent' – with another objective when the realization of the first objective makes the realization of the second easier. It is not necessary that they are identical. Likewise, objectives are conflicting when realization of the one makes realization of the other more difficult and independent when realization of the one does not influence the difficulty of realizing the other. The cognitions were also in accord, which, together with the overlapping motivations, explains how the water authority could easily link the Breakthrough to the area plan when they were in talks with the province in the governmental steering committee.

In terms of resources, even when the water authority would not have particularly liked the provincial objectives, the critical dependence of the water authority on the provincial government actually offered the latter the opportunity to increase its influence by cooperating in linking the Breakthrough to the local planning. In fact, linking the National Ecological Network policy with the Breakthrough was done in the expectation that this would increase efficiency. The provincial government was also motivated by financial considerations when the Breakthrough was given a place in a land use re-ordering project for an area through which the Breakthrough would pass, while they linked the timetable for this re-ordering project to the timetable for the amendment of (national) land re-ordering policy. This had to be done, since funding from the planning policy could only be used for the Breakthrough if the project were to be undertaken under the amended land re-ordering policy.

6.3.2 Detailing and Presenting the Plan

In this process it is especially the triple presentation of the new, more detailed plans to the public that deserves attention. It is clear that this was done differently compared to the first initial presentation. The actor constellation consists of the steering committee that guided the elaboration of the plans, the water authority that not only took a strong role in the detailing but also in the presentation and the audience that responded generally with constructive remarks in this phase.

It seems that the water authority had a genuine motivation to discuss the plans in a rather open way with the audience and that the audience perceived this to be the case (cognitions). In fact, this could be a well-understood self-interest on the side of the water authority. This method worked better than a strict develop-announce-defend strategy, as learned by the water authority. However, the adaptations made as a result of the meetings also support the idea that the openness was more than just tactics. In the background, the considerable power for the people to hinder the progress of the project with the resource of legal objections might nevertheless play an important role.

6.3.3 Dealing with Physical Planning in the First Part of the Trajectory

The third interaction process analyzed is that by which the Breakthrough linked up with the Wierden local authority's spatial planning policy. It is described above in Sections 6.2.2 and 6.2.6 under the headings 'Fear for nature' and later 'Bypassing the physical plan for the first trajectory'. The actor constellation consists of the Wierden local authority, the water authority, an alderman from Wierden, landowners and the local council of Wierden. Its interactions can be understood in terms of the characteristics of the alderman, the local council and the landowners, in the local authority's area, with the water authority's characteristics included as background.

Alderman

The alderman responsible for planning exerted the most positive influence on the link between the Breakthrough and planning policy in Wierden. His positive influence can be understood first of all in terms of his motivations. The goals of the water policy that the Breakthrough would fulfil partly matched those of the alderman's planning policy: countering drought. The nature goals associated with the Breakthrough also fitted in with the alderman's planning goals. His support for the Breakthrough also linked up with the alderman's desire for good external relations with other tiers of government. The motivation here stemmed in part from his own goals, as well as from the realization that the Wierden local authority often depended on, and would continue to depend on, other levels of government, including the water authority.

Moreover, the alderman shared with the water authority the view (cognitions) that the Breakthrough in fact would counter drought in Wierden, while he appreciated that his function and personal character were resources he could use to link the Breakthrough to the Wierden planning policy (self-effectiveness assessment). The match between his goals and cognition with those of the water authority, and his position as resource, explain the support offered by the alderman.

Landowners

Given the favourable configuration of motivation, cognition and resource position, the alderman's cooperation was understandable, but was in itself not sufficient to forge the link between the Breakthrough and the Wierden planning policy. This needed both the local council and to some degree also the landowners. The landowners were initially against the Breakthrough which, given their characteristics as actors, can be explained as follows. They were in principle in favour of a link between planning and water policy by means of an amendment to the zoning plans. The water policy goals matched their own, which clarifies their motives for supporting that part of the plan. Nevertheless, most of the landowners were on balance against a link between the Breakthrough and their zoning plan, due to the other policy that linked with the Breakthrough.

In their perception (interpretation of reality – cognitions), the link with the National Ecological Network would bring restrictions to their business practices, while most of them regarded their agricultural businesses as a serious resource, which most wanted to expand. In this regard, their cognitions differed from the water authority's, which saw no reason to fear any such restrictions.

The link between the Breakthrough and the Enter village land re-ordering project was not a problem for the landowners as such, but linking the timetable for this project to amendments in parliament certainly affected their motivation adversely, since it meant postponing the land re-ordering project's implementation. The risk of regulation and postponement of the land re-ordering weighed particularly heavy in the view of the landowners because they perceived that the provincial government could also site the ecological corridor elsewhere, where it would pose no threat to their farming.

So both the motivation and the cognitions of the landowners differed greatly from those of the water authority, which offered little chance that the landowners would easily cooperate in the linkage.

There was little chance that they would cooperate, either, due to the unequal distribution of resources between the landowners and the water authority. The water authority had no resources to compel cooperation, since a condition of the cooperation with Wierden was that the Breakthrough would be incorporated into the land re-ordering project, provided the landowners agreed voluntarily. The landowners, however, did have a resource available by which they could make the water authority keep its distance. By expressing their dissatisfaction directly to the local councillors and the media, they exerted an adverse influence on the motivation of the local councillors. It was not electorally favourable for them to support the linkage, while their cooperation was indispensable. It was they, after all, who would have to approve the change to the local zoning plan. They utilized this resource right up to the point when the alderman succeeded in persuading the landowners that it was also in their interest to link the local zoning plan to the Breakthrough.

Councillors

The local councillors were initially less enthusiastic than the alderman, thanks to the adverse influence of the landowners, which affected their motivation to work on linking the Breakthrough with local zoning policy. Their objections dissipated when agreement was reached with the landowners, who ceased to express their resistance to the councillors. Nevertheless, this was not enough to motivate the councillors, since two objections to the link remained. It was, in fact, inherent to the link with planning policy via the local zoning plan that planning blight compensation would have to be paid. The costs involved would legally have to be borne by the local authority. The second objection was the cost of changing the zoning plan. In the councillors' view, the council was unjustified in tapping its own resources for a project that, in fact, served the interests of other tiers of government. The water authority agreed to bear these feared costs itself.

That changed the councillors' perceptions about linking the Breakthrough to their zoning plans. They expected no further adverse consequences for the Wierden local authority, which offered them sufficient motivation to agree.

6.3.4 Dealing with Physical Planning in the Second Part of the Trajectory

The fourth process analyzed is composed of the interactions by which the Breakthrough was linked to the Almelo local authority's zoning policy, including the regional business park and the building of a new residential area. This process has been described above in Sections 6.2.3 and 6.2.7

under the headings 'Hot land' and 'Nature against nature'. The link between the Breakthrough and the Almelo zoning policy was forged again mainly via interaction of the alderman with the council and the landowners with the water authority in the background.

The Almelo alderman's interest in this case was only tepid at best, because of his cognitions. He did not initially acknowledge that Almelo had anything to gain from the Breakthrough, presented as it was as a solution to nature and water budget problems, while the Almelo alderman saw himself as responsible for urban issues. Nor was he entirely successful in picking up the signal that the water authority expected him to recruit support for the Breakthrough from his constituency.

The high water levels in 1998 increased the perception of risk and did affect the alderman's interpretation of what the project could achieve positively. Therefore, when the provincial government tied the Breakthrough's construction to the establishment of a regional business park in Almelo, the alderman's motivation rose to the point where he cooperated on the Breakthrough. The increase of motivation continued when it turned out that sand released by excavating the Breakthrough could be used for building a housing estate. Thanks to a link between the Breakthrough and the zoning plan, they would be able to save money.

The agricultural landowners in the city of Almelo were at first not sufficiently motivated by the link between the Breakthrough and the zoning plan to offer their support. Just like their peers in Wierden, they too were wary of the regulations under the National Ecological Network. They also assumed that they would suffer from over-irrigation, an issue on which their cognition differed from that of the water authority. When the water authority sought intensive contact with these landowners, suspicion declined with regard to the research that formed the input to the water authority's cognitions. Some landowners even became motivated by the Breakthrough when it turned out that the regional business park would be built quite near their farms and land. In comparison to the alternative scenario, in which only the regional business park would be built, which would destroy their view (and maybe could even threaten to swallow their lands in the future), the alternative with the Breakthrough acting as a buffer was suddenly a relative improvement. Another positive cognitive change influencing their motivation was that they acknowledged the water authority's openness in linking their individual interests to the Breakthrough. For example, an extra bridge was added to the Breakthrough to preserve an existing footpath.

The local council was in these circumstances quite hesitant and postponed the decision until there was sufficient relaxation of the objections of at least part of the residents/landowners. Clearly, it had the legal resources to force a decision but was not motivated to do so at all before this point.

6.3.5 Getting Funds

The next process, and the last one to be analyzed, comprises the interactions between the project leader and the Water Authority Council, project leaders of foreign water authorities and the office managing the European Interreg subsidy, which linked the Breakthrough to the European subsidy. It was described above in Section 6.2.5 under the heading 'Gold rush'.

The project leader's characteristics played an important role in this actor constellation. He showed an intrinsic motivation and interest in the world of subsidies, which focused his cognition: it made him very receptive to information on this subject. His self-confidence and experience formed a significant resource, which helped him forge links. He was bold enough to apply for subsidy funding, even when it was uncertain whether the Water Authority Council would offer the necessary support if and when the subsidy was actually made available. The council was uncertain since they had the perception that the Breakthrough might not be financially feasible, which hindered them from offering their total support to the project. These doubts disappeared when the council became aware that subsidy funding had already been obtained. This changed the perception about financial feasibility and thus also the motivation to cooperate on the link with the subsidy by making resources (credit) available for the Breakthrough.

The motivation for two foreign water authorities to link into the project stemmed from the perception that the funding they needed to achieve their goals would reduce thanks to the subsidy, combined with the knowledge that the subsidy was conditional on cooperation and knowledge sharing between water authorities from different countries.

6.4 BOUNDARY JUDGEMENTS AND THEIR IMPACTS

Boundary judgements are definitions of systems and problems that underpin conceptual models. For the purpose of our case study they can be defined as socially constructed definitions of the domain of relevance (in terms of relevant scales, problem and policy sectors and time and change aspects – see Chapter 2). Boundary judgements that differ among actors can cause incoherence and can even be a source of conflict: boundary judgements that are too narrow for the adequate use of the innovation or so wide that complexity becomes unmanageable and can also stop all progress.

In this section we will consider what kind of boundary judgements of the actors involved can be observed and how they could have influenced the actor characteristics and the resulting processes. Some relevant boundary spanning has already been mentioned as instances of linking. The project combines the water policy goals of (1) separating rural and urban water by re-coupling a natural creek system to the main stream of the region, (2) drought prevention, and (3) flood protection and the goals from other policy fields of (4) ecological highway (nature), (5) land re-ordering (agriculture), (6) buffer zone (industry) and (7) landscape and recreation. Some of these linkages did not really have the character of boundary disputes over the relevant domain while there actually was not disagreement about the linkages. However, there are more boundary judgements that are recognizable and had an impact on the process. As in Chapter 2, we discern spatial, sectoral and temporal aspects of the domain.

6.4.1 Spatial Aspects of the Domain

In this case we have seen that the area where the options for the trajectory of the new river were searched rather quickly reduced to only one trajectory. At that time this happened without much debate. It was the product of a multi-criteria analysis, thus the kind of decision that most of the actors considered suited for rational (analytical) decision making, not a complex or wicked problem. To some degree it is the nature of water itself combined with the wish to create something natural that seem to dictate the route. On the other hand, even the trajectory chosen has to pass (under) a major shipping canal. Clearly this decision of the majority of actors conflicted with the preference of the agricultural association. But one can doubt whether this can be labelled a boundary judgement conflict, or whether it was not just a matter of conflicting interests. Nevertheless, different boundary domain perceptions were involved. Most farmers concentrated on what the project would imply for their own lands, while the water authority's perspective of linking a creek system to the east of the area with the main river to the west of the area implies a much larger area considered as the relevant spatial domain.

Somewhat later, the spatial domain of the project was greatly expanded in a way by the coupling to the ecological main structure that ultimately links nature areas in large parts of the country or even Europe by corridors. This domain specification was clearly not understood when opponents wanted to take the natural banks of some part of the project and compensate this by offering to create nature elsewhere. Initially even some provincial councillors were lured into regarding this as possibly a fair deal, while it completely missed the point.

At the same stage and place, another development led to a significant extension of the spatial domain deemed relevant by the population. This was the regional business park for which the Breakthrough would provide a strong and wide buffer zone. This extension greatly helped to relax the objections.

6.4.2 Sectoral Aspects of the Domain

As listed above, several policy sectors ultimately contributed purposes to the project, apart from the water quality and two sided water quantity goals. In the course of the case story the emphasis between these three shifted now and then, but none was excluded. While the included water goals were almost non-contested, such as the addition of landscape and recreation, and the function as a buffer zone for industry was even welcomed as soon as it was recognized as part of the sectoral domain of the project, nature and agriculture (land re-ordering) were less generally accepted.

At first one sees a very smooth addition of nature purposes to the water project, when the water authority and the province wholeheartedly welcomed each other's sectors in the project. They regarded this clearly as a win-win option for which it was not difficult to open up one's minds. But the relation with the sector of agriculture became stressed by this addition. This was only reinforced by the linkage of the project to land re-ordering (a sector rooted in agricultural infrastructure improvement policies). In fact this tension can also be viewed as a boundary judgement conflict in which the farmers held the wider definition of the domain. Because, it was the farmers who included all European and national habitat protection rules into the relevant domain, as interlinked with the inclusion of the ecological main system – an inclusion contested by the water authority.

6.4.3 Temporal Aspects of the Domain

The coherence of the different time frames of the sectors and procedures involved was also in this case a serious problem. Inclusion of land re-ordering could only provide new resources for the project when a change of the law was awaited, even though this hampered the progress. The long time horizon of the EIS procedure was successfully made more coherent with the project's development by splitting the assessment in two.

Like in the North and South Meene case (see Chapter 5), the requirements of the European subsidy strongly complicated the time management of the project. Demands to realize concrete action in the short run are actually conflicting with the lengthy procedures of spatial planning. When successful, one can say in hindsight that such pressures have speeded up the process. But they also create great risks for the project, because when a deadline is not met, the completion of the project might become unaffordable, while it is too far ahead to be stopped either.

An interesting spatio-temporal issue in this regard is also the split of the project in different phases, of which in this study two have been dealt with (a third one is also essential for the project, a planned fourth one concerns a side arm). The point here is not that the actual building of the waterway is split into phases, but that also the project is starting to be actually realized on one spot while the development of ideas, resources and permissions continues for another part of the trajectory. This might seem a risky style, yet the project managers have learned that it is the only way to realize such projects. This strategy is not only used on the level of phases (stretches of the trajectory) but also on the more detailed level of plots of land that can be easily obtained because a farmer wants to retire and welcomes the nature development adjacent to his farm house. This creates examples that are used later to convince neighbouring farmers that the results are worthwhile and helps to present the project as inevitable and even already happening.

While it is clear from this description that boundary issues are abundant, all in all one could state that in this case the water authority, the province and most municipalities have shown a sufficient degree of openness towards each others' domain specifications to enable progress in the project.

6.5 COHERENCE AND FRAGMENTATION IN THE GOVERNANCE CONTEXT

The inputs into the process and the characteristics of the actors involved are not isolated. They have a context at several scales that can all directly have an impact on the process.

The structural context consists of the elements of public governance and the property and use rights that are not specifically developed for the processes studied. This implies that the extent of relevant elements of governance has to be widened. The real boundary spanning challenge, however, is not the widening of the extent, but the protection or regaining of the coherence within and between these elements. To what degree was the degree of governance coherence a troublesome context for the process?

The levels and scales context shows all levels involved, from the European (directives, subsidies), the national (policies, finance), the provincial (for example, main actor for nature development), the regional water authority, the local (for example, physical planning), and groups of citizens and farmers, including individuals (for example, landowners).

While the European and national levels were not directly active as actors in the process, their policies inspired much of the action and they have been contacted as sources of finance. A national administrative agreement on water management between the relevant state, province, water authority and local authorities has created some degree of clarity at least for the water quantity issues involved. The province took quite an active role to use the potential of the project as nature development and to accommodate the planned regional business park. The linkage of the development of the business park to the project also created an extra motivation supporting the project with the municipality of Almelo. More complicated was the relation between the national and local level. In search for financial resources, it was decided to link the project to the land re-ordering policy scheme. While the national law governing such land re-ordering projects was about to be changed in such a way that contributions to the project were made possible, it effectually led to postponing the already agreed upon land re-ordering project (to the regret and thus de-motivation of local farmers). A third issue here was the relation between the European and national level (nature policies) and the group and local levels, when citizens, farmers and even council members proposed to interrupt the wide natural river banks for some miles and proposed alternative nature development elsewhere. Though initiated from an interest (motivational) perspective, this clearly had a cognitive side, since it was rooted in a misunderstanding of the whole point of creating an ecological infrastructure.

There was no ready networks and actors context from which just a regional subgroup could be tapped and activated for this project. The initiator was clearly the water authority. The addition to the project by the province, using the project for the ecological main network, made both the area and the budget much larger, giving in principle the province, not the water authority, the role of prime actor. Nevertheless, the water authority kept playing that role in practice, maintaining and sometimes creating relations with all necessary governmental and non-governmental organizations and groups. The province, however, at key moments stood actively aside to further the progress of the project. In the part of the trajectory where the larger municipality of Almelo was a key player because of its physical planning powers, the rural orientation of the project (land, nature, creeks) did not fit well with the urban aspirations of the city, causing some disinterest. Later the inclusion of a large part of a rural municipality into the urban municipality of Almelo made the extended municipality open up to the rural issues at stake.

With this already the next governance context is touched, that of the relevant problem perceptions and goal ambitions. To start with a positive issue: the vision of integrated water management, in which quantity and quality issues but also nature protection, finds a place and openness towards other issues as part of the vision has been accepted among most actors and has certainly helped to merge problem perceptions, leading to quick joint boundary judgements in the cognitions of the water authority and province (see above). The easy linkage of nature development with the initial water project can serve as an example of this. Nevertheless, local authorities have often problem perceptions of their own that might or might not be reconcilable with those of integrated water management. Among groups and individuals (and sometimes their local councillors), such inclusive views are often lacking. The water authority as project manager has sometimes responded by its marketing strategy. For instance, when the high waters of 1998 were creating high awareness of this risk among the public, the purpose of the project – one of several – to mitigate such risks was quickly placed in the spotlight.

The strategies and instruments context shows a lot of incoherence, especially in connection to the responsibilities and resources for implementation context. A project such as the Breakthrough has to rely on many instruments that are designed for purposes that represent only part of its own array of goals. Clearly, this is the case with the dependency on the local authority's cooperation to acquire rights under the zoning plan to dig the Breakthrough. Having to satisfy the requirements, time schedules and preferences of implementing actors simultaneously resembles for the project manager playing a simultaneous chess game in which one not only has to win all, but even all at approximately the same time. The best hope one can have under such circumstances is that the web of resource dependencies is sufficiently mutual to give all involved a stake. The institutional distribution of responsibilities, resources and instruments explains the interdependence that arose between the provincial government and the water authority in the implementation of national government policy. Framed within the problem perspective that the quality of nature was ascribed to water quality, the province was partly dependent on the efforts of the water authority, which was responsible for water goals. This is, however, far from always true, creating great risks for the project. Thus, project managers of such a project are urged to become masters of adaptive implementation. Much of this adaptive action could well be labelled boundary spanning.

6.6 MANAGING COMPLEXITY BY BOUNDARY SPANNING

In many respects the Breakthrough case shows very quick adaptations of actors to wider boundary judgements of others. The water authority started off in this sphere by seeking the involvement of various parties. The provincial initiative to link the project with nature development was welcomed as an opportunity and not as a threat by the water authority. They were, however, not the only actors that mattered. So far this strategy was successful; however, of interest were the strategies when boundary judgements clashed. There were two issues over which boundary judgements really clashed. The first one is the role of agriculture versus nature development in the project, with all kinds of spatial consequences. The other consists of the different time frames of the various sector rules, like EU subsidies and physical planning procedures. In fact, these clashes merged in practice into one, since the time pressures from the EU subsidy regulations were most threatened by the tension between farmers and the nature development ambition of the project that was a condition *sine qua non* for the province and became a clear goal for the water authority. The project was, however, also linked to creating the national ecological highway structure, not only with a different spatial scale of consideration, but also with potentially conflicting rules and values. The water authority responded with a whole array of strategies (see also Chapter 2).

New actors and arenas were used:

- hiring an independent chair with own interesting network connections;
- appointing a singular spokesman to deal with the press, keeping away from failure and inviting press at successes;
- using the land re-ordering steering committee as a platform;
- making as much use as possible of allies, such as the province in some cases and local aldermen in others, thus avoiding being central in every game.

Some can be labelled creating new cognitions and trust by open communication and exchange:

- quite open and also very active communication to the inhabitants, including home visits;
- actually using as much of their proposals as could fit in;
- showing off with small realized plots to gain support and momentum.

Others are a bit more manipulative, or should we say steering communication that is directed somewhat closer to influencing motivation, be it still with predominantly communication:

- marketing the project on the basis of the purposes closest to the hearts of the inhabitants in a certain place and time;
- playing down the risks of habitat protection rules applying to the area sooner or later.

The last category consists of facilitating and compromising, where the water authority really transfers resources to make the project more attractive to (potential) critics:

- commissioning an external consultancy to prepare a draft zoning plan for a municipality;
- promising to take some risks on board that were frightening opponents, such as planning blights;
- at an essential moment compromising to let agriculture continue for the first seven years.

In these ways gradually much of the opposition was overcome.

6.7 CONCLUSIONS: THE TWO CASES COMPARED

In Chapters 5 and the present chapter two cases are studied in some detail. Though in many respects their problems are comparable, they were not completely simultaneous in time. The North and South Meene case was mostly evolving in the period 1998 – 2002, while the bigger and more complex Breakthrough case started a bit later, but mostly evolved from 2000 onwards and to a large extent is still continuing. This chapter has been written in 2008, while the planning aims at completion in 2014.

This has some relevant implications for the structural (governance) context of these processes. The quantitative water task overview of WB21, the National Administrative Agreement on Water (between all relevant authorities) and the fully felt pressure of the requirements of the European Water Framework Directive and the national and European ecological highway policies were not yet present or influential in the North and South Meene case, while they certainly are in the Breakthrough case. In many respects North and South Meene was a pioneer project of its sort. Overall, the structural governance context has improved.

A second difference is that the water authority of Regge and Dinkel in the Breakthrough case was much better prepared to face the complexity – and even to look for it when these sectors, actors and rules seem to be unavoidable sometime in the process – than the water authority in the North and South Meene case that more or less stumbled into it (no wonder, pioneers as they were). The inclusion of more purposes into the water management which initiated the Breakthrough project – even to the extent that formally it is now as much a nature development as a water project – was met with a very adaptive attitude. In the concluding chapter, we will revisit the characteristics and requirements of such an adaptive approach that could enable water authorities to become good boundary spanners.

7. The Dutch land use re-ordering process as a multi-stakeholder management strategy

Katharine Owens

7.1 INTRODUCTION

To address contemporary water issues in a balanced manner, without unduly impacting society, managers need receptive and adaptive strategies to synthesize the goals of disparate sectors. Managers need the ability to connect what may at first appear to be the incongruent goals of, for example, agricultural and nature conservation sectors. Rejecting isolated work and instead building connections between and among different actors and sectors can enable and fortify relevant and appropriate decision-making processes. Embracing this boundary work involves engaging in adaptive governance and yields integrated and interactive management solutions.

The Dutch land use re-ordering process (*landinrichting* process) is a linking strategy attempting to bridge policy subsectors to work together in envisioning the future development of a given area. This chapter explores two cases of wetland policy implementation involving the land use re-ordering process, evaluating its application in these cases and highlighting the successes and failures in each scenario.

In Section 7.2 the concepts boundary organizations and boundary objects are introduced, followed by the characterization of the land use re-ordering process in terms of institutional type in Section 7.3. In Sections 7.4 and 7.5 the Contextual Interaction Theory is described as it is used to analyze the cases, including variable specification and methodology. In Section 7.6 the descriptions and analysis for the two cases under scrutiny in this chapter are presented. In Sections 7.7 (discussion) and 7.8 (conclusions) the author details how the specific characteristics of the land use re-ordering process influence its usefulness as a boundary linking strategy.

7.2 BOUNDARY ORGANIZATIONS AND BOUNDARY OBJECTS

When evaluating social interaction processes in wetland policy, our attention is drawn to the organizations working on the boundaries, particularly between interests and scales. Cash and Moser (2000) describe boundary organizations as institutions mediating at the interface of science and decision making at multiple scales. In particular, they and others (see Guston, 1999) focus on the boundary between science and policy makers, though they argue this conceptual framework is also useful when envisioning boundaries 'between different scales and functional levels' (Cash and Moser, 2000, p. 114). For this treatment (following Kearney et al., 2007) we envision boundary work as not limited merely to the interface between science and policy, but instead capable of being used to describe boundaries between actors at different scales, representing varying sectors with different interests. Namely, boundary spanning over the sectors of nature and security/flood protection in our first case and the sectors of agriculture and nature in the second case.

Boundary organizations hold a particular role in interaction processes. Cash and Moser (2000, pp. 115–16) write that boundary organizations can serve functions including brokering information, communicating salient research needs, insulating from cross-boundary pressures, providing neutral discussion fora and building long-term trust. They are not described or envisioned as necessarily cooperative. Boundary organizations are not in the business of fostering cooperation for cooperation's sake. Cash and Moser (2000, p. 115, my emphasis) find the function of a boundary organization is 'maintain[ing] and facilitat[ing] both the connection *and separation* across boundaries'. Swart and van Andel (2007, p. 6) state that boundary spanning strategies may also incorporate excluding actors from the process, in an effort to 'control the process of mediation', though they remark that this may ultimately prove an unwise strategy. The role of the boundary organization is to facilitate interaction. Boundary organizations provide an area for the junction of multi-scale 'interests, ideas, disciplinary languages and perspectives' (Cash and Moser, 2000, p. 115). One way they do this is via the production of boundary objects, an item of value on either side of the boundary, allowing 'cooperation, debate, evaluation, review, and accountability' (Star and Griesemer, 1989 and Guston, 1999 in Cash and Moser, 2000, p. 115). Star and Griesemer (1989, p. 393) eloquently describe boundary objects as 'both plastic enough to adapt to local needs and the constraints of the several parties employing them, yet robust enough to maintain a common identity across sites'. Therefore boundary organizations and boundary objects may not always facilitate cooperation, but should facilitate interaction across scales, sectors and interests.

Boundary spanning is seen as particularly applicable to social interaction processes that deal with environmental issues. Cash and Moser (2000) find boundary organizations, coupled with interactive and adaptive management, helpful in addressing multi-scale environmental problems. Medd and Marvin (2007, p. 6) apply boundary spanning to water management, finding it especially salient when working in a field defined by 'ecosystem boundaries' as opposed to 'institutional boundaries'. They write: 'translating sustainable water management into practice within the region has to pass through a multiple set of scales, between regional and network space, and across different sets of social, environmental, and economic interests' (p. 10). It can be argued that any environmental problem potentially may jump the boundaries of nation, state or municipality given the fact that air, water, wildlife and other resources fail to follow national, state or municipal boundaries. In this way boundary spanning can be crucially important in environmental decision making. Medd and Marvin (2007, p. 16) find that 'strategic intermediaries play a critical role in reconnecting the multiple spatialities of water'. This is certainly true for wetland restoration projects as a subset of water projects. Wetland projects often involve multiple actors, working at various scales and representing government, business, environment, recreation and many other potential interests. Occasionally when dealing with wetland restoration policy and projects in the Netherlands, one encounters the land use re-ordering process being used as a multi-actor management strategy. Land use re-ordering programmes, managed by the provincial level of government, are large-scale projects that seek to solve a number of planning and development issues in an area by enabling land swaps and sales. The underlying concept is to promote the best overall scenario for all parties by bringing relevant actors together for discussions. In such a process land can shift between these uses as actors discuss options, make compromises, and ideally create collaborative scenarios that satisfy all the actors involved. In evaluating the Dutch land use re-ordering process we ascertain whether it serves as a facilitator of linkages, an adequate controller of the mediation process, and if the boundary work performed by the land use re-ordering organization is capable of enabling satisfactory decision making for the actors involved.

7.3 CHARACTERIZING THE LAND USE RE-ORDERING PROCESS AS A BOUNDARY OBJECT

Using Ostrom's (1999) institutional rules as a guide this section seeks to classify the land use re-ordering process in a meaningful way as an institution type. As described thoroughly by Ostrom (1999, p. 53), rules-in-use are often not available in writing, and perhaps not even understood as rules by participants. This attempt to classify the land use re-ordering process takes the concepts behind Ostrom's rules and channels them into an understanding of the land use re-ordering process.[1] The land use re-ordering process can be described as a legally supported interface for deliberation and conflict resolution, but let us consider this definition in terms of more specific rules.

Who is involved in the process, and what defines those allowed to take part? (Entry and exit rules)
Those with a stake in a land issue may participate in this provincial level programme to foster integrated development. As the province manages these processes, it is in their interest to include several actors – allowing more issues to be discussed, and a greater pool of land available, potentially yielding more trade opportunities. It also appears that provincial managers wait years to accumulate parties interested in participating in these interactions. It appears highly unlikely that an actor without a legal stake or interest would be allowed to participate. Specifically, this is not a forum comparable to a public meeting; average citizens apparently do not participate in this process. Instead, this is an accumulation of land policy actors (for example, local and regional governments, water boards, nature organizations, property and tourism development organizations, famers) with relevant interests in a given area.

What differences exist between general members and those with specific tasks or greater power? Is it possible to change positions? (Position rules)
Early in the land use re-ordering a process committee is formed, which is headed by a chairperson. The committee members are stakeholders in the process. It is not clear whether the chairperson is elected by the committee or appointed by provincial process managers. It is clear that the chairperson is a stakeholder, and not a provincial-level bureaucrat or politician. The committee chair remains as chair for the duration of the process; there is no indication that the chair has more formal power than the other process participants; of course they might be influential in agenda building and summarizing conclusions. It is likely the chair holds a level of informal power in the process.

Are there limitations on areas that are off-limits, are there constraints about who can annex which resources? (Scope rules)
Actors must agree within the context of the process to a land trade or a change in land use. Agreement by all parties is a necessary part of the

process, meaning that any area an organization deems off-limits would be considered as such in the process. That being said, the purpose of the process is to take seemingly unsolvable issues and use a larger pool of options to negotiate a win-win situation for all parties. It is important to note that even with this limitation in place, the spirit of a negotiation can be subverted, as shown in the Ameland case, and described in the discussion section.

What are the regulations about what is considered mandatory, authorized or forbidden within the process? (Authority rules)
The parties involved are key players in the process. They decide together what changes to make and how to create win-win scenarios. Nothing would necessarily be considered mandatory or forbidden within the process, if the parties agree. Authorization rests with the committee and its chairperson.

Do some actions require permission or agreement from others? (Aggregation rules)
In a land use re-ordering process, actions require agreement of all parties. The essence of the process is creating a space where actors can solve problems through mutual agreement.

What consequences exist for breaking rules? How is rule compliance supervised? Who enforces compliance? How stringently? Can rewards be granted for certain behaviours? (Payoff rules)
In theory, the land use re-ordering committee has the authority to enforce consequences when rules are broken. In practice, this is true, but this authority was utilized in a surprising manner in the Ameland case to in essence subvert the process (see further below). This committee of stakeholders supervises the process; the stringency of enforcement differs from case to case, as dictated by the individuals involved. Within the legal context of the land use re-ordering process there is apparently no specification of how stringently rules will be enforced. Actors continue to take part in land use re-ordering agreements, which indicates that there is a level of trust in and respect for the process. In practice, there is no indication that rewards are given for certain behaviours. Actors are not penalized if they choose to reject a proposal. Instead, the format is meant to include stakeholders in developing a plan that all can agree to.

By classifying the land use re-ordering process via Ostrom's institutional rules we see that, as an institution, this is an arena for a process in which not the general public, but relevant stakeholders in land policy participate.

We also find that in the land use re-ordering process a chairperson, who is also a stakeholder, heads the committee and that authority to enforce rules rests within this committee. The core of the land use re-ordering process is that of mutual agreement; any actor can set an area as off-limits, and nothing would be considered necessarily mandatory or forbidden. Actors are not penalized if they reject a proposal. Through exploration of two very different cases, we can illuminate how the characteristics of this process influence its usefulness as a boundary organization.

7.4 ANALYSIS VIA THE CONTEXTUAL INTERACTION THEORY

These land use re-ordering cases are evaluated via Contextual Interaction Theory, which assesses actor characteristics of motivation, information and power to understand their influence on implementation. The theory provides an analytical tool for evaluating cases in a consistent way as implementation scenarios, describing how the actor characteristics influence the likelihood to implement at all and the adequacy of implementation.

Contextual Interaction Theory (CIT)[2] focuses analysis on the implementation stage of the policy process, simplifying an implementation situation into the interaction of two actors: policy implementer and policy target. It evaluates the core actors to determine the manner in which their motivation, information and power influence two aspects of a policy process: the likelihood to implement at all and the adequacy of implementation. This designation captures two distinct moments within the policy process: whether an implementation begins in reality and whether an implementation that begins accomplishes the intentions of a given policy. Theory application assumes any actor type (governmental, private or other) might play a role of implementer or target, as dictated by the policy in question and the actor's stakes. CIT utilizes scores for motivation, information and power to create hypotheses about how actors will interact in an implementation situation (see Bressers, 2004 for an extensive theory description).

7.4.1 Independent Variables

CIT draws connections between actor characteristics and degree of cooperation in an implementation situation. When applying CIT, the independent variable of actor characteristics is in its 2004 version (Bressers, 2004) defined in terms of the motivation, information and power of both target and implementer. This section describes the concepts underlying the definition of motivation, information and power within this study.[3]

Motivation can be conceptualized as the way the implementation of the project is understood to play a part in the achievement of an actor's objectives. The variable of motivation incorporates themes such as an actor's own motivation and potential sources of external pressure. Building a composite of an actor's own motivation includes aspects such as compatibility with the goals of implementation, work-related motivation, the actor's attitude to the implementation objective, attitude to the target group and self-effectiveness. Understanding potential sources of external pressure includes examining normative, economic, social and political influences.

Information includes general knowledge about the policy and how to comply, accessibility to materials, and the transparency of the process for both targets and implementers. General information encompasses aspects such as policy awareness for relevant actors, including an understanding of policy requirements and benefits, and knowledge of other stakeholders and their role in the process. Transparency incorporates accessibility and the level of documentation available to process participants or interested parties. It also touches on the simplicity or usefulness of this information, and uncertainties that may affect the process. In the most recent version of CIT in Chapter 2 the information variable is referred to as cognitions, emphasizing the subjective character of knowledge believed to be true. In this chapter we will use it in its 2004 specification.

The conceptualization of power, used in this application of the theory includes aspects of capacity and control. Power may be associated with capacity or resources such as inputting finances, personnel or time. Capacity or resources have the ability to strengthen or weaken the position of a given individual, organization or agency. Power as control divides further into formal and informal facets. Formal power is that given to a group, individual or agency through legal channels or areas of responsibility. Examples of positions of formal power or responsibility in wetland restoration projects include project initiator, decision-making roles, reporter of results, project or site monitor, project financial supporter or fulfiller of policy requirements. Informal power may derive from roles as site users or stakeholders, or actors having the ability to use expertise, coalitions or media to their advantage in a process. Informal sources of power may also stem from the ability to convince others to comply with one's own goals. When considering formal or informal power, it is important to reflect on the difference between power and a reputation of power. Reputation of power involves how actors perceive each other in the process. In essence, the reputation of power is real in its consequences unless later experiences prove to others that the reputation is not grounded in reality. For this reason, it is extremely important to understand how the actors comprehend their own power in relation to that of others in the process. It is critical to appreciate who has the formal power to implement a given project, and to what degree, to observe how actors try to build power through the process, and to recognize who actually exercises power in each case. In the most recent version of CIT in Chapter 2 the power variable is referred to under resources, which provide both capacity and power. Again, in this chapter we use the 2004 specification.

7.4.2 Dependent Variables

Policy implementation normally involves interactions between implementers and the target of the policy. It cannot be assumed that implementation happens automatically, no matter who is responsible for seeing implementation takes place. CIT considers the likelihood to implement at all the primary result of an implementation process. Given various combinations of the three variables within the first phase of analysis, the theory provides a prediction for the type of interaction which will occur, and a hypothesis about each. Potential interaction types include cooperation, opposition and joint learning. Cooperation may be realized as active (actors have a joint ambition, though this is not necessarily proper implementation of the policy), passive (one party is impartial about this policy implementation) or forced (a forceful actor compels passive cooperation). Opposition stems from one actor attempting to inhibit the other actor from implementing the policy. Joint learning is seen as a scenario in which only deficiencies in information block application. Finally, no interaction, or the absence of an interaction is also a possibility – however this situation eliminates the likelihood to implement at all. One example of a theory prediction for likelihood to implement at all is:

> If application of the instrument would contribute positively to the objectives of one actor, while the other actor is negative, and the information of the positive actor is sufficient, then the character of the interaction process will be dependent on the balance of power between the actors. Dominance of the positive actor will lead to (forced) cooperation. (Bressers, 2004, p. 32)

Initiation of implementation does not automatically lead to the envisioned changes in target group behaviour. When an implementation situation is seen as progressing successfully through the first phase (that is, likely to implement), the next step is analysis of how well actual implementation meets policy intention. This may include dynamic adaptations, ideal in reflexive and flexible policy implementation, which ultimately strengthen or support policy intentions.

Considering adequacy of implementation (phase two), the types of predicted interactions are different than those for likelihood to implement at all. In general, the second phase represents an increase in complexity as actors work to physically address a real world problem, perhaps including negotiations, reworking of plans, or other interactive problem-solving exercises. This often means that motivations, information and even the power balance might need to be assessed differently when considering adequate implementation instead of just whether there will be any form of implementation at all. Potential interaction types include cooperation, opposition and symbolic application. Cooperation may involve active constructive cooperation (actors have a joint ambition, here implying that the goal is to implement the instrument) or active obstructive cooperation (both actors benefit from improper implementation; this can also happen in passive cooperation when one or both actors wish to implement as a matter of form, but have no actual interest in adequate implementation). Opposition may incorporate negotiation (both actors work to maximize their goals via compromise) or conflict (most often the target group ceases communication; displaying power by, for example, bringing the policy's legality into question). The final possibility is symbolic application (the policy is realized through bureaucratic channels, but only weakly in a physical sense) which has potential to incorporate learning over time to alter the interaction. One example of a theory prediction for likelihood to implement at all is:

> If adequate application of the instrument would contribute positively to the objectives of at least one actor, but it/they have insufficient information for adequate application, then there will be initially symbolic interaction, but also learning by the positive actor(s), leading later to other situations. (Bressers, 2004, p. 33)

Analysis via this theory illuminates how stakeholders at the core of the policy process influence policy implementation. It provides a consistent way of looking at wetland restoration cases to evaluate the utility of the land use re-ordering process.

7.5 METHODOLOGY

The implementer is the actor promoting the given measures; the target is the actor necessary to bring the measures to fruition. The instances of land use re-ordering processes depicted here represent two cases taken from a larger comparative study. Case descriptions were built by interviewing two relevant actors per case (the policy implementer and policy target). Interviewing is one way to understand more about participant motivations, information level and the power balance. It also gives insight into how participants connect meaning with events (Berg, 2001). The semi-standardized interviewing method was used, which entails asking predetermined questions in a systematic manner, but also includes an expectation that the interviewer probe beyond answers given (ibid.). The interviewees provided unique and beneficial information about local history, plan development and process interactions. Extensive notes were taken during each interview to ensure proper documentation of responses. Each interview was analyzed to determine motivation, information and power scores. All respondents seemed willing to participate in interviews and keen to share their experiences.

7.5.1 Measuring Variables

These three independent variables represent dense concepts. The researcher must carefully connect interview questions with the concepts to create adequate variable estimates. Transforming broad concepts into numbers provides both advantages and disadvantages. It generates a consistent and practical system for comparing actor characteristics, though could potentially offer a less comprehensive understanding of actor traits. With this in mind, interview instrument development included multi-faceted variable conceptualization. Systematically asking all relevant questions and triangulating responses (by asking for details or substantiation for claims) creates thorough analysis. The researcher also critically assesses the responses of actors who may offer highly variable descriptions of a common event. This methodical, organized treatment translates the various facets of each variable described above to produce an inclusive picture of the interviewee's characteristics and experiences. The researcher determined motivation, information and power scores by calculating responses to interview questions and incorporating these scores into a quantification tool (see Owens, 2008 for thorough description). Target and implementer scores funnel into the CIT formulation to produce a prediction based on the combination of characteristics. This allows comparing the theory prediction with observations of the degree of cooperation in each case.

CIT measures actor characteristics to understand their influence on implementation. When utilizing the theory in other studies (see ibid.), the goal is to understand how theoretical predictions compare with interaction observations. In this chapter we use the theory results to compare the degree of cooperation between the two cases of interest. In other words, how far along the process of implementation did each case progress? Or, how successful are the two cases? CIT envisions the dependent variables as two phases of implementation: the likelihood to implement at all, and the adequacy of implementation.

As these are broad ideas, it is essential to clearly state what they mean in the context of this research. For this study, it is most important to understand the role of the land use re-ordering process in facilitating cooperation. To better understand what influence the land use re-ordering process might have, we focus on two cases: one in which the implementation succeeded through to the second phase, and one in which the implementation failed in the first phase. Stated another way, we demonstrate the land use re-ordering process by showing cases of both success and failure. This is not to say that the land use re-ordering process, present in both cases, should be considered irrelevant. Instead, we use this comparison to pick out the useful elements of this process as an institutional form by comparing the successful to the failed implementation. In this analysis a case that does not progress from initiation, or one that fizzles out immediately is considered a failure. A case that progresses through the implementation and addresses policy goals is considered a success. As these cases involve wetland restoration policy, it is important to understand how this context influences implementation success.

Restoration ecologists continue to debate how to define success in ecosystem restoration; assessment criteria can be complex and extensive (Hobbs and Harris, 2001). While the ultimate policy goal may be (explicitly or implicitly) long-term ecological sustainability, here we do not measure the success of wetland cases against an ultimate outcome of sustainable long-term ecosystem restoration. Instead, success is based on adequate implementation from a policy perspective. More specifically, we determine whether implementation as discussed and agreed upon by actors is enacted. If this action is taken and completed, the implementation is considered a success. For each case, we highlight the present state of the process and discuss how it has met the challenges of each phase of the process.

7.6 CASE DESCRIPTIONS AND ANALYSIS

These cases represent two very different instances of land use re-ordering processes. In the first case the actors have similar motivations and work together to enable the successful implementation of a wetland restoration project. In the second case the actors hold contrasting goals for the restoration of an area. After describing the cases in detail, we will evaluate what role the land use re-ordering process plays in linking sectoral boundaries in these two cases.

7.6.1 The Bargerveen Project

The nature area Bargerveen is found in the north-eastern Dutch province of Drenthe. Investigations by the Dutch State Forestry Service (Staatsbosbeheer) from the early 1990s indicated groundwater level was too low and that managers lacked control of surface water levels in this nature complex of 2089 hectares (5162 acres). The Forestry Service then built approximately 40 kilometres of small peat dams to attempt to control the area. In 1998 the region received severe rainfall, inundating these peat dams and threatening the village of Zwartemeer. At this time Bargerveen joined a land use re-ordering process. When a province proposes a land use re-ordering they must seek ministry approval from the Ministry of Agriculture, Nature and Food Quality, then an Area Portioning Commission (Deel Gebieds Commissie) is installed as a temporary form of government to direct the activities of the land use re-ordering. In this case the Service for Rural Territory (Dienst Landelijk Gebied) was hired as project leader by the Portioning Commission. Wetland policies applying to the area include the European Union Natura 2000 Network, via the *Bird and Habitat Directives,* and the Netherlands Nature Policy Plan, National Ecological Network. The project proposal involved creating a new dike as well as water retention areas within the Bargerveen, stabilizing area water levels and encouraging peat and moorland growth. The plans gained municipal level support both because of the recent flooding and because they would bring clean water to the area in an inexpensive way. EU LIFE funded 60 per cent of the project, while the Forestry Service contributed 20 per cent, the regional water board contributed 10 per cent and the Portioning Commission contributed 10 per cent. The project was implemented in phases from 2003 to 2006.

The Service for Rural Territory is charged with managing land to the satisfaction of the project partners, and plays the role of implementer in this case. The State Forestry Service owns this land, but they must rely on The Service for Rural Territory to lead the process in a way that will help restore the complex's active raised bogs and wet heathlands. The State Forestry Service is here regarded the target for analysis. It is the organization that has to adapt the current situation to realize the goals of the wetland restoration part of the relevant policies. Both implementer and target are positively motivated toward the project. The implementer describes it as a win-win situation while the target states no one had something to lose. The target is motivated to protect and restore the nature on its land while the implementer is motivated to conduct the process in a way benefiting the participants. Both the implementer and target display high information levels. They are both knowledgeable of actors and their qualifications, aware of the multiple levels of policy applied to this site, and report no problems with information sharing among actors. The actors met almost monthly, for a total of 20 meetings over two years. Information levels of both actors increased over the course of the project. The implementer has a low power score while the target has a high power score. In this case the target holds the balance of power. Given the actor scores quantified in analysis, the CIT hypothesizes for the likelihood to implement at all that the interaction process will have the character of cooperation. More specifically, predicting that when both actors are positively motivated active cooperation will transpire.

When comparing theory predictions to observations, the hypothesis rings true: these actors cooperate to make a plan for the restoration of the Bargerveen within the greater plans of the land use re-ordering. The Forestry Service has formal authority for this area but trusts that the administration of the Service for Rural Territory will benefit their goals in the long term. It is important to note that the Forestry Service remain as active participants in the process. When asked about decision making, the target states that there were rarely problems, and not a lot of difference of opinion. The implementer describes decision making as occurring via a committee of stakeholders, and finds that they usually had something in common. In this case, once actors became involved with the land use re-ordering process, they worked to make it successful.

The scores do not change greatly for the second phase of analysis, the adequacy of implementation. Again, both target and implementer are positively motivated toward the project and have high information levels. The implementer's motivation score increases slightly, while the target's motivation remains consistent between the phases of analysis. Actors worked together to solve problems during the process, including an unforeseen difficulty with increasing levels of aluminum in the area's waters.

In one natural process associated with peat and the acidic water found around peat, when digging in a peat area one can produce aluminum silica. Though this is a natural by-product, it remains a polluting substance. Actors became aware of increasing aluminum levels about four months into implementation, through notification by a local factory which tests water quality. To solve the problem, implementation was put on hold and eventually reinstated in the winter months when the risk of producing aluminum decreased. This unforeseen risk was a costly misstep for the project partners, but was eventually handled in a satisfactory way. Both target and implementer experience an increase in information levels during the second phase of the process. This can be attributed to increasing actor knowledge as they dealt with the aluminum problem. The implementer and target scores for power remain consistent during the process.

The power scores do not change, with the target continuing to hold the balance of power in this phase. Given the quantified actor scores, the theory predicts that constructive cooperation will evolve, and that if both actors are positively motivated, then active constructive cooperation will occur. When comparing this theoretical prediction with observations we find that this is an accurate description of the interaction. Throughout the implementation process the actors cooperate in a constructive manner to ensure implementation.

7.6.2 The Ameland Dune Fringe Project

This case takes place on the Dutch Wadden Island of Ameland, which is part of the Northern Province of Friesland. In the late 1980s and early 1990s the Ministry of Agriculture, Nature and Food Quality (Ministerie van Landbouw, Natuur en Voedselkwaliteit) created a Re-ordering Commission (Herinrichting Commissie) to manage a land use re-ordering project on the island. Several levels of policy apply in this case including the Netherlands Nature Policy Plan, National Ecological Network and non-specified provincial-level nature plans. Purportedly this land use re-ordering sought to shift land from agricultural use to create approximately 400 hectares (988 acres) of nature on the island and to develop a hotel and golf course complex. The golf course and hotel project was implemented immediately while the nature development project still awaits implementation despite 17 years since project inception. The nature project goals include restoring the inner border of the dune area and building a buffer between a recreation area and the nature reserve Ameland Dunes. The buffer zone, essentially a wetland, will prevent people from crossing the nature reserve by taking a short cut between the recreation area and the beach front. When the project was conceived, the nature reserve was important as a breeding and foraging area for the hen harrier (*Circus cyaneus*) and the short-eared owl (*Asio flammeus*). The reserve was considered by some the most important area within the Netherlands for the short-eared owl. Now there remain only four breeding pairs of hen harrier and no short-eared owls within the reserve.

As stated above, the source of land for both projects (tourism development and nature) was primarily agriculture. Yet not everyone involved in this plan has an interest in the nature aspect of the land use re-ordering. Farmers on the island supported the goals of the development project but not the nature project. As the Re-ordering Commission includes representatives of farming interests, these individuals used the process to enable tourism development but did not allow completion of the nature development aspect of the project. Since the project began, one piece of land within the target area for nature was sold privately to the Re-ordering Commission Chairman, who then proved unwilling to sell this land for nature development. In this way, not only farmers in general, but also leadership within the Re-ordering Commission are in favour of actively supplanting the nature goals of the land use re-ordering. This project represents a case of a wetland restoration that has not yet been implemented.

The ministry and the province of Friesland are implementers in this analysis, as their organizations direct the land use re-ordering at different times in the process. Since the project began, the land use re-ordering process has changed from being administered by the ministry to being administered by the provincial government. The implementer interviewee worked for the ministry when the project began and now works for the Province of Friesland. The Working Group for Ameland Nature (Natuur Werkgroep Ameland) within the land use re-ordering process works to designate nature goals in the process, and is the target in this analysis. The target aspect is based on an interview with an individual who was a member of the Working Group for Ameland Nature and is employed by the Ameland Nature Center. When doing the case study this seemed to be a reasonable choice as they are committed to the area. However, later – as we will show – the most sensible issues arose in the relation between nature, on the one hand, and agriculture (farmers), on the other. So we ended up using both interviews to get information on the position of that alternative target.

The implementer displays a neutral motivation score in analysis. This reflects that in many instances the implementer interviewee spoke in terms of how the farmers perceived the issues, and about the interests of the farmers. For example, he states that as island dwellers, any loss of farmland for nature is seen as a social and economic risk for the farmers. He finds that the farmers felt their interests were more important than the project realization. While formally charged to implement the land use re-ordering, this interviewee also understands and articulates the interest of the farmers within the process. The target interviewee (from the Nature Center) displays a positive motivation score. While this actor also acknowledges the social pressure from locals who did not support the project, his role in the process is promoting nature protection and conservation on the island. He finds protection of bird species as well as development of nature tourism a long-term benefit for island dwellers. The implementer has a high information score while the target has a low information score. Both actors are knowledgeable of actors and their qualifications. The implementer describes few problems with information sharing, accessibility and documentation during the project. The implementer states only that the timing was off and reports some uncertainties knowing the interests of farmers. In contrast, the target describes a lack of information, stating: at first it seemed okay, but after some years, when the golf course was finished, nothing was heard of again. The target interviewee finds communication between actors was limited, and accessibility was very bad. This actor continues to have questions about how money was spent on the project, particularly funding sources and the whereabouts of money intended for the (wetland) nature aspect of the project. Both actors have similar moderate power scores, neither definitely holds the balance of power in this process.

Given the actor scores quantified in analysis, the CIT hypothesizes for the likelihood to implement at all that a joint learning process will evolve that will sooner or later create another situation. Does this prediction agree with observations? Yes, it is true that the positive actor does not currently have the information to apply the instrument. However, the positively motivated actor (representing nature interests) describes being effectively shut out of the process. In this way, the current interaction is one with little information sharing. As we learned that the real issues were with the farmers, who had a negative motivation, it makes sense to review the process also with them as specified targets.

According to both interviewees, local farmers hold immense power in determining how this project proceeds. In such instances theory predicts obstruction of all progress even when the implementer's motivation is regarded as positive and simply no action at all if the implementer's motivation is regarded as indifferent. In his interview, the implementer describes attempts to restart the project since the original land use re-ordering. On one occasion, the deputy of the province of Friesland attempted to restart the process but did not succeed. Within the last year representatives from both the municipal and provincial levels of government attempted to revive the process, and also failed. The implementer also remarks that even one farmer refusing to sell land within the target area jeopardizes the entire project. According to the target interviewee, the people of Ameland are against the project and the power of the province and ministry are not enough. Due to the complications found in this project, plans for nature and recreation are now more closely linked from inception, then presented and financed as one plan. Clearly this project has served as a learning experience for implementers in future projects, but stakeholders are also concerned about whether the nature aspect of this project will ever come to fruition.

The theory predicts this case will not produce an interaction as the variables currently stand. No action on the nature aspect of the project is being taken. As the actors in this case do not move forward from planning stages, it is not possible to evaluate the second phase of analysis, the adequacy of implementation. This case is considered a failure from an implementation perspective.

7.7 DISCUSSION

Bargerveen and the Ameland Dune Fringe project do not represent randomly selected cases from a greater population. Instead, these two cases were chosen as examples of relative success and failure of wetland restorations incorporating land use re-ordering processes. Is it possible to compare these cases in a way that allows us insight into the utility of this process as a linking strategy between boundaries? The Bargerveen case represents the intersection of nature protection and flood control. The actors describe this case as not involving a great deal of differences in opinion between the actors. While this certainly plays into the project's success as a land use re-ordering process, this case was neither simple nor without complications. Though the tone throughout could be adequately described as cooperative, complex issues arose during the process. In particular, the contamination of the area by a natural aluminum by-product led to renegotiations, increased costs and the addition of time to the project. This case is characterized by communication, with actors using the framework of the land use re-ordering process to meet regularly to discuss viable options, and troubleshoot issues throughout the process. This case shows that the land use re-ordering process can serve as an adequate linking device between disparate sectors such as flood control and nature conservation, each with their own actors, procedures, goals and resources. In essence, the land use re-ordering process created a channel for spanning these boundaries in a complicated and complex wetland restoration project.

In comparison, the Ameland Dune Fringe project has not proceeded despite the formal checks and balances that should be a part of the land use re-ordering structure. The island has experienced important species loss while this issue remains unresolved by actors. This case involves actors representing conflicting goals from nature, farming and tourism. The land use re-ordering process should provide a neutral body linking across these boundaries, but this did not occur in this case. This case is characterized by a lack of communication between actors, with the target in particular describing a perception of being excluded from communication channels within the process. According to the implementer interviewee, to famers on the island, changing farmland to nature is seen as a social and economic risk. The structure of the land use re-ordering should allow formal channels for actors to support their varied goals. However, in this instance, members of the land use Re-ordering Commission itself supplant the purported project goals by privately buying land and refusing to sell it for nature development. In this case the implementers represent governmental and political organizations at multiple scales. Clearly the Ameland constituency deserves the representation of farming interests as well as nature interests by their elected officials. However, as the implementers of national and international environmental policy, they also represent a player within the process which could enable project implementation. The Province of Friesland and the Ministry of Agriculture, Nature and Food Quality have dual and sometimes conflicting goals to balance – as representatives of citizens and as implementers of policy; as promoters of both local economic prosperity and international environmental protection. Kearney et al. (2007, p. 14) describe effective cross-scale linkages as featuring 'a respected, authoritative, independent body that acts as the facilitator for the linkage arrangement'. One characteristic of the land use re-ordering process is that it is not independent, but instead comprised of stakeholders. In this case, the process committee did not foster linkages in practice. The province could take on the role of the respected, authoritative body/facilitator, but has not done this to date. In this case the structure of the land use re-ordering process fails to link actors in a way that allows them to communicate across interests and scales.

Cash and Moser (2000, pp. 115–16) write that boundary organizations can serve functions including brokering information, communicating salient research needs, insulating from cross-boundary pressures, providing neutral discussion fora and building long-term trust. In terms of the Bargerveen case, these issues were addressed through the land use re-ordering process as they arose. It served as a structure for building effective communication channels, allowed for communicating salient research needs, provided a neutral discussion forum and served in some way as the actors built connections of trust during the process. It is not clear that cross-boundary pressures became a problem in the Bargerveen case, as actors held similar motivations for the project. When assessing the Ameland Dune Fringe case, we see that the land use re-ordering process was not able to (in itself) serve as a tool for effective communication, broach cross-boundary pressures or build long-term trust among actors. It may have provided a neutral discussion forum and allowed the communication of some research needs, but arguably not in an in-depth manner.

7.7.1 The Influence of Land Use Re-ordering Characteristics

To what extent do the characteristics of the land use re-ordering process play a role in the results of the two cases? When motivations are congruent, as in the Bargerveen case, the land use re-ordering process may serve as a medium for fostering mutual goals and motivations. The process gathers all relevant parties into a forum of communication, as well as one seeking mutual agreement through discussion and compromise. Those with a stake in the process are brought together to create solutions to not only the problems of others, but more importantly, to solve their own problems. As a committee is formed by stakeholders, this allows those with the most relevant stakes in the process an ability to effectively communicate. Linking these primary stakeholders has the potential to even improve information among actors. As shown in the Bargerveen case through the quick reaction to and resolution of the aluminum silica issue, everyone who was needed to solve the problem was in place and communicating. In addition, the process constraint of mutual agreement can help foster trust among actors, making participants feel as if they have the power to protect their own stake and goals within the process. This, as well as the fact that nothing would be considered mandatory or forbidden within the process, if agreed upon, makes each actor feel as though they can enter the process without committing to potentially losing their stake. As noted, authority and the power to enforce consequences for rule-breaking rest with the committee and its chairperson. In the Bargerveen case, this structural element did not negatively influence results. When motivations are incongruent, as discussed below, this aspect may prove damaging to the process as a linking strategy and even make it susceptible to misuse by actors that only want to harvest what is in it for them.

We have determined what about the process may fortify a process in which actors share similar motivation, but how might the characteristics of a land use re-ordering influence a process where motivations contrast? Despite motivations, the process will gather those with relevant stakes and put them in a position to communicate and create compromise. In the Ameland case we see that how the actors choose to interact in this format may not be necessarily mutually beneficial. In the Ameland case, actors agreed to devote some land for tourism, and that change was implemented. The process proved ultimately unsuccessful when actors failed to continue the sentiment of the agreement by also purchasing and devoting other land to nature use. As with the Bargerveen case, all relevant parties are involved in the process, but in this case the committee, particularly its chairman, work to subvert the spirit of the agreement by halting action after the tourism project is implemented, but before the nature project is implemented. In this case the chairman himself bought agricultural land for sale and refused to sell it on to the province for the nature aspect of the land use re-ordering project. As described by case interviewees, even provincial authority has proven unable to change the results of this case to date. As mentioned above, the process aspect of mutual agreement can help build trust among actors, making participants feel as if they have the power to protect their own stake and goals within the process. It is important to note that the subversion of the Ameland case took place within the context of this constraint. The actions were agreed by everyone. All actors were initially satisfied, only later did the committee 'fail' to continue to implement or move forward with a part of the project they found less important. That the committee is the enforcer of the rules is most significant in this case. It also seems clear that on some level other committee members, all stakeholders, support the committee chairman's actions. Whether they fully support this is unclear, but they do support it to the level that they choose not to force the chairman into implementing the nature plan from the land use re-ordering process. The authority in the process rests with the committee, to the detriment of nature interests in this case. The province interviewee remarks that their own policy has changed since this case, and that now plans for nature and recreation are more closely linked from inception, then presented and financed as one plan. It is likely that the results of this case have impacted trust among stakeholders regarding land issues in Ameland.

7.8 CONCLUSIONS

In these cases we see that the land use re-ordering process has the potential to serve as a facilitator of linkages, a controlling influence on the mediation process, and has the capability of enabling satisfactory decision making. That being said, it is also clear that while creating channels for communication and agreement, the process still has the potential to be subverted by actors who are seeking to denigrate the process. In particular, the process aspect that lays the primary authority within the committee of stakeholders proved to be a path for subversion in the Ameland case. The Ameland Dune Fringe project shows us that the land use re-ordering process is not sufficiently robust as a boundary object to singularly carry a complicated process along when actors work to subvert the project goals. That being said, it is hard to imagine a boundary object capable of such a task in every situation. These two cases of Dutch wetland project restoration feature water bodies that span sector boundaries of flood control, nature, tourism and agriculture. Water resource managers may necessarily have to navigate goals rooted in such varying sectors as the environment, social issues, tourism, security, transportation and economic development. The land use re-ordering process can provide an adaptive, useful linking strategy to connect actors in water management issues, but naturally has limitations. Though perhaps not always fully effective, land use re-ordering processes do have some potential as boundary organizations to allow water managers to address contemporary issues in a balanced way. Though incapable of overcoming all constraints, their pros and cons as analyzed here may still serve as inspiration to design institutional arenas that provide valuable tools for managers as they problem solve in cases of water management. As the present institution is designed now, it is only helpful when motivations are congruent and/or power is balanced.

NOTES

1. Note that in each case the original rule concepts, shown in parentheses, are from Ostrom (1999) and the specifications are taken from Ostrom's specification in terms of common pool resources and applied to the context of the land use re-ordering process.
2. Hans Bressers (1983) originally developed the Contextual Interaction Theory as 'instrumentation theory'; it was then expanded via Bressers and Klok (1987), Klok (1991) and Bressers (2004), and tested in Owens (2008). See also Chapter 2 of this volume.
3. The concepts described in this and the following sections are based on Bressers (2004).

8. Linking natural science-based knowledge to governance strategy: a case of regional water depletion analyzed

Mirjam van Tilburg

8.1 INTRODUCTION

This chapter is focused on the boundary between natural science-based knowledge and decision-making processes in water management. Handling complex water issues in a rational manner requires both in-depth knowledge of water systems and transfer and adoption of that knowledge in policies. In a narrow view it is often assumed that natural science-based water system knowledge facilitates water governance. On the one hand, seen from this perspective, more information leads to better decisions. On the other hand, water managers have to line up with actors in society and their cognitions and motivations in order to be able to collect the needed resources for policy interventions, such as money, legal rights and support.

When science is considered in a broader view, it might also be used by water managers for persuasion or for rallying support in interaction processes. Also stakeholders might choose to juggle science in order to influence, delay or obstruct decision making.

In this chapter the use of natural science-based knowledge as a strategic instrument in policy-making processes is elaborated. Core questions that will be addressed are:

- What is the position of scientific models that are limited to relations that link interventions to (improvements of) water system conditions?
- What happens when scientific knowledge is out of the hand of scientists and used as a tool by policy makers in participatory processes?
- What are the lessons with regard to the use and exchange of natural science-based knowledge and participative processes?

In Section 8.2 the relationship between science and policy is discussed. In Section 8.3 a case in which water managers decide to use natural science as a strategy is introduced. In Section 8.4 the motivations and resources of the actors and their impact on the process are described. In Section 8.5 the observational tool that is employed to analyze the case is described. In section 8.6 the analysis is widened by focusing on converging and diverging boundary judgements. In section 8.7 the lessons learned are presented.

8.2 KNOWLEDGE IN THE POLICY PROCESS

The relationship between science and policy has been a point of interest for a long time. Scholars like Price (1967), Snow (1951) and Lasswell (1971) tried to reconcile the relationship between science and politics without undermining the independent and pure status of both worlds. Others focused on the role of scientists as adversaries and the dependency of politicians on experts (Schooler, 1971; Jones, 1972; MacRae, 1976). This being said, the complex nature of interactions between science and politics has more sides: actors' interests are interwoven with knowledge creation (Bloor, 1976; Barnes, 1977) and the attribution of the status fact to knowledge is a result of social processes (Latour and Woolgar, 1979; Knorr-Cetina and Mulkay, 1983).

The idea that science and policy are closely intertwined is firmly rooted in general thought on the relationship between science and policy. In determining water policy, natural science-based knowledge is vital in a traditional technocratic perspective on the science-policy interface. It is used to monitor the condition of water system (in terms of water quantity and quality), to design water engineering projects, to predict water system conditions and so on. It is a traditional technocratic role of science in the policy-making process. Research provides data on which policy can be built. The role of science can be described as production of neutral knowledge as a basis for decision making (Hoppe, 2002; Arquit Niederberger, 2005).

The focus of attention is still on the relationship between science and policy, but this relationship is no longer perceived to be exclusive. Scientific knowledge is just one of many factors that come into play in the decision-making process (Jasanoff, 1986, 1990). Several studies show that the image of the unbiased, objective and non-partial scientist is a myth, scientific advisers behave like any other stakeholder in a policy process (Nelkin, 1979).

Nowadays, the use of scientific knowledge in the policy process is considered to be quite normal. As Weingart (1999) suggested, few people remember that 30 years ago the relationship between science and policy was considered to be a dangerous liaison. Research on science and policy relationships has developed a broader scope, especially the societal context and stakeholder involvement linked to the science-policy interface.

Another, though closely linked, topic is what is called the democratization of science and the scientification of democracy (Weingart, 1999; Ravetz, 2001; Liberatore and Funtowicz, 2003). Democratization of science refers, on the one hand, to the increasing accessibility of scientific research for the public. On the other hand, it points at the tendency of involving the public in decisions concerning controversial and/or ethical questions raised by or derived from scientific research. The general public is more often invited to share their opinions, feelings or knowledge about topics including controversial issues in spatial planning or water system management. Another effect of the democratization of science is the loss of status of science. Incidents and the fact that science cannot bring absolute certainty in risky or uncertain situations have led to this loss of status. Scientific propositions are no longer thought of as neutral facts but are open for debate. Still, science plays a very important role in everyday policy and everyday life; there is hardly a move we can make without relying on experts (Jasanoff, 2003).

Because water managers have to line up with actors in society, the traditional technocratic science-policy interface needs to be adjusted to suit policy-making processes in a more dynamic environment. Using science in the policy process, specifically when interacting with stakeholders, can be tricky. First of all, the use of scientific knowledge is not always visible (Weiss, 1979), research itself can unintentionally have a political stance (Weiss, 1973) and policy problems do not always fit a research paradigm and vice versa (Schon and Rein, 1994). Also, scientific knowledge is not always understood because of different discourses and cultural differences (Dryzek, 1997; Siegel et al., 2004). Uncertainty about cause and effect and risks is also a complication in the use of scientific knowledge in the policy process.

So, with all the risks and pitfalls in mind, how should science be used in a interactive policy process? Well, there is not an easy way to determine in what manner science can be helpful and successfully applied in the policy-making process. Especially, when policy makers are the ones using the scientific knowledge in the interaction process with stakeholders. But there are some clues in the literature on how science can be more successfully used. First of all, stakeholders have all kinds of stakes and concerns regarding the policy issue at stake. One possible strategy is to link the stakeholder concerns to the scientific models that are used. Assuming that not all stakeholder interests and concerns can be incorporated into a scientific model, the interaction process itself plays an important role (Borsuk et al., 2001). For this reason, using scientific knowledge produced in interaction with an existing relevant social network improves the chance that the knowledge is used effectively (Siegel et al., 2004). Another way of linking science to actions and participants is integrated assessment (see Kloprogge and van der Sluis, 2006 for an overview of methods). Although the role of science and scientists in integrated assessment and other participatory processes is well described, the use of scientific knowledge in the hands of policy makers in such processes is a topic that is still quite invisible.

So, what happens when scientific knowledge is out of the hands of scientists and used as a tool by policy makers in participatory processes? One way of finding an answer to this question is focusing on what happens in the interaction process when natural science-based knowledge is introduced. For this, a case of water depletion will be analyzed, for which we explain our framework.

Knowledge might be of interest for optimizing decision making; however also for persuasion or for rallying support. This means, first of all, that there is more than one rationality to take into account. With regard to the mechanisms through which knowledge of policy makers and stakeholders is influenced, the participants' cognitions are of great relevance. Cognitions are about the information actors consider to be true and the filters actors use to determine what knowledge to take into account, what knowledge to consider as truth and what knowledge to reject. When explicit knowledge is presented, people will (unconsciously) use a frame of reference (or filter) to make sense of that knowledge. When explicit knowledge is processed through those mental filters (frames of reference), we have interpretations. Figure 8.1 illustrates the outlined mechanisms. It can be seen as a part of and an addition to Figure 2.3.

So, why is it important to know what role knowledge plays in an interaction process between water managers and stakeholders? 'Here are my conclusions, now find me some facts' is a well-known one-liner that illustrates how cognitions, motives and perhaps also resources can be intertwined. Interaction can go both ways, and which is dominant is an often disputed question. In this chapter, where we seek to understand strategies for the use and exchange of natural science-based knowledge and participative processes, those strategies have to take both possibilities into consideration.

To achieve productive interaction and effective policy making all actors need to have or be willing to develop some pooled perception on what is respectable knowledge with regard to the issue at stake. In our case knowledge was used as a strategy to create pooled perceptions with the

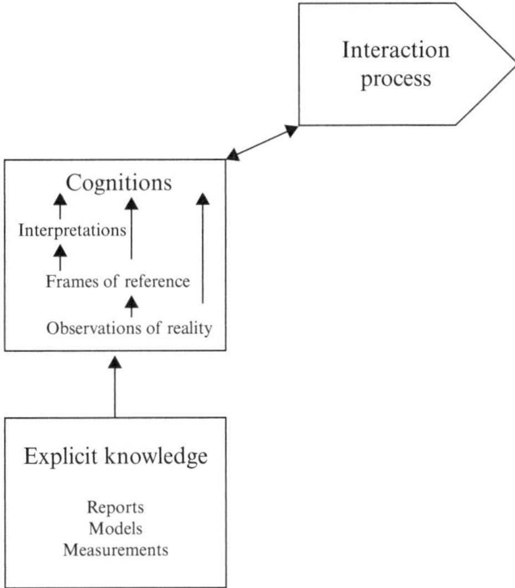

Figure 8.1 Position of cognitions

farmers. The regional water authority wanted to show the farmers the urgency of the regional water depletion problem by presenting state of the art natural science-based knowledge about groundwater, groundwater models and decision support systems. By showing the farmers that the water managers' measurements of groundwater levels (and conclusions about water depletion) are accurate, the water authority hoped to persuade the farmers and get their support for its policy. The central argument is found in a natural science-based model that argues that water depletion causes much more (economic and ecological) damage than damage caused by too much water (water damage), also for the farms. Because hard science facts instead of political arguments are used to convince farmers, disagreement can easily be overcome, they reasoned. The knowledge presented can therefore be viewed as a strategy to alter the participants' cognitions.

As shown in Figure 8.1, cognitions are made up by observations of reality, frames of reference and interpretations. To analyze the role cognitions play in the interaction process, and whether the knowledge presented by the regional water authority changes anything in the cognitions, an observation tool has been developed. This tool helps to monitor the way knowledge travels when knowledge is exchanged between a water authority and the actors. The tool consists of items that need to be observed and analyzed. Our tool includes four dimensions:

1. Knowledge itself: the first item deals with the explicit knowledge that is being brought into the process. Explicit knowledge is a type of knowledge that can be characterized as focal and presented as objective. Because of the use of symbols, this type of knowledge is easily communicated and diffused. The way the knowledge is shaped and presented is examined as is the issue of who presents what knowledge.
2. Knowledge processing: the second observation issue is about how the knowledge is processed by the various actors. Not only the degree to which actors understand and internalize the information is observed, but also whether the knowledge fits the actors' way of thinking, their frame of reference.
3. Interpretation of knowledge: third, attention is paid to the number of different interpretations of the presented knowledge. What is being left out? How much is simplified? But also what is overstated and repeated?
4. Influence on process dynamics: a fourth item that needs to be observed is the direct (visible) influence of knowledge in the interaction process. What images and storylines are constructed based on the knowledge presented? Has the presented knowledge changed anything in the participants' cognitions and consequently in their positions and actions during the interaction process?

8.3 WATER DEPLETION, THE EFFORTS OF THE REGIONAL WATER AUTHORITY AND MURPHY'S LAW (CASE)

Preventing water depletion is in general an important policy goal for water managers in rural and natural areas. An area suffers from water depletion if the groundwater levels are too low or the seepage is not strong enough to sustain the ecological value of this area. This includes the situation in which water from other areas needs to be channelled into the water system in order to compensate for low groundwater levels. Water depletion problems are often linked to areas with a nature destination. However, water depletion also occurs in farming land and can have effects on other sectors in society. Especially regarding the water levels within a water system, there are many competing interests that require conflicting water levels.

Farmers normally like the water levels to be a bit low, so that they can farm their land earlier in spring; in summer they want to retrieve water from the same water system easily to sprinkle the land. Some industries need higher water levels because they need water for cooling. The shipping trade needs deep water in order to be able to sail. Drinking water companies would like to extract groundwater for drinking water because that is cheaper than purifying surface water. Nature protection organizations want relatively high levels to protect bogs and marshes. Conflicts over water levels are quite common in Europe. Although water depletion is a more visible problem in Spain, for instance, it is also a problem in Western Europe where, just like in the Netherlands, water depletion is a relatively invisible but severe problem.

Water managers can prevent or influence water depletion by using two strategies. First, water managers can decide to let more water into the water system. Second, they can physically modify water streams, for instance, by reshaping straight water streams into streams that meander, and perhaps allow the surrounding land to be periodically flooded. The latter strategy is well known as river restoration. In this case the regional water authority wants to enlarge the amount of retention in the vascular system, the creeks that feed the river. Retention is the temporary storing of water in the water system and catchment areas. Enlarging the amount of retention in the vascular system of the water system means that the water levels in small creeks and ditches bordering agricultural land will rise. Under agricultural land groundwater levels will therefore also rise. Farmers are very opposed to higher groundwater levels because the soil stays soaked longer after the winter season. As a consequence, farmers will have to wait longer when they want to work the land with machinery in springtime. Generally, farmers in the case area focus on water surplus damage, not on damage because of water depletion. Our case focuses on the battle over water levels in a region which is situated in the eastern part of the Netherlands and is adjacent to Germany. Of course, in many other areas similar preferences of farmers can be found.

Traditionally, farmers have a significant influence on the regional water authority. Furthermore, the water authority and the farmers are mutually highly dependent participants. Many elected water authority members are farmers. Also, farmers have a well organized lobby and have considerable influence on the provincial government. In addition, the water manager often needs farmers to cooperate when implementing several types of policy measures.

The regional water authority would benefit in this case when farmers could be convinced that water depletion is a bigger problem than water surplus damage. More specifically, the water authority needed to convince farmers that more retention (leading to higher groundwater levels) would be profitable. And the water authority anticipated that it might just have the right hard natural science-based data for that. The water authority staff developed a decision support model that they used to test intended policy. The essential elements of the model are a regional groundwater model that predicts the changes in groundwater levels when various interventions in the water system are being done. Data on various aspects of interaction in the water system are included, as are precipitation models and data about actual groundwater levels in the region. The natural groundwater situation from 1850 in the region is used as a reference. Specifically for agriculture, other factors (land use, crop, type of soil) that have impacts on groundwater levels were included in the model. Finally, the economic effects of the planned policy were also calculated.

So, no arguments against selling this policy on the basis of providing knowledge were anticipated. It was just a matter of sharing the knowledge with the participating farmers, and the objections against the policy would vanish. The water authority decided to organize a conference about regional water depletion, in order to explicitly use knowledge as a means to persuade the farmers.

The fact that the water authority was engaging in a debate with farmers was not new; the strategy of showing the core data, modelling and assumptions on which the water depletion policy rests was new. By presenting their state of the art knowledge about the causes and consequences of water depletion including the groundwater models and the decision support system, the water authority hoped to settle this dispute.

Traditionally, policy measures to prevent water depletion, such as retention capacity or raising water levels in small creeks, are quite strongly opposed by farmers. From the farmers in a low-lying delta point of view, their land is already too wet and the quality of the soil is at stake. The referred to measures would cause their land to become more moist.

The conference took place in the fall of 2006. It was an open conference, all interested stakeholders were welcome, but the conference was aimed specifically at farmers.

Now, what happened? Well, the conference did not exactly turn out the way the water authority hoped. Possible explanations will be explored later, but it is safe to say that the case of water depletion in the region shows that explicit, natural science-based knowledge, such as groundwater models, and their underlying assumptions are not easily accepted. The farmers proved to be very capable of dealing with technical and natural science-based knowledge. Furthermore, many arguments made by farmers against the models and the underlying assumptions were grounded in technical or natural science-based knowledge itself. So, the fact that farmers do not accept the models is not to be considered as a result of misconceiving the knowledge presented. If misconceiving is not the problem, then what is?

When we apply our tool for analyzing the use and processing of knowledge throughout the interaction process, we will describe in detail what events took place that day and what led to the failure to meet the objective of the conference. But, first, we will briefly examine the motivations and resources of both the water authority and the participants (compare with the Contextual Interaction Theory model discussed in Chapter 2).

8.4 A SMALL DETOUR: MOTIVATIONS AND THEIR PARTIAL BASIS IN RESOURCES

8.4.1 Distinguishing Between the Role of Knowledge and Other Actor Characteristics

In Section 8.2 we described the relationship between science and policy, and the problematic nature of using knowledge in the policy process. We wondered what happens with natural science-based knowledge when it is applied and used by non-experts in the policy-making process. The case of water depletion is a case in which natural science-based knowledge is used by non-experts and did not create common ground between the water authority and the farmers. Using hard science facts instead of political arguments did not prove to be useful in this case to convince farmers to support the policy measures the water authority wants to implement.

When we try to reconstruct how the knowledge travelled through the interaction process, what role the natural science knowledge played and what impact that knowledge had, we can apply the tool that we described in Section 8.2. Applying this tool may shed more light on what happens with natural science-based knowledge in the hands of non-experts. Analyzing what role cognitions play in the interaction process, and if the knowledge presented by the regional water authority changes anything in the cognitions, we have to take the context of the case into account.

Parts of a policy process, such as the conference on water depletion the water authority organized, can be considered as an interaction process. Various factors may have an influence on the interaction process, but only and as far as they change the relevant characteristics of the actors involved. The core characteristics of the actors are their motivations, their cognitions and their resources. These three characteristics are influencing each other, and can, in turn, be influenced by other factors from outside the process. The actors' characteristics shape the process but are in turn influenced by the course and experiences in the process. Therefore, they can gradually change during the process. Also, the border context of the governance regime influences the actor characteristics. Finally, the broad (societal) context has some influence on the actor characteristics (see Chapter 2).

In other words, if one wants to analyze the use of knowledge as a tool in a multiple stakeholder-policy process, the core characteristics of motivations and resources need to be examined too. This way, the role of natural science-based knowledge can be disentangled from other dynamics in the interaction process. This serves the validity of the analysis. Describing the water authority's motives and the relevant resources for using natural science knowledge as a means in the interaction process helps us to understand what happens in an interaction process. It is not only knowledge that influences actor cognitions, the actors' motives and resources also have an impact on cognitions.

8.4.2 Motivations and their Partial Basis in Resources

What were the underlying motives of the water authority to engage in an interaction process and use natural science-based knowledge as a means to convince the farmers of the necessity of their policy measures? The most important reasons for using natural science-based knowledge were:

- meeting policy goals;
- improving existing relationships;
- avoiding costly procedures;
- meeting organizational goals.

Meeting policy goals

The first and most obvious motive for the water authority is the obligation or will to achieve existing policy goals. The prevention of water depletion, not only in nature reservation areas but also in regions with agricultural land use has become an increasingly important policy issue. After almost a decade of silence, water depletion is firmly back on the national and regional agendas. The water authority is responsible for implementing measures to achieve national and regional policy goals. The water authority experienced some external pressure from higher governments to at least make an effort to achieve the policy goals concerning water depletion. Establishing and implementing water depletion policy is not easy. Not only the farmers in the region opposed those measures, the water authority's own elected governors were at least sceptical when water depletion policy proposals were put up for voting. Convincing the farmers of the necessity of the policy measures is important because they own much of the land that suffers from water depletion. Or, in other cases, if the water authority decides to elevate water levels to reduce water depletion in nature areas, the bordering farmland will be affected too. This being said, farmers hold a very important resource, which is land.

Improving existing relationships

The water authority greatly benefits from a good relationship with their stakeholders, whether they are farmers, nature preservationists, drinking water companies, industry or individual citizens. But being on friendly terms with farmers is especially important to the water authority; they are the largest group of landowners, but also because many elected officials in the water authority and in the provincial government have strong ties with farmers. So there is an incentive structure for professionals in the water authority to try to convince farmers of the necessity of their water depletion policy measures.

Avoiding costly procedures

Cooperation and goodwill from the farmers in the region is important to the water authority. Also, when implementing policy measures other than those for water depletion, the water authority heavily depends on the willingness of farmers and other stakeholders to cooperate. This is because the water manager is not the owner of the land surrounding the water system they govern. The farmers, again, have resources to influence the water authority. For instance, for maintenance of the water system, such as mowing or dredging, the water authority needs permission to cross someone's private property in order to get to the water stream. Additionally, in cases where the water authority needs to acquire land to realize a water project, the water authority trades land with farmers, instead of buying them out. The water authority could use several legal procedures to force farmers or other landowners to cooperate. But that takes up a lot of time and money (important resources for the water authority) and its approval in possible court cases is uncertain. The legal procedures have to be followed meticulously. One little error might produce legal failure. There are many examples of governmental organization plans that were blocked by administrative courts.

Meeting organizational goals

In our case area the water authority also uses knowledge as a means of persuasion because it fits the (long-term) organizational strategy. Soon after 2000, the water authority adopted a new strategy in dealing with its social environment. The changes in water system management confront water managers with an increasingly complex and dynamic policy field, as described in Chapter 1 of this volume. This is not only because various governmental organizations need to cooperate and different policies need to be attuned, but also because more actors get involved. The water authority acknowledged the changes in water management, and the need to be better attuned to its social environment. Action was taken by introducing the concept of contextual water management in their long-term policy. Contextual water management meant in this case simply making sure that the water authority takes into account the needs, positions and interests of stakeholders when formulating policy or doing routine maintenance. But it also meant that the water authority made sure that its own interests and needs were heard. By sharing the knowledge that is the foundation of their modelling and policy measures, the water authority hoped to establish two-way communication with its stakeholders, thereby living up to its new management style.

Now that we have some insight into the water authority's motivations and resources to use natural science as a means, we can focus on what should be directly influenced by natural science knowledge: cognitions.

8.5 APPLYING THE TOOL FOR ANALYSIS: COGNITIONS

In this section the tool for describing and analyzing the way knowledge moves or travels through the interaction process is applied to the case of water depletion. This will help to understand what happens when natural science knowledge is used as a strategy in a policy-making interaction process. Relevant motivations and resources, as described previously, will be highlighted in the analysis.

Cognitions refer to the actors' interpretation of reality. They determine how facts are dealt with, how value and meaning are attributed to observations and the interaction between core belief values and knowledge. These activities are undertaken on the basis of knowledge, memory, logical thinking and intuition: the frames of reference as included in Figure 8.1.

8.5.1 Knowledge Itself

Knowledge, in any way, shape or form, is presented in the interaction process by a certain actor and has by itself an impact on the actors' cognitions. Also, who presents what knowledge is considered relevant. The water authority chose to have the conference to be moderated by a consultant from a consultancy firm. The core argument for this was the fear of appearing manipulative, even before the conference. The knowledge was presented by presentations. A policy maker from the water authority presented the method used by the water authority to measure whether water depletion causes damage and what type of interventions in the water system would be suitable to deal with water depletion damage. The explicit knowledge that was shared with the farmers consisted of a technical description of the groundwater models, the models linked to the groundwater model and the decision support system. Also, a lot of attention was given to loss of earnings because of water depletion, the differences in the nature of damages caused by water depletion and those caused by humid soil and the long-term effects of water depletion. The presentation was a solid display of what the water authority perceived to be facts, very technical, with the use of many formulas, maps and graphs.

8.5.2 Knowledge Processing

The key relevant issue is whether the natural science knowledge which is presented alters the actors' cognitions, not only in terms of understanding but also in terms of fitting their frame of reference. Most of the audience seemed very able to comprehend the knowledge presented. Farmers are familiar with groundwater models and modelling in general and asked specific questions about scales of measurement and applications. The core of the discussions was about the way the models were constructed, and according to the farmers the calibration needed to be improved.

A distinct difference in reasoning between farmers and the water authority could be observed. Farmers draw from their own practical experience, knowledge about the farmland and business economics. The water authority primarily argued from a hydrological and technical approach. It proved difficult to reach agreement on whether certain measurements were acceptable. The criticism from the farmers' point of view was also that the models did not take negative side effects of increasing use as retention into account. Those negative side effects were mostly described in terms of business economics. The farmers brought much technical knowledge into the discussion about the models. Although they reasoned in economics language, their arguments were based on technical or natural science-based knowledge as they perceived these. Farmers tend to perceive water depletion less of a problem, because it is manageable through sprinkling the farmland in case of dry weather. The present method of evaluating the effect of measures on the groundwater levels does not take sprinkling as a measure into account (obviously because it is wanted at times when the water systems already experience deficit problems).

Also, farmers argue, water damage is a much bigger problem than the water authority perceives because the water authority forgets to take into account the negative impact of wet soil on the ability to work the farmland in early spring. When the soil is wet and the farmers use their (heavy) equipment to access and work the land, its structure gets damaged.

The farmers also have a problem with the water authority not taking into account the fact that if a part of the parcel is too wet, the entire parcel becomes unusable, and that grass from early spring (when the soil is usually quite wet or too wet) is more nutritious for cattle and therefore more valuable.

An additional (important) critique was that the water authority's measurements are not detailed enough (1 : 50 000). Due to this, important differences within a parcel are not visible. Or to cite a colourful expression of a participant: the water authority measurements imply standing with one leg in a freezer and with the other in a fireplace . . . and concluding that the average is good.

Finally, the farmers touched upon broad perspectives: they combined technical and natural science-based knowledge with knowledge about the local environment, experience and business economics.

8.5.3 Interpretation of Knowledge

Now that we know how the natural science knowledge is presented and processed, we need to examine the way the knowledge is interpreted.

During the conference the farmers repeatedly presented economic and technical or natural science-based arguments about why the models of the water authority are incomplete. They also intensively expressed their doubts with regard to the claim that water depletion causes more damage to their business than swampy soils. Strangely enough, the conference moderator and the water authority representatives listened politely to the farmers' arguments, but then continued their story. Since water authorities are very aware of the difference in interests and frames of reference between the water authority and the farmers, one would expect the water authority to address the different views on reality. Instead of seeking consensus, it seemed like the water authority tried to force its own arguments.

The farmers applied different frames of reference compared to the water authority. Farmers perceived water depletion and water damage in business economics terms. The water authority approached the issue from a hydrological and technical point of view. Farmers rejected the water authority's groundwater models because, in their view, variables of importance are left out. The water managers proved stuck in hydrological and technical arguments during the discussion. Farmers, on the other hand, combined their technical arguments with arguments based on tacit knowledge about their farmland and the region and made a more flexible and comprehensive impression.

The water authority repeatedly tried to resume its line of argumentation. Both the explicit knowledge and the tacit knowledge presented by the farmers were not addressed. During the interaction process it seemed that the water authority had more problems connecting to the farmers' frame of reference and positions taken than the other way around.

8.5.4 Influence on Dynamics

Has the presented natural science knowledge changed anything in the interaction process? Because the water authority representatives in the conference did not respond to the farmers' contra expertise some storylines developed that did not have a lot to do with the knowledge presented. Instead of discussing and acknowledging the different types of knowledge, and reasoning in terms of knowledge and measurement (the apolitical approach the water authority aimed at) farmers started to vent their displeasure with the water authority's policy measures taken in the past. These comments developed into storylines about how the water authority never listens to farmers anyway, the water authority not being willing and able to take into account specific situations of specific parcels, and the water authority being rigid and arrogant.

At the end of the day the atmosphere at the conference was not very delightful. The conference moderator of course managed to gracefully formulate an (empty) conclusion. Unfortunately for the water authority, the natural science-based knowledge about groundwater, groundwater levels and groundwater models did not create the common ground with the farmers the water authority hoped for. It also failed as a tool to show the farmers how urgent water depletion is as a problem for both the water authority and the farmers themselves. The interaction process was negatively influenced as old sores were repeated over and over again. However, it was not the knowledge that led to this unfortunate outcome, but the water authority's (lack of) response to knowledge that triggered the farmers to become irritated. Were both parties actually talking about the same domain of relevance?

8.6 EXPANDING THE TOOL: ADDING BOUNDARY JUDGEMENTS

The analysis regarding actor characteristics applied within the framework of our tool, which helped us to monitor the way knowledge travelled, helped us to understand what happened. The role of motivations, cognitions and resources that played a role in the interaction process in the water depletion case were highlighted. However the analysis has to be pushed further, the results yet are puzzling, for instance: why the water authority failed to adequately respond to the farmers' knowledge claims and objections? Investigating what role boundary judgements play in the motives, cognitions and the interaction process may shed some more in-depth light on the likely explanations by enriching the analysis of the dynamics that appeared. In Section 8.6.1 we will repeat the concept of boundary judgements briefly and analyze our case. In Section 8.6.2 we will elaborate our findings in terms of converging and diverging boundary judgements.

8.6.1 Boundary Judgements: Letting the Outside In

Boundaries exist between policy sectors, scales and time perspectives (see Chapters 1 and 2). Boundary judgements are socially constructed definitions of domain of policy sectors in terms of relevant sectors, scales and time perspectives (Bressers, 2007). Boundary judgements are part of the actors' frame of reference and work like a mental filter through which the actor determines who or what is part of their domain, who or what is of significant importance and how to act. Boundary judgements are a small but important part of actors' cognitions, because they determine the actors' view on who is allowed to say what and what is relevant within an interaction process. Boundary judgements are not necessarily a result of a conscious deliberation. They mostly lie dormant in the frame of reference, and are activated or disputed as soon as actors come into contact with one another. Judgements with regard to the aspects of a domain can have a strategic value. Influenced by their motives boundary judgements can be activated, stakeholders can choose to broaden or narrow their boundary judgements, thereby including or excluding other actors and issues. When boundary judgements differ amongst actors, they can disturb the interaction process and even be a source of conflict.

In this case it is interesting to see whether the knowledge presented by both the water authority and farmers changed anything in the boundary judgements, and whether the boundary judgements, in their turn, changed anything in the stakeholder characteristics such as motives and cognitions. Before assessing the influence of knowledge on boundary judgements, the boundary judgements themselves need to be explored. What boundaries were crossed and what are the boundary judgements of the water authority and the farmers to begin with?

Boundary judgements: sector and scales

Sector: The farmers perceive the water authority focusing on soil instead of water, what they think should be their core business. And, even worse, the water authority is trying to tell them what is happening on their farmland all of a sudden. In the eyes of the farmers, the water authority makes a twofold shift: from water jurisdiction to water and soil, and from the public domain to private property. The water authority perceives their interference with private property as something that cannot be avoided, because the water system in the region is branched off in so many small streams that all water policy measures impact private property.

Scales: Scales refer to both geographical scales (what geographical area is the issue about) and administrative scales (which governmental body should be involved). It seems quite obvious that the geographical scale where the issue is about is regional. This region falls under the jurisdiction of the water authority, so the water authority being the obvious governmental agency involved is not very surprising. At first glance, the boundary judgements seem convergent. The water authority and the farmers are well aware of the jurisdiction of the water authority in both geographical and administrative terms. But are they?

The water authority is responsible for water system management. And yes, water depletion is an important policy goal. But water depletion is most often linked to nature reservation areas. So, why is the water authority concerned with water depletion in farmland? From the water authority's point of view, there is no real reason why they need to be worried about farmland. It just wants to heighten the water levels in the water vascular system. But because the water authority knows that the farmers will oppose that measure, they try to convince the farmers of the necessity of that measure by pointing out the damage that water depletion does to their farmland.

8.6.2 The Role of Knowledge: Building Bridges or Freezing Up?

This section describes how the water authority tries to bridge the gap between their own policy goals and the interests of farmers by using knowledge as means in an interaction process. This attempt to convince farmers of the importance of water depletion as a problem, and win their support for the proposed policy measures was not successful. It was not the knowledge itself that created a problem in the interaction process, all participants were very able to understand and process the natural science-based knowledge presented. The lack of success can be attributed to the water authority's inability to cope with the way the farmers responded to the knowledge presented. Did boundary judgements play a role in this?

Who is considered to be an expert about what? What sources are reliable? Now, the water authority considers itself as an expert on water. This means that they can make an authoritative knowledge claim regarding surface water, groundwater, water chemistry, hydrology, water ecology, water biology, and other technical and natural science-based knowledge about water. This knowledge claim is not contested by farmers. Farmers, on the other hand, view themselves as experts when it comes to running an agricultural or cattle raising farm. They make an authoritative claim on knowledge regarding the business of running a farm and the characteristics of their land. This knowledge claim farmers make is not only an academic claim, it relates to a deeply rooted sense of ownership of their business and their land. Or as a farmer puts it: you cannot tell a farmer who has been working his land for over 40 years what to do with his land.

In the case of water depletion the water authority was crossing boundaries in three ways: they expand their sector from being primarily concerned with water system management to concern about effects of water depletion on the water system and soil. Second, the water authority is moving from the public domain (water systems) to private property (farmland). Third, the water authority makes knowledge claims about water and the effects of water depletion or water damage on farmland and on the farmers' business. While especially the last issue of crossing a previously held boundary was meant to be a strategy for boundary spanning, it might have aggravated the cleavage. It was felt more as trespassing rather than spanning boundaries. Farmers consider their land and their business to be their field of expertise. As shown in Table 8.1, it is possible to link the problems that were encountered in the interaction process to this boundary spanning and diverging boundary judgements.

The overview in Table 8.1 shows that the boundary judgements of the water authority differ from the judgements made by the participating farmers. Diverging boundary judgements can create problems in an interaction process such as the one in the case of water depletion in the region. It is plausible that in the farmers' perception, the water authority was illegally crossing boundaries without even knowing it. This was not only felt in terms of scales, but also in terms of expertise. The water authority might have been able to smooth things over if the knowledge claims the farmers made were adequately acknowledged and responded to. But because the water authority was probably unaware that they were reasoning from another domain perception and were not spanning but just crossing the boundaries that were emphasized by the farmers, the farmers' response to the natural science-based knowledge of the water authority was mistaken for stubbornness or lack of knowledge, instead of a knowledge claim to emphasize their boundaries. When the water authority persisted in their own line of argumentation, it is quite possible that the farmers' underlying negative motives to participate in the interaction process surfaced. These motivations, disagreement over the problem at stake and general reservations against water depletion policy because of the nature status of

Table 8.1 Linking boundary judgements to knowledge

Boundaries Crossed by Authority	**Boundary Judgement Water Authority**	**Boundary Judgement Farmers**	**Knowledge Treatment by Farmers**	**Knowledge Treatment by Water Authority**
Sector: Water management → soil	Concerned about water depletion and its effects in the broader sense. Aiming to solve problem with approval of farmers	Water authority should stick to its mandate, the water authority implements water policy, the province and the private owners decide about land/soil	Denying water depletion as the bigger problem at stake, focusing on water damage that can be managed if water authority sticks to its task (managing water levels in water systems). Not a groundwater problem, but surface water	Presenting precipitation tables and groundwater models to prove water depletion is a bigger problem than water damage
Scale: Public domain → private property	Just pointing out benefits of policy measures for both parties	Governmental organizations have no jurisdiction over private property	Not accepting models because of scales and specific conditions of parcels	Persisting in scales presented and general assessment. Not paying attention to need for customized assessment of specific conditions
Scale: Water knowledge → knowledge about farmland, business	Numbers and models do not lie; they show without a doubt that water depletion is a bigger problem for farmers than water damage	Water authorities have water experts, they have no knowledge about the specific conditions of our farmland or business	Not accepting models because of incompleteness (not taking into account business indicators). Offering contra expertise regarding condition of soil and effects of business	Not acknowledging contra expertise. Focusing on hydrological arguments, not including knowledge about other aspects as relevant

the issue may have reinforced the farmers in their boundary judgements, causing them to freeze up. In that case, real boundary spanning, creating common ground by sharing natural science-based knowledge as a means to win over the farmers and get them to support water depletion policy measures becomes virtually impossible, because the knowledge, being hard science, is no longer a neutral means.

8.7 LESSONS FROM THE CASE

In this chapter we found that by using the observational tool described in Section 8.2, it is possible to reconstruct the way knowledge is used and understood in an interaction process. Identifying the underlying motivations and resources enables us to focus on the impact of natural science-based knowledge on actors' cognitions without confusing it with these actor characteristics. The case of water depletion shows that the strategy to use natural science-based knowledge as a way to create agreement about a policy issue can be contra productive. When boundary judgements are added to the analysis, we find that instead of creating common ground by using a neutral instrument such as hard science facts, the water authority caused the diverging boundary judgements to freeze up. Boundary judgements make up for a substantial part of the explanation of the dynamics in the interaction process.

With regard to the use of natural science-based knowledge in the policy process by non-experts, three lessons can be learned:

Lesson 1: Be aware of sensitivities

The most important lesson that can be drawn form this case, is that sensitivities which go along with boundary spanning, even in a sub-category such as knowledge, should be thoroughly investigated before entering an interaction process. This includes more than exploring the common opinions about the issue at stake; it involves doing some research into the boundary judgements of stakeholders. The case of water depletion shows that problems could have been avoided, if the water authority had known it was trespassing (personal) boundaries in the farmers' perception. The case also illustrates that sensitivity for signals, that actors emphasize boundaries while interacting can be essential.

Lesson 2: Make sure you are accepted to say something on the subject

Discussing boundary judgements could be a way to clear the air before an interaction process takes off. Although the water authority in this case puts a lot of time and effort into making sure that all stakeholders had the same amount of knowledge, the water authority forgot to make sure that all stakeholders agreed about what subjects are under discussion and who is allowed to say something about what. In the case of water depletion, the farmers felt that the water authority had no authority to make knowledge claims about their land and their business.

Lesson 3: Acknowledge contra expertise

Nothing is more frustrating than sitting in a room, having to listen to someone talking about your business, and not being heard when you have something to say too. This means that there needs to be enough flexibility in the interaction process, to allow others to make knowledge claims, and seriously exploring those claims. Politely listening is not enough. Serious information deserves to be seriously discussed.

9. Rethinking boundaries in implementation processes

Jaap Evers

9.1 INTRODUCTION

Implementation of ambitious water management projects is often hampered by conflicting interests arising from the complexity of the governance system. There might be some possibilities for improvement that deserve consideration. In this context two approaches towards project implementation will be presented in this chapter and the pros and cons assessed: among others, by presenting a case study in which a serial perspective on implementation got stuck by unforeseen dynamics and, in the end, was amended by elements of parallel implementation. The approaches are called serial and parallel implementation.

The general debate on parsimonious and redundant policy approaches in water management, which began in Chapter 1, will be applied and elaborated specifically with regard to its implications for implementation. This issue has been previously discussed by Geldof (2001, 2004) when he introduced the concept of interactive implementation which is considered to be a synonym for parallel implementation. The emerging phenomena during implementation will be investigated in this chapter by an analysis of the role of boundary judgments and boundary spanning as assumed by the two approaches. No single solution is offered in the sense that one approach is always better than the other. What can be offered is guidance in when to apply which approach, to what extent they can be combined and some strategies and notes on personal competences.

In Section 9.2 the serial and parallel approaches towards implementation will be introduced and positioned. In Section 9.3 the implementation case will be presented and analyzed. In Section 9.4 analysis of the role of boundary judgments and boundary spanning in the two implementation approaches is presented and some guidance with regard to strategies and competences is given. In Section 9.5 the conclusions are presented.

9.2 SERIAL AND PARALLEL IMPLEMENTATION

In this section the two contrasting approaches towards implementation of integrated water management projects will be introduced. The focus is on the differences between them, although admittedly countless in-between positions can be imagined. The differences have implications for the domains that are created by the involved actors in the processes. Through negotiations, consensus seeking and decision making often implicit boundaries are created on who, what, where and when certain people or aspects are part of the implementation process as it develops.

The traditional serial approach starts with the idea that implementation is an activity that is basically executing the plan, endorsing the obvious, starting with a construction plan. In this view, executing the plan implies serial and predictable activities in a setting in which dependence of the relatively stable context is minor. In this context, activities can be structured, chopped into steps and controlled. In a serial perspective the different phases of the implementation process are thus dealt with step by step. The implementation serial is divided into phases and intermediate products (Figure 9.1). A step by step approach in which the subsequent phases are known beforehand seems, for instance, appropriate for the (re)construction of a weir in a secondary canal. A firm grip on the implementation is achievable by creating a plan in complete detail. All outcomes that do not conform to this plan are perceived as failure. This approach qualifies for relatively simple implementation tasks (see Section 1.4 in Chapter 1).

From the boundary spanning perspective the serial implementation perspectives' most striking characteristic is the fact that, as the process within the serial proceeds, the number of boundaries under discussion declines. In the phase of planning many boundaries are discussed. The plan describes the measures to be taken to handle the observed problem. The plan is passed on to the designers who narrow the boundaries down by creating a construction plan in which they specify, for instance, the amount of cubic meters of concrete, sand and so on. Subsequently the construction company reduces the boundaries under discussion by setting the exact location and the method of digging and construction within the trajectory. When the project is delivered there is thought to be no boundary issues left. However, since society and policies change over time, it comes as no surprise that new boundary issues will arise, even in the phase of operation and maintenance (Figure 9.1).

Parallel or interactive implementation might be thought of as being more suitable for complex implementation tasks (see Section 1.4). Complex in this context assumes the absence of strings of serial activities. Instead the activities are considered to be recurrent and substantial uncertainties

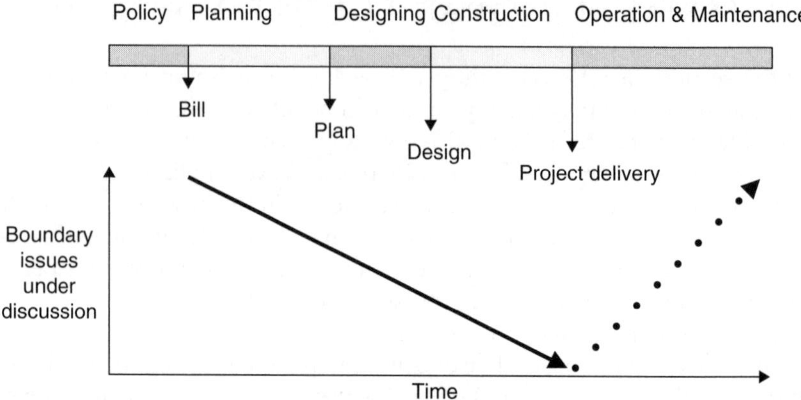

Source: Geldof (2004).

Figure 9.1 Serial approach and the amount of boundary issues under discussion during the implementation steps

and dependencies are involved. The context of recurrent implementation activities is considered to be dynamic and unpredictable. This implementation strategy comes with different implications with regard to boundary spanning and especially with regard to the time boundaries involved (see Chapter 4).

Parallel or interactive implementation suggests blurring the boundaries between the phases of the implementation serial (Geldof, 2001, 2004). This implies that the activities in the context of processes or steps are not serial to each other in the sense that the previous one has to be finalized before the next can start and can be shaped. This implies that the phases of the implementation process are not serial by definition, but exist, develop and interact alongside each other to deliver the policy outcomes. As referred to above, they are considered to be recurrent.

This might easily lead to misunderstandings. Recurrent does not imply that random patterns can be expected. Logic ordering of activities and their interactions still exist; they are just hard to predict and record beforehand. What is meant is that every step in implementation is now considered to consist of subsequent and often recurring rounds of decision making (Teisman et al., 2001). By deviating from the idea of deterministic serial activities some benefits can be harvested. For instance, decision making with regard to design can benefit from the first rounds of elaboration of a program for operation and maintenance. And lessons with regard to construction options might lead to a change of design or even a change

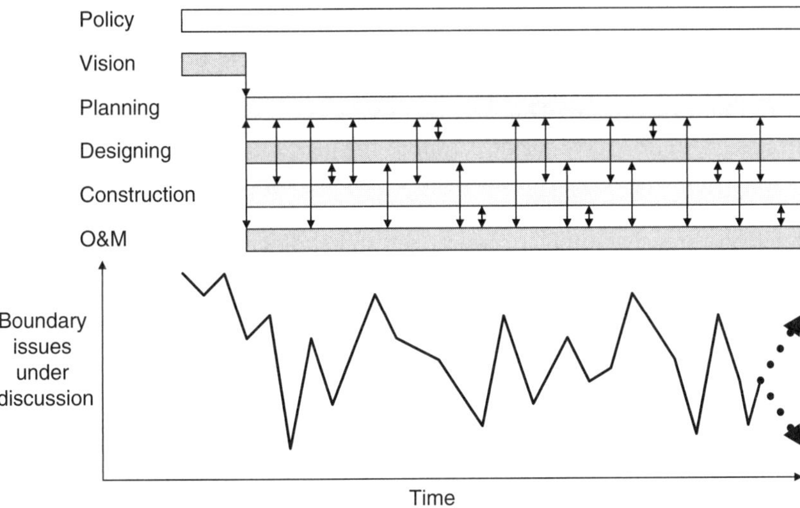

Source: Based on Geldof (2004).

Figure 9.2 The parallel perspective on implementation. The activities are shown on the vertical axis; on the horizontal axis the time. The amount of boundary issues are under discussion during the implementation process

of policy. Parallel implementation implies that, as much as possible, every step or phase in the implementation serial benefits from an advanced understanding in other steps or phases. The outcome is that the boundaries between these sub-processes will be spanned. Maximizing the extent of parallel activities and linking advanced understanding to other phases is done by involved actors and requires craftsmanship. It requires communication and initiating and managing actor constellations across actors that dominate different phases of the implementation process, implying that the phases will be less autonomous arenas. This is being said to avoid misunderstanding. There is nothing mythical or physically illogical about this approach. The evaluation criteria on success and failure differ from the serial perspective. Implementation is no longer defined as putting policy into effect. It is now defined as getting something done that makes sense. Performance is then the main objective and compromise a means of achieving it (Barrett and Fudge, 1981 in Hill and Hupe, 2002). Figure 9.2 expresses implementation processes as joint learning processes in which the actors are able to anticipate the surprises and uncertainties the process will surely bring. This implementation strategy might be better equipped especially with regard to the handling of complexity related uncertainties in the fields of engineering, hydrology, morphology or ecology or in dealing with the divergent preferences of actors involved, or both.

In Figure 9.2 the implementation process starts by creating a vision. It is necessary to first have the direction of the process clear. A vision is necessary to make people enthusiastic; it shows the direction, but leaves plenty of space for other stakeholders to bring in their own ideas. For creating a vision extensive interaction between stakeholders is not essential. After the process of developing a vision the processes planning, designing, construction and operation and management evolve parallel to each other. Here substantial interaction between the actors of the different phases is needed. In the concept of interactive implementation the word interactive mainly deals with the interaction processes of planners, designers, constructors and managers. A joint learning process leads to advanced understanding in each of the processes. In the serial perspective these actors work independently from each other (see Figures 9.1 and 9.2). Still, we see in Figure 9.2 a gap between the policy process and the phases of the implementation process. This is explicitly done because most of the policy is created at higher levels of government and the water authorities are mostly responsible for implementing these policies (such as the European Water Framework Directive). It does, of course, not imply that there is no interaction between lower levels and higher levels of government when policies are created. In the end policies are formulated to improve field-level situations and are based on field-level observations.

9.3 THE IMPLEMENTATION CASE: EPERBEKEN

One of the contemporary goals of water authorities is to restore channels into a more natural state. The projects in this context are often called restoration projects. The case to be analyzed with regard to implementation issues and the two presented implementation approaches is about a system of water courses, channels and brooks. In this section two specific events are presented and analyzed that emerged in a water project called Eperbeken of the regional water authority Veluwe. Restoration was one of the goals aimed at. The analysis is taken from a more comprehensive case study (Evers, 2007). The boundary issues under discussion in the different phases of the implementation process will be highlighted and linked to the implementation approach. In the first event the water authority clashes with a foundation that represents the historical values of the regional brook systems. Due to a serial implementation process this conflict resulted in a delay of the whole process. The second event discusses the construction phase of the project. Both events are first elaborated in a short narrative and followed by an analysis of the interaction processes.

9.3.1 The Eperbeken Case: Planning Process and Appeal

The first event happened in an attempt to join the intersection of two brooks in the neighborhood of the town Epe. Most of the brooks in the system are man-made. Channels served as water suppliers for watermills before the industrial revolution in the Netherlands. The channels lost their function and became neglected. With, among others, the introduction of the European Water Framework Directive the policy is now to restore the ecological values of the watercourses. Ecological values are not the only aspect relevant for restoration projects. The brook system represents crucial cultural-historic values and functions in water management in rural and urban areas. There are many actors and many stakes involved, which make these projects quite complex. The split level intersection of the two watercourses referred to represents a unique phenomenon in the Epe water system. It reflects great cultural historical value; it shows the ingenuity and creativity of the former mill owners in mining and transporting water to their mills.

The planning phase of the implementation process started in 1994. The work group that led the planning process consisted of representatives of the different levels of government (national, provincial, municipal and water authority) and a representative of a regional non-governmental organization (NGO), the Brook Foundation. The project leader was a representative of the water authority. The planning process resulted in an effort to join the two referred to brooks. Connecting the two watercourses would result in more water carrying days in any of the brooks. It would not only improve the ecological characteristics of this water course, but would also improve the spatial quality of the town center of Epe. Although the split level intersection of the two channels was a unique feature, the work group chose in the plan to connect the watercourses. Ecological values were thus prioritized over cultural-historical values during the planning process. The final concept of the plan was published for any stakeholder that might appeal against (parts of) it. Despite the fact that the Brook Foundation was represented in the work group planning, it was the Brook Foundation (by its board) who appealed against the plan of connecting the two watercourses. First, the board of the Brook Foundation sent their comments to the water board that rejected the arguments. The foundation then appealed by an appeal procedure of the province. The province judged in favor of the Brook Foundation. The intersection of the two watercourses was considerd to be a unique feature of the Eperbeken system and of high

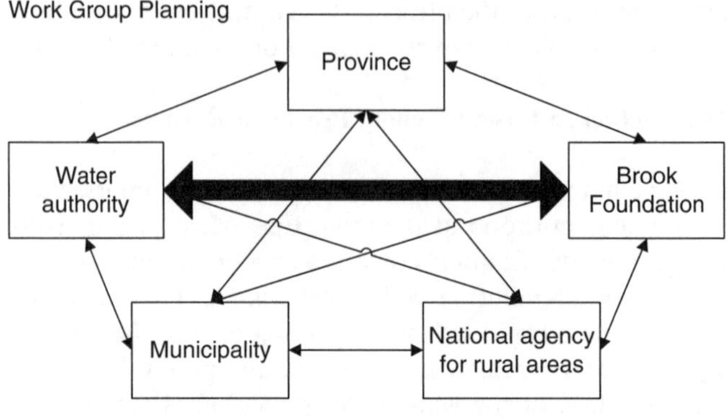

Note: ↔ Interactions actors; ⟷ Crucial interactions actors.

Figure 9.3 Actor constellation planning process

cultural-historical value. Next, based on the provincial mill Act, a downstream water mill had rights to receive water that would be diverted away by joining the two brooks. Therefore, the split level intersection had to be maintained. In May 1997 the modified plan, without the connection of the two watercourses, was approved by the province.

Actors and interactions in the planning process and the appeal procedure

The representative of the water authority was the project leader. Different to normal situations in which hydrologists were active, this project leader represented one of the first project leaders with an ecological background. It is not unthinkable that this ecological background influenced the choices in the process. The province was the third party in this process as it functioned as subsidizer and had to approve the final plan. Although in the planning work group representatives of the municipality and the national agency for rural areas were also present (Figure 9.3), they are not regarded as crucial in this process.

The water authority preferred more water carrying days for one of the brooks in order to improve the ecological quality and spatial quality of the watercourse. The representative of the Brook Foundation could best be described as a brook ecology enthusiast. The Brook Foundation, however, gave priority to the cultural-historical value of the split level intersection and thus did not want to join the channels. So, first of all, there was some miscommunication between the representative and the board of the Brook Foundation. The organization that was expected to play a central role in the last phase of the process, operation and maintenance, was thus not adequately represented in the planning and design phases. Although the other actors described a good and equal atmosphere in the work group, the representative of the Brook Foundation perceived his position as submissive to the other governmental representatives. Given the perceived dominant position of the water authority within the work group, the representative of the Brook Foundation felt forced to cooperate in the idea of connecting the channels. The representative of the province in the planning work group considered his role in the work group more as a process manager and hardly with the goals on the content of the plan. This illustrates the significance of the difference between organizations and individual representatives of organizations and the importance of intra-organizational communication. One has to conclude that the Brook Foundation, by appealing, was able to get hold of another power resource, dominant to the water authority. But this was a later intervention. A more adequate representation of a crucial operation and maintenance actor in the planning phase could have softened this kind of conflict later on. Before dealing with boundary issues and different layers of context within the planning process, first, the construction process of the Eperbeken project is discussed.

9.3.2 The Eperbeken Case: The Construction Phase

The construction phase of the Eperbeken project started in 1999 due to a shortage in personnel and a merge and reorganization of the regional water authority. To finance the construction phase, the project applied for a European subsidy (Interregional Rhine Meuse Activities (IRMA) subsidy) in September 1999. Shortly after, the subsidy was assigned to the project. The subsidy prescribed a public tendering of the construction project before the end of 1999. Due to time constraints not all activities were sufficiently prepared in the budget. This led to deviations between costs and budget afterwards. The constructor submitted new construction contracts for every piece of extra work.

The construction project started in February 2000 and it was expected that the project would be delivered in the summer of the same year. The deadline for the construction delivery to effectively grant the subsidy was set on 31 December later that year. After some delays in license procedures during the spring, the weather conditions during the autumn and winter were also unfavorable for construction. Work was hampered and stopped. The project requested an extension of the subsidy deadline. The subsidy administration approved the request and the deadline of the construction project was postponed to 31 December 2001. In March 2001 the construction activities started again. However, due to an outbreak of foot-and-mouth disease, all activities came to a standstill again. By the end of March the region was put in quarantine. A prohibition on livestock transport was enforced. By the outbreak a general distrust with regard to government settled in the agricultural community. In July of the same year the construction preparation restarted for the third time. In August the activities resumed. Again bad weather conditions influenced the construction activities. Construction activities took more time than expected and extra facilities were needed, resulting in extra costs. In the autumn of 2001, in some channel sections wooden lining was replaced and watersides were widened in the town center, a few water retention sites were also created in the more rural areas. Overall, compared to the plan, not much had been done yet.

Furthermore, a study showed that a certain trajectory of 6 kilometers was polluted. The construction of this trajectory was, therefore, cancelled and postponed until proper sanitation of the (sub)soils of this trajectory could be managed. The causes of contamination are related to the original functions of the watermills, being copper smithies, paper producers and washhouses. Also, soil stored at a storage site was contaminated. An additional temporary storage site had to be created. In 2006 a project plan was created for dismantling the storage site (Van der Meij, 2006). At the end of September a new proposal was created with respect to the temporary storage site.

Within the construction project a coordination group was created. It consisted of the same members as the planning team plus the supervising engineering consultancy and the constructor. During a coordination meeting in October 2001 the situation of the construction project was discussed. Because of the bad weather and terrain conditions, some trajectories were still not constructed. The consultancy and constructor suggested a different construction approach to speed up construction. However an additional hindrance concerned the frozen relationships between the (agricultural) inhabitants and the government after the foot-and-mouth disease. The project team had to build trust again with the agricultural community in order to restart construction, as they were dependent on their cooperation. In the end, the landowners had the power position in the construction process, because without their cooperation the project would automatically fail.

The winter of 2001–02 was terrible for the construction process. It was extremely wet and there was hardly any frost. It made the terrain inaccessible for the heavy machinery. The weather conditions again resulted in delay and extra work. It became clear that a new appeal for postponement of the European subsidy deadline had to be sent to the subsidy administration. The administration granted the postponement to 31 March 2002, which in March was again postponed finally to 31 May.

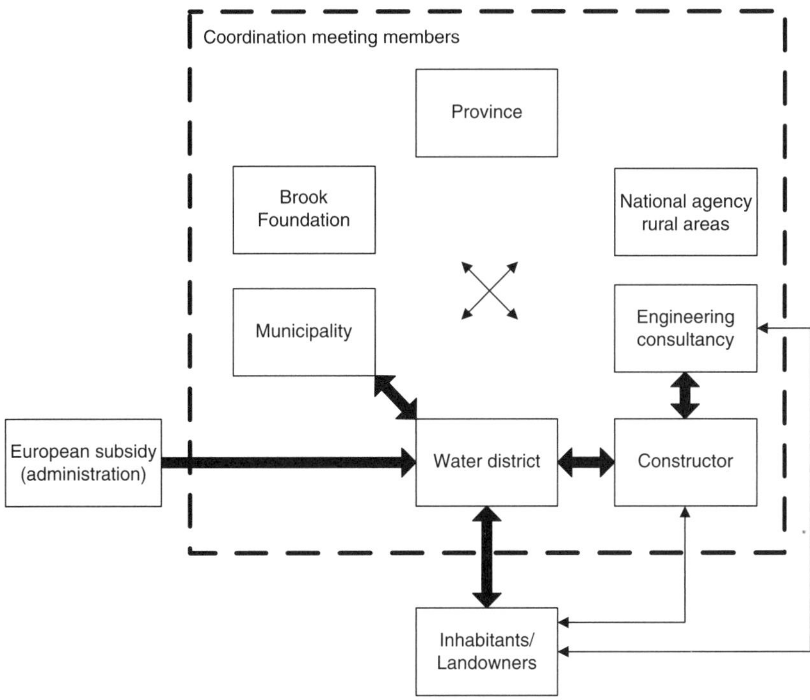

Note: ↔ Interactions actors; ⟷ Crucial interactions actors.

Figure 9.4 Actor constellation construction process project Eperbeken

In April 2002, at the end of the construction phase, all sorts of opportunities were grabbed to construct extra work. For example, an extra retention pool was created. One could say that in this last period of the construction phase the project team used an adaptive approach. These characteristics of this final period resulted in quite a lot of work done, but also in extra costs. On 22 May the construction project was officially delivered. The water authority does now use this water system as an example of restoration projects, because the system over time developed into a system where cultural-historic values are very well combined with ecological values.

Actors and interactions in the construction process of project Eperbeken

The construction process of the integrated water project was characterized by a few crucial interaction processes (Figure 9.4). The main causes of delay and extra costs of the construction process were the permits procedure, the foot-and-mouth outbreak, the weather conditions and the IRMA subsidy. The latter influenced the hasty development of the (incomplete) budget and part of the work being done under bad weather conditions, which resulted in frustrations and extra costs.

Permits procedure spring 2000

The exact reason why some permits were not granted during the early spring of 2000 is not really clear. However, it is obvious that it had enormous consequences. The delay lasted the complete scheduled construction period and permits were granted by the end of the summer of 2000. Simplifying, one can say the permit granter (the municipality) did not have a positive motivation for the construction, and had the authority (resources) to delay the process by not granting the construction permits. Therefore, the project was delayed and the process here is best described as obstruction. This resulted in working in unfavorable weather conditions, but there was the perception of pressure to have to work, because of the European subsidy.

The European subsidy

The intention of a subsidy deadline is to put some pressure on the speed of the process to reach targets within the granted budget. However, it did not really serve this function here. It certainly did put pressure on the project team to continue the work, and also when the weather conditions put constraints on construction. Because of the European subsidy the costs of construction were higher than the budgeted costs (which was construction in spring/summer weather conditions). The incomplete budget was also the result of the hasty public tendering of the construction plan to a constructor, which was obliged by the subsidy. In both autumns of 2000 and 2001 preparation and construction were planned shortly after one another. So, every delay in preparations immediately resulted in delays in construction. The result was many frustrations among the different actors, especially between the consultancy and the constructor.

In this phase we have seen a lot of misfortune. To what extent could this have been avoided or better accommodated by a more parallel implementation? Certainly, with some of the bad luck, this was not the case. But in a more parallel implementation, the construction process would have started earlier; grabbing opportunities at partial trajectories would have seen relatively fewer problems. That way some of the difficulties would have surfaced sooner in the process, giving the project managers more time to accommodate them. Only in the last instance and under extreme pressure was such an adaptive strategy developed.

9.4 BOUNDARY ISSUES IN IMPLEMENTATION

In the previous section it became clear how a serial perspective on implementation got stuck by unforeseen dynamics and in the end was amended by elements of parallel implementation. In this section the potential for blurring boundaries between implementation phases by implementing them in parallel will be assessed as well as some notes on strategies and competences to achieve this. First, the perspective of time boundaries will be addressed as changes in temporal boundary judgments will automatically induce changes in boundary judgments in scales and sectors.

9.4.1 Boundary Issues With Regard to Time Perspectives

The implementation process of integrated water plans is all about time and change. Change starts when the present situation of the water system does not comply with the contemporary norms and values and actors feel the urgency to act. Bringing the system into a situation in which the water system that does comply with the contemporary norms and values then gets on the policy agenda. With regard to implementation there is a fixation on the future. However to change effectively one has to take notice of the past, especially on the most detailed level at which implementation takes place (Geldof, 2004). On the lowest level of scale history is strongly connected to the system. Preventing obstruction beforehand at this level may very well imply taking history into account (respecting the stories told by local stakeholders). If one does not take the past into account it is assumed that one will meet resistance to plans for change more often and more strongly. This was also the case in the Eperbeken project.

Most of the channels in the Eperbeken system were man-made. The oldest were created in the seventeenth century. The watercourses transported water to the water mills. After the industrial revolution most water mills went out of production and the water channels deteriorated. In the 1970s the Brook Foundation was founded and its volunteers decided to take up the maintenance of the brook systems. In the mid 1980s the national and provincial governments and the regional water authority decided that the management of the brook systems came under the responsibility of the water authority. With the introduction of integrated water management, ideas of 'good' water management in these systems changed over time: from a single purpose of water transport to the mill to a multifunctional system concept. All the actors still influence the process. The seventeenth century copper smithies influenced the layout of the system and the copper pollution in the soil bed. The Brook Foundation is still an important advisor with specific knowledge of the brook systems.

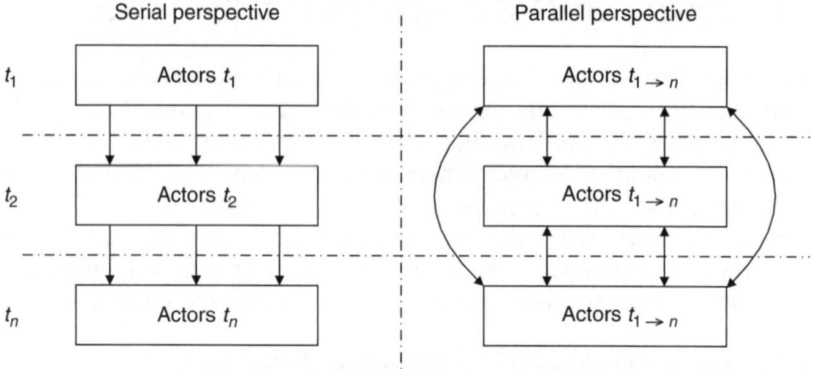

Figure 9.5 Schematic representation of the differences between the serial perspective and parallel perspective of dealing with time perspectives

In the early 1990s ecology entered the integrated water management plans of the water authority. In the planning process of the Eperbeken project the historical and cultural values of the system were regarded as of less value than the ecological values of the system. In this case one can notice how time changed the perspectives of the water authority on premium water management. The foot-and-mouth outbreak also changed the attitudes between the actors during the construction process. Single independent events can be of major influence on the process.

The serial perspective is like a relay race: the next runner will reconsider the virtues of the baton before moving on in what could be a somewhat new direction, hoping to be able to link to the next runner over there. This is also shown in the left side of Figure 9.5. Note that t_1 is just a moment in time. In this figure it is the start of the implementation process, but there is of course time before t_1.

A technique to clear up the past is called harvesting history (Geldof, 2004). A joint negative past has to be cleared up first and must become negotiable. The actors have to choose a new start, without forgetting the past and without bearing a grudge. Alongside, space has to be created for people to tell their stories. It shows that different people can have strong divergent stories about the same water system. As well as bad experiences between people and organizations, positive values of the water system are addressed. These are valuable to the process. In this manner a connection is made through time, the history of the system (both technical aspects as well as relationships between people) are taken into account in the process of change. In complex projects the art is to give processes the time that they need. This is different from scheduling an amount of time in which the task has to be done as in the serial perspective. Visions must not be translated into fixed goals too fast. It is, of course, not advisable to hurry in realizing the goals. On the other hand, progress is still obviously desired. Stakeholders do not want to be kept in suspense and get the idea of stagnation of or exclusion from the process. It is important to keep the right pace, to make the optimal decisions at the right moments (Geldof, 2004). Making the right choices at the right time asks a different concept of time. And a different approach of time requires a different approach of process management. Most actors do not feel the necessity to constantly participate in the process. However, neglecting their voice at the wrong moments can have negative consequences in the future process. This includes all kinds of stakeholders, from citizens to administrators. Success of sustainable development cannot be defined in terms of short-term time perspectives of deadlines.

9.4.2 Boundary Issues With Regard to Scales

It is obvious that when time boundaries are spanned between actors, boundaries across scales and sectors might also be blurred. A multiplicity of policies proved to influence the Eperbeken case. As in all other integrated water projects, these policies originate from the European level to the local level of the municipality. It is at the local level of the water system that all these policies have to be integrated into a coherent set of measurements. Boundaries between policies of different scales are thus spanned into a joint domain of locally specific governance. This policy domain is the basis of the specific context that included previous decisions on, for instance, targets, instruments, resources and time choices (Bressers, 2007). In the planning process of the Eperbeken case it is recognized that the actors of the project team formed a coalition which agreed on ecological boundary judgments (a preference to join the channels resulting from framing the decision in the context of ecological optimization). The board of the foundation and the province, however, had different boundary perceptions, framing the decision making around protecting the historic situation in their boundary judgments. Both these domains run across different scales and levels of government. It was the dominant power position of the province to the water authority that the latter domain was accepted. Geldof (2004) argues that by working in parallel it is possible to be active at different scales alongside each other. At every level different sorts of processes and structures are taken into account.

The conventional serial perspective is not able to adapt to the changes at other levels, because the boundary judgments are set in an early stage of

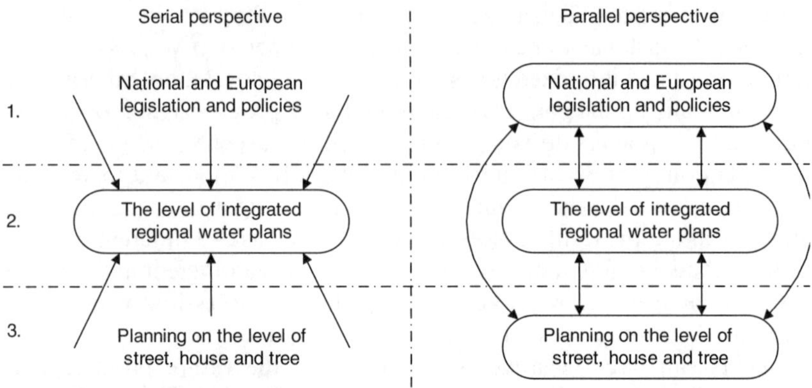

Source: Geldof (2004).

Figure 9.6 Schematic representation of the differences between the serial perspective and parallel perspective of dealing with different scales and levels

the process. It is not uncommon that when a plan enters the construction phase it is already outdated. In the parallel perspective the implementation process is able to adapt its boundary judgments to these developments at higher, but also at lower levels. In the serial perspective of implementation of integrated water plans it is unusual to work (or think) on different levels of scale, especially not on the level of the street, house or tree (Figure 9.6). However at street level, plans are often even more integrated than policy plans at governmental levels, because at the lowest level integration is natural (Geldof, 2004). In this prospect the biggest innovation task is in regional integrated water projects, to adjust and fine-tune higher level plans to the plans and ideas of the street, house or even tree level. Designers are more familiar with this concept of designing through scales. Designers can create solidarity between relations of the stakeholders and decision makers (Geldof, 2004; Hajer and Sijmons, 2006).

Typical for the serial process is that it is assumed that legitimacy of the plan results in legitimacy for the next process phases. Many interactive planning processes go on behind closed doors, involving only a select group of actors. These actors represent stakeholder organizations most of the time, such as nature or agricultural interest groups. The negotiations of the planning phase are often not transparent to local inhabitants. Local landowners, however, are very relevant when the water authority needs to buy land to be able to widen watercourses. The parallel perspective suggests interaction between actors of all levels, for the reasons described above. This needs a careful preparation and organization of the participation process. The interaction between actors of different levels enables the exchange of information. Knowing the ins and outs of different perceptions of different levels can lead to enhanced understanding of each others' goals. It can contribute to public acceptance and legitimacy for the implementation of the water plan (Van Ast and Boot, 2003). It is necessary to involve people at least in the situations in which they offer the largest added value to the process. For most local people it is the scale of their living environment. Where local governments most of the time think and talk in terms of measurements to take, people on the lowest level think and talk more in terms of how the system should be operated and maintained (Geldof, 2004). The parallel perspective suggests speedy construct measures that are supported by all relevant actors (for instance, in just a part of the area) and not to wait for legitimacy for all measures in a plan. Spanned time boundaries create flexibility in boundary spanning activities between levels.

9.4.3 Boundary Issues With Regard to Sectors

The participatory process not only spans boundaries between actors of different levels, but also between sectors. Integrating sectors creates the potential for a higher quality solution. The interaction between sector actors enables exchange of sector-specific information and goals. This can lead to a better understanding of the different sector-specific problem perceptions. This often leads to a broader legitimacy among the different sector actors.

During the planning process of the Eperbeken case representatives of several sectors were asked for their opinion within participatory groups. This linked the planning process to sector-specific stakes and goals. Sector actors were only offered the opportunity to be heard, to comment on the plan and finally to appeal to it. The project team created the integrated plan based on their position and knowledge and the other inputs as referred to. Typical for the serial perspective, the interaction and discussion of boundary issues with sector actors was only done in the planning phase. In the following phases the emphasized boundaries will be contested nevertheless; however there is no room left for discussion, negotiation and consensus building on sector boundary issues. This easily leads to resistance and blocking behavior.

In the parallel perspective of interactive implementation (sector) boundaries are under constant discussion, and sector actors are in principle constantly involved in every aspect of the implementation process (planning, designing, construction, operation and maintenance) (Figure 9.7).

Due to a process of consultation, negotiation and consensus building

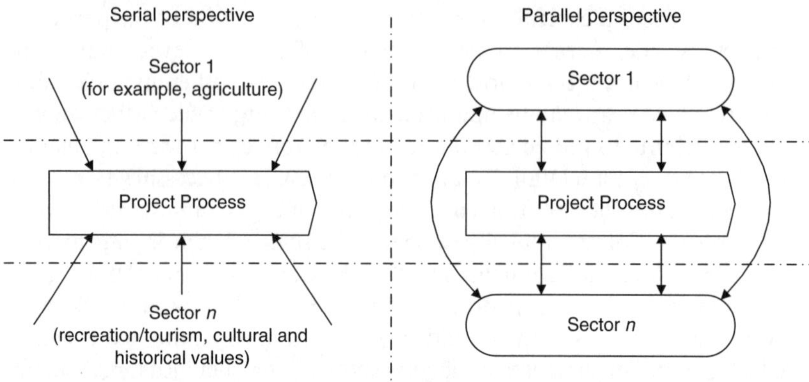

Figure 9.7 Schematic representation of the differences between the serial perspective and parallel perspective of dealing with different sectors and aspects

new sector boundary judgments are shaped. Of course the craftsmanship is in finding an optimal balance in involving sector actors not too little and not too much in the process. Geldof (2004) argues that in the implementation process a distinction has to be made between actors with a formal task in decision making (governmental organizations) in water management and other stakeholders of the water system. The arena of negotiation and consensus building with sector actors has to be separated from the arena of decision makers.

This implies that with the participation process representatives of sectors have their platform of negotiation and consensus building and decision makers also have a platform. Representatives of national, provincial and local governments are integrated in the decision-making process. The water manager has to link to both arenas and needs smart process management to make sure that the arenas interact with each other. Integrating the actors in the process expands the knowledge base of the implementation process. In the parallel perspective, for instance, the local maintenance team is involved in the planning phase. The knowledge base is thereby increased by specific local knowledge about the possibilities to maintain certain water management solutions. Vice versa it provides the maintenance team with knowledge and perceptions of planners about the problem perception and the desired situation. For sector actors identical arguments are relevant. Sector actors have specific system knowledge that can be added to the knowledge base of the implementation process in every phase. This might increase the potential of constructing a legitimate and high quality problem solution.

9.5 CONCLUSIONS

This chapter discussed the choice between parsimonious and redundant approaches in water management, with a focus specifically on implementation. This was done by introducing two approaches, serial and parallel implementation, presenting them as extremes and then illustrating the pros and cons by assessing a case in which a serial perspective on implementation got stuck by unforeseen dynamics and in the end was amended by elements of parallel implementation.

In a boundary spanning perspective, the serial perspective emphasizes strong boundaries within the implementation process. This leads to the co-existence of different and rather unlinked domains within the implementation process, a domain being an environment within boundaries (see Chapters 1 and 2). While implementation proceeds, the boundary judgments that created domains of earlier phases are constantly contested in the following phases. This happens because other relevant actors with different boundary judgments were excluded from previous implementation domains. This difference in boundary judgments of those actors in the process and those out is crucial. The lack of consensus building with regard to diverging boundary judgments related to these issues results in conflicts and obstruction of the process. In the parallel perspective the boundary issues are constantly under discussion. The actors negotiate and build consensus about who, when and what, where and with what and by that strive for converging boundary judgments. In the parallel perspective the water manager facilitates the open (adaptive) implementation process. This asks even more boundary spanning activities of the water manager than within the serial perspective. Still it also leads to more converging boundary judgments.

It is also clear that, depending on the situation, there is no one universal optimum between elements of the two perspectives. It is obvious that simple situations could be well served by serial implementation while many hampering implementation processes in complex situations might well be served by applying principles of parallel implementation.

10. Guidance schemes for the boundary spanner

Jan van der Molen and Kris Lulofs

10.1 INTRODUCTION

In this chapter we present guidance for operational management of boundary spanning efforts. This will be done by introducing four guidance schemes. In order to be able to clarify and illustrate how the schemes could be used in practice, a boundary spanning case across national borders will be presented. The core questions elaborated by the guidance schemes as presented in this chapter are: what kind of process conditions and circumstances should be paid attention to; which choices can be made; how can choices on relevant aspects be brought in balance and be lined up with the ambitions?

The presented guidance schemes, the choice of the seven differences and the suggested ways to cope with them are based on the literature (Otto, 2000; Kaats et al., 2005) and ideas and personal boundary spanning experience of the authors.[1]

In Section 10.2 the case of cross-border boundary spanning in the Vecht river basin will be introduced. Briefly the characteristics of the river basin and the core characteristics of public administration systems at both sides of the border will be summarized. Also the history of efforts on cross-border cooperation as far as relevant in this chapter will be summarized. In Section 10.3 four guidance schemes will be introduced, explained and illustrated based on the literature (Otto, 2000; Kaats et al., 2005) and ideas and personal boundary spanning experience of the authors. In subsections the following topics are outlined:

- managing out, the external perspective on boundary spanning;
- managing in, the internal perspective on boundary spanning;
- managing up, the political perspective on boundary spanning; and
- managing through, the accounting perspective with regard to boundary spanning.

In Section 10.4 seven differences between regions across national borders are presented which we consider as potentially critical for successful boundary spanning across national borders. Furthermore we illustrate how boundary spanners might cope with each of these seven differences. In Section 10.5 some observations and conclusions will be presented.

10.2 THE STORYLINES OF THE VECHT BASIN

The river Vecht originates in the German federal state North Rhine Westphalia, streams through Lower Saxony and then enters the Netherlands. From origin the Vecht was a strongly meandering river, shallow and with large areas that frequently flooded. Between circa 1800 and 1950 most of the hardly accessible swamp and peat bogs that surrounded the river were cultivated for agricultural use. Gradually channels provided alternatives for shipping and the completion of another channel in 1858 marked the end of commercial shipping at the Vecht. Alone on the Dutch side of the border 69 bends were removed and the river was shortened by 30 km. In order to avoid droughts and further cutting into the surface, weirs were constructed in the second half of the twentieth century. The Vecht is now a middle sized lowland rain river with solid banks and weirs. Its contemporary problems concern flooding, droughts, minor water quality issues and the need for restoration activities. Policy sectors with a substantial position in the Vecht basin are water, nature, physical planning, agriculture, tourism and cultural heritage.

There are large differences in the structure of public administration at both sides of the border. The Netherlands has a system that broadly consists of three levels. National government, province (regional), municipality (local) and water district boards (local). The German public administration system is characterized by more levels: federal government (national), the federal states, regional (the *Bezirke* and smaller *Kreise*) and local (*Gemeinde*). So even between the German federal states there are noticeable differences. For a few years there have been no *Bezirke* in the federal state Lower Saxony.

The Dutch public administration culture tends to be rather informal and horizontal. In water management the hierarchy between central government and de-central governments only exists in matters of national importance. And even in such cases a consensual policy style is preferred (Lulofs and Coenen, 2007). The German system is relatively more hierarchical and provides strong separation between policy making and implementation. There is a more fragmented allocation of legal power and responsibilities. Furthermore the German policy culture also includes a strong position for professional expert views and exhaustive analysis. Dutch policy culture tends to be relatively more pragmatic.

Most concrete activities in cross-border cooperation with regard to the Vecht and its management take place in the context of three arenas. Each can be considered as the institutional sediment of an occasion that asked for action to be taken and the relevant boundary perceptions of the actors involved. The characteristics of these three arenas differ substantially (cf. ibid.). The third one, the border spanning activities with regard to the new communal Vecht Vision, will be used to illustrate the guidance schemes presented in the next section. However, basic notions of the preceding two arenas of cross-border cooperation are needed for a good understanding since these efforts will be referred to sometimes.

10.2.1 The Permanent Border Waters Commission

The permanent German-Dutch Border Waters Commission is the oldest arena and started in 1960 when a bilateral treaty was signed between the two countries. The primary driver for the treaty and the commission was the need for a possibility to record agreements between the two countries on water issues. Often the downstream partner, the Netherlands, initiated these issues (Keetman, 2006). The downstream Dutch water managers involved felt the urge to have the issues on a transnational agenda; the German constitutional situation led to the conclusion that it should be a treaty and a legislated commission. The Border Water Commission thus reflects the needs of Dutch water managers and the procedures and culture of German water managers. The commission meets annually. The preparatory activities for this commission are organized in sub-commissions. Now seven sub-committees are active along the border of Germany and the Netherlands. The Vecht is covered by one of them: the sub-commission Vecht-Dinkel.

10.2.2 The Implementation of the European Water Framework Directive

By the European Water Framework Directive (WFD) the water basin became the central object of water management. When a water basin crosses national borders some cross-border coordination is required. Major subsequent work packages are precisely described and concern the ecological characterization of the river basin, the development of a surface water quality monitoring system, the preparation of a programme for improvement and finally the development of a river basin management plan. According to Lulofs and Coenen (2007) coordination was far from perfect; the involved water managers acted relatively autonomously. The preparation of the river basin characterization report in the two federal German states and for Dutch territory proved out of phase and the approach and concepts varied substantially. Rather substantial inconsistencies appeared in the three sub-reports produced that were relevant for the Vecht basin. Due to time constraints the sub-reports were integrated pragmatically and afterwards many corrections were needed. Some blame the steep learning curve that had to be climbed and others think that national regimes and problem perceptions were dominant in explaining why coordination was far from perfect. Subsequently WFD required a surface water monitoring system that included chemical and biotic indicators. A work group of Dutch and German water managers addressed this issue for the relevant area. The work group discussed the differences and possibilities for cross-border calibration. Completely identical systems proved impracticable due to the impact of national and federal requirements. Calibrating the systems proved possible and now German and Dutch data can be converted. This enables upstream water managers to interpret downstream data in their own system and reversed (2007).

10.2.3 The Communal Dutch-German Vecht Vision

The third arena that configures transnational cooperation in the Vecht river basin concerns the development of a strategic and indicative plan to push the development of the Vecht. In 1997 a Dutch indicative plan was made for developing the Vecht and its basin in the coming decades. The ambition is a semi-natural controlled lowland river. In such a river system processes of erosion, sedimentation, meandering and forming of river dunes are relevant. The indicative plan for the Vecht does not only span boundaries within the water sector and across geographical boundaries, it also tries to link to other policy sectors in order to create synthesis between water goals and goals in other societal sectors. Since 2005 the Vecht is no longer a state river and the responsible Dutch water authorities, two water boards, decided to update the 1997 plan. The previous effort to produce such a vision across the national borders failed due to diverging boundary judgements with regard to time horizons. This being said, also diverging ambitions with regard to integration of sectors played a role. Water board Velt and Vecht initiated a process in order to develop this Dutch-German indicative plan on the whole Vecht. The necessary preparatory activities were already largely finished by the spring of 2008. The aspired situation for the year 2050 is described. The ambition is huge and the strategy of imposing and enforcing, as applied in the implementation of the European WFD, is absent. The border spanning activities with regard to the new communal Vecht Vision is the case we will use to illustrate the models presented in the next section.

10.3 GUIDANCE FOR THE BOUNDARY SPANNER

In this section some foci of attention are presented in order to guide the boundary spanner. Some basic notions on reflexive water management introduced by Westley (2002) reflect our position (see Section 1.3 in Chapter 1). She assumed that adaptive management of ecosystems implies that water managers have to juggle four balls: the political ball (also referred to as managing up), the bureaucratic ball (managing in), the societal ball (managing out) and the scientific ball (managing through). Our central assumptions furthermore include that further development of cooperation depends on spanning of boundaries and might stop when crucial boundaries cannot be spanned. The third central assumption is that for creating and maintaining stable spans it is necessary that the four perspectives are kept in balance by the tactics and strategies of the boundary spanner.

The perspectives will be introduced in the following four subsections. Subsection 10.3.1 will deal with managing out, the external perspective on boundary spanning, Subsection 10.3.2 will deal with managing in, the internal perspective on boundary spanning, Subsection 10.3.3 will deal with managing up, the political perspective on boundary spanning and Subsection 10.3.4 will deal with managing through, which we will call the accounting perspective with regard to boundary spanning.

10.3.1 Managing Out, the External Perspective on Boundary Spanning

Managing out is about establishing actor constellations and cooperation between those actors. The task for the boundary spanner is to assess who the partners in cooperation should be, how they could be activated and motivated and which windows of opportunity might occur or might be created to bind the actors together. This leads to the phases, subjects and aspects as presented in Figure 10.1 (van der Molen, 2001).

The model distinguishes five phases. Take off is an idea that spanning certain boundaries might be in the interest of several actors that for this reason might be potentially willing to cooperate. Or alternatively, by using some supporting instruments to influence cognitions and motives, some actors might be convinced that cooperation might be in their interest. This calls for an assessment of the environment including a global check on feasibility of the idea, and thus also on the needed competences to realize the idea in reality. In the case of the communal Vecht Vision it was well known that previous efforts to span the national borders in this context failed for several reasons as described in the previous section.

Seeking the appropriate partners reflects the second phase in this model.

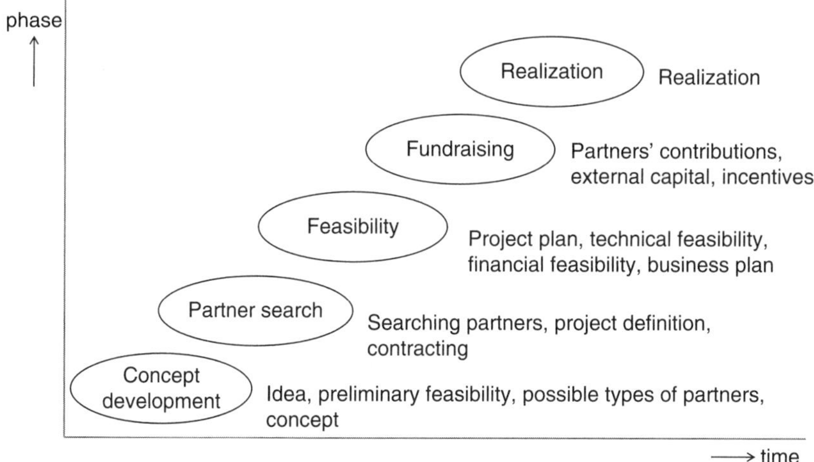

Figure 10.1 Phases, subjects and issues for managing out, the external perspective on boundary spanning

Selection is based on the needed competences and dependency towards certain partners. Sometimes the needed networks already exist. With regard to the Vecht Vision there pre-existed some linkages, for instance, within the mentioned Border Waters Commission and in the context of the European WFD. However these contacts were not considered by definition sufficient to realize the cross-border Vecht Vision. For instance, the boundary judgements with regard to time horizons of actors did certainly not include 2050 nor was integration of sectors a real issue. The Border Waters Commission handled predominantly urgent problems and short-term issues while the WFD focused on 2015.

However there was a fortunate process condition that made it easier to influence the scale dimension of boundary judgements. It was clear that the introduction of WFD influenced actors' boundary judgements in the direction of some opening up towards larger scales. Still networks were not instantly available. And initiating the right actor constellations was not easy due to the large number of actors involved in Germany and the strong separation between policy making and implementation. This might not look like a problem since the Vecht Vision represents an indicative strategic plan. However Dutch actors involved think local and are aware that the real integration of sectors is not realized in policy but in implementation and projects. Without feasible implementation options Dutch actors involved tend not to be satisfied, and this certainly included the Dutch boundary spanner.

In the third phase the technical and financial feasibility is analyzed in depth and, if applicable, a business plan is written. On this basis capital, risk capital, loans and subsidies will be collected. If this succeeds realization starts in phases four and five.

So what were, besides the already mentioned facts, the highlights of the cross-border water management case with regard to this model? The involved boundary spanner proposed to potential partners was to integrate water and other relevant policy sectors in the Vecht basin. With some well-known partners the idea was discussed, a global budget for some activities was elaborated and some written material was produced (phase 1). The written concept was presented to and discussed with the potential partners at both sides of the border during the actual partner search in phase 2. At that moment a network of eight organizations was already established. Some agreements were reached with regard to how to proceed. Programming (phase 3) and fundraising (phase 4) started more or less at the same time. The Dutch water authority decided to take the risk and pre-financed activities, among which were consultancy activities of a German-Dutch alliance of consultancy firms. These acted as a project office and scanned chances for cooperation relevant for the Vecht Vision and its implementation. The alliance produced a more detailed project plan and a detailed budget. The idea was to finance the project by a subsidy, however the most designated funding programme was not yet open. The nine core partners then decided to pre-finance some of the activities of the project plan. Among others, it was assessed which actors at both sides of the border should participate in the Vecht Vision process in order to realize the integrated water resource approach (cf. Chapter 1) that was strived for. Forty organizations were approached which covered various sectors. After the subsidy scheme became active and the subsidy was granted, the implementation of the second part of the project plan started.

Of course the important process variables concern the arenas to be created and the cognitions and motives of actors. In this case the boundary spanner preferred to invest some seed money and every now and then persuade the actors to come together, get them involved and get them familiar with the types of boundary judgements needed to create a joined Vecht Vision.

Using the model focuses the boundary spanner on carefully selecting partners, developing a joint perspective on the project at hand and the needed process; it provides clear go/no-go moments and reminds managers of the necessary steps and the logical sequence. In the switch towards the next section it might be helpful to remember that managing out is about the inter-organizational aspect, establishing and maintaining inter-organizational relations in order to get the right coalition.

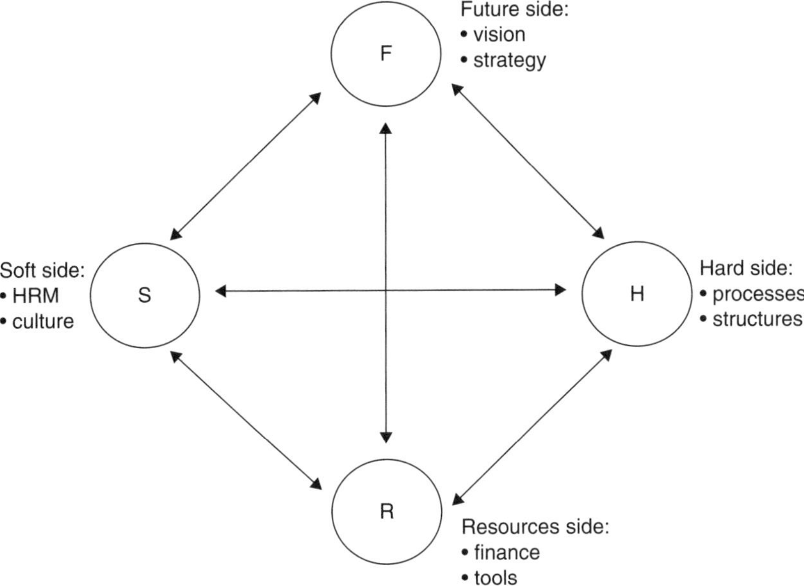

Figure 10.2 Managing in, the internal perspective on boundary spanning

10.3.2 Managing In, the Internal Perspective on Boundary Spanning

Managing in is about developing the coalition towards a collaboration that is well equipped to make progress. For managing in, the following model is used that is derived from change management (Figure 10.2) (Korringa and Van der Molen, 2005).

This model's first central assumption is that the four aspects play crucial roles in the development of organizations as well as in the development of actor constellations created in the context of boundary spanning. The second central assumption is that the four aspects interact and an organization or actor constellation can only function well if the aspects are in balance and tuned. Adding structure and organizational design, at the right side of Figure 10.2, makes, for instance, sense above all if it is based on shared vision and mission, to be found at the top of Figure 10.2. A vision can, for instance, only be converted into strategies if resources are present, below in Figure 10.2, and people are willing and competent to cooperate, the left side of the model represented in Figure 10.2.

In water management practice many people have a technical profile and, for instance, hydrologists and morphologists embrace an engineering work attitude. These practitioners are often biased towards the right hand side in the model. Discussions are then about content and structure, for instance, work groups are installed. However we think that improvement of organizational competences and progress in boundary spanning depend strongly on the interaction between the left side and the top of the model in Figure 10.2. Design of structure at the right side only follows the previous argument. After all it is people that act, not structure. Only if people know where to go and are competent to move can progress be harvested with regard to establishing purposeful structure. Besides, the question of how to structure is in most cases not the most difficult one, and often the necessary resources somehow can be collected. If the existing vision and strategy of an organization proves contra-productive for boundary spanning, chances for success are small, unless political momentum can be found for the boundary spanning initiative. For vision and strategy, managing up, the political ball to be discussed in Section 10.3.3 can play a decisive role.

So what were the highlights of the cross-border water management case with regard to this model? The implications of this model can be illustrated by all three cross-border initiatives as described in Section 10.2. With regard to the Border Waters Commission, the dominant perspective is the right side of the model. The balance with regard to the other dimensions of the model was never developed. Strategy and vision was lacking, the delusion of the day was dominant. Also with regard to the left side of the model the Border Water Commission and its sub-commissions were not well developed, with the exception of a few motivated and trained civil servants. Finally, resources were limited, and the few really motivated civil servants in sub-commissions tried to expand activities and tried to finance these by subsidies. However this proved to go against the tide.

Regarding the European WFD, the situation with regard to the model was quite different. The obligations were well described, the deadline was well known, and action was unavoidable and an issue in politics. The top of Figure 10.2 proved the dominant perspective, quickly followed by attention to the right side of the model. The model under these circumstances tells us that it would be logical to focus upon the competences of the people involved, the left side of the model. And if this proves not to be problematic, the bottom perspective of the model, the resources, would become extremely important. Furthermore, if something essential changes with regard to one of the four dimensions, the model tells us to reassess all four dimensions in order to check whether the dimensions are in balance.

With regard to the Vecht Vision such influential external events were not present. Therefore the departure position was found at the left side of the model, by motivated people with open minds and converging boundary judgements. These people and their organizations should drag the

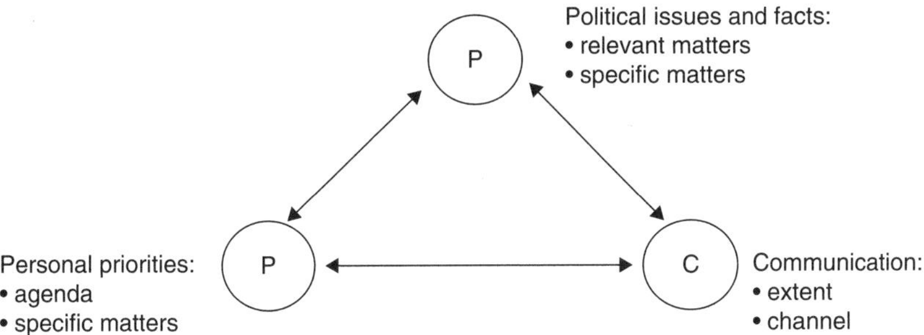

Figure 10.3 Managing up, the political perspective on boundary spanning

initiative along. The mentioned eight organizations, with a central role for the Dutch water authority, developed a vision, strategy and to some extent political support. Only thereafter the right side and bottom side of the model were developed.

10.3.3 Managing Up, the Political Perspective on Boundary Spanning

It is important to realize that within public administration the strategic choices and priorities are often set by the board of governors. This also holds true for boundary spanners that try to develop cooperation. Within the political setting often one governor is responsible for the initiative; however that does not necessarily imply that the responsible politician is motivated for the cooperation and the boundary spanning initiatives. Of course the craftsmanship is to evoke positive impacts from the relevant politicians.

Three variables are relevant for assessing the potential of the political perspective. The scope of issues that are considered political issues and facts represent the first variable, the personal priorities of the relevant politicians is the second variable and the communication towards relevant politicians is the third. Depending on the extent and procedures for notifying, enlightening, apprising and advising the relevant politicians, politicians will react using the set of political issues and facts and their personal priorities as filters (Figure 10.3). Of course these filters are driven by boundary judgements.

There are a couple of issues that need to be understood with regard to political reality. If politics is directly involved, for instance, if the responsible governor participates in a steering committee, conditions are good beforehand. Under these conditions relevant communication and information can be handled easily by personal contacts. Governors often consult a limited number of advisors, so to open up to them and influence them either directly or through their advisors is as much a skill as it might seem to depend on power and luck to those who are outsiders. This being said, a change in position of governors might easily threaten as well as facilitate boundary spanning. In general the actions of governors can overcome barriers; however, as easily, inappropriate actions can lead to new boundaries being created. Intuition for how the old boys' network functions might be as rhetorical as valuable.

If the relevant politician is not directly involved it is likely that the scores on the crucial variables of political issues and facts and personal characteristics are less positive. Access to political support in this situation is more difficult. Of course the first option would be to activate politics and get them directly involved. However access for the boundary spanner and other representatives of the organization towards the political arena might fall short. Besides, just communicating and informing will most likely not change reality if the political agenda or personal characteristics prevent politicians from playing a more positive and supportive role. Changing the boundary judgements of relevant politicians might help under these circumstances. In Chapter 2 it was described that such dynamics could be expected from new actors, new arenas, new cognitions and new resources and power. For managing up, given these basic options, one might consider activating another governor who embraces a more positive personal characteristic towards boundary spanning. Also activating politicians from outside might be an option. Otherwise new governors after elections might result in new options. Changing cognitions, motivations might also be done by reaching out for new resources. For instance, at higher scale levels policy programmes often subsidize boundary spanning activities. However, linking a boundary spanning initiative to larger scales can also be beneficial because larger scales might not only facilitate boundary spanning but might use power. In the case of establishing cross-border cooperation between German and Dutch water managers the European WFD and its obligations played a crucial role. Local politicians are likely to open up if substantial outside resources become within reach; these are considered politically interesting chances. They can activate political pressure and enable active political support for boundary spanning. Raising pressure from the outside by activating public concern is not a realistic suggestion; typical boundary spanning themes do not easily activate civilians. With regard to the Vecht Vision some storylines with regard to political issues and facts and personal characteristics come down to personal involvement. Especially within the board of governors of the water management authority motivation for cross-border cooperation was found. This explains the fact that the central boundary spanner also worked for this water authority and it was also this water authority that was willing to pre-finance some of the needed efforts.

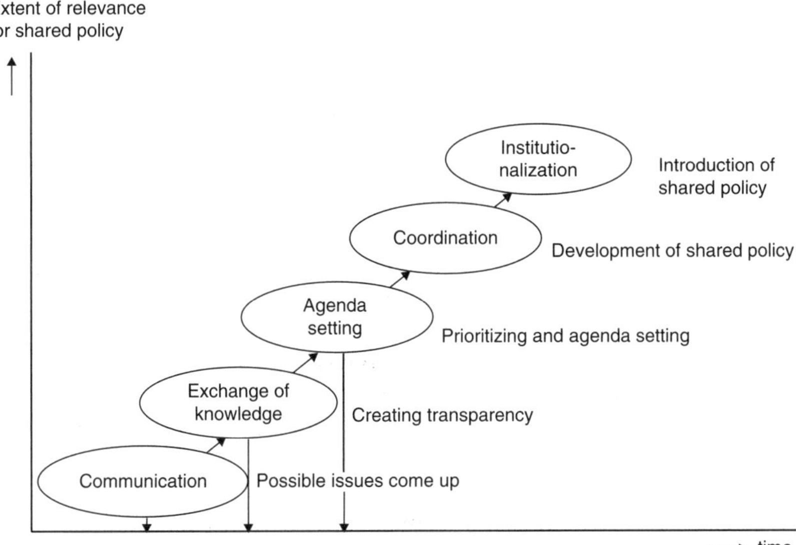

Figure 10.4 Managing through, the accounting perspective with regard to boundary spanning

10.3.4 Managing Through, the Accounting Perspective with Regard to Boundary Spanning

In the previous three subsections, suggestions for setting and managing the process conditions of boundary spanning were introduced, described and illustrated. In the end, success of boundary spanning is what counts, and all important process guidance has to be considered secondary. Success of boundary spanning is measured by indicators such as policies brought together, plans across boundaries being made, joint implementation across boundaries being started, and also stable, preferable institutionalized boundary spanning linkages to continue cooperation and progress.

From a process monitoring perspective it is therefore of interest to think about a model that enlightens the successive steps and the level of progress. We use a phasing model that is deduced from earlier work on modelling cross-border cooperation (Figure 10.4) (Verwijmeren and Wiering, 2007).

Although the original model did not assume a set of sequential steps, the proposition that each step taken implies more substantial cooperation can easily be read. However not all issues need to pass all phases. For instance, if in phase 2 it becomes obvious that an exploration of the problem is not necessary, what does that imply for the quality of the cooperation? Not much, it might imply that the issue is found not relevant any more after exchange of information. This might be the case if knowledge and expertise is distributed dissimilarly over organizations. It might also be the case if the issue has meanwhile been dealt with to a satisfying level. In both cases one might conclude that actors were capable of stopping when that seemed the right thing to do and no resources are wasted on starting new forms of cooperation that are not needed.

Meanwhile we think that this model functions most productively if one interprets it as labels that reflect possible sediments of interaction patterns between partners in cooperation. The first phase is that of communication. In order to process to the next phase converging problem/issue definitions have to be developed. This involves either emphasizing the already shared boundary judgements or, alternatively, careful development of converging boundary judgements with regard to the relevant scale, sector and time dimensions. In our case it was clear from history that progress was blocked by diverging judgements on sector and time dimensions. At both sides of the border the awareness of benefits of integrating sectors and a long time perspective was lacking. In this perspective the arrival of the European WFD was exploited skilfully in order to overcome these hindrances. These events illustrate that assessing the past can help us to learn and focus, especially when this can be linked to external conditions, which open a window of opportunity.

During the second phase fact finding and learning is dominant. Only if this process reinforces the idea that by development of joint policy brings benefits to all, progress is possible. As already explained within our case, cross-border cooperation was started with a relatively small group of eight actors that developed ideas first and learned. It is, however, also obvious that new problem/issue definitions can enter the arena in this phase.

During the third phase the shared problem/issue definitions should reach the political agenda. Commitment to develop shared policy should be harvested. Political support is a boundary spanning aspect that needs attention right from the start. At this point, political support and commitment should be explicated. In fact it took some pre-financing in our case. This being said, what brought actors together was a promising concept and the chance to get the next steps financed by an external subsidy scheme. Our case illustrates that political commitment does not necessarily imply legal commitment nor is it a yes or no issue.

During the fourth and fifth phases a shared policy should be reached out for, as was done in our case. The fact that this is only an indicative strategic plan overruled the traditional national sovereignty argument that often blocks progress. Finally, the challenge to anchor established cooperation emerges. This requires boundary organizations or boundary objects (see Chapter 7).

A final remark with regard to this model is that it makes sense to think in multiple problem/issues definitions and multiple policy issues that move through the model simultaneously, and in different phases of the model. Some might never reach subsequent phases regardless of the efforts and the skills of the boundary spanners. Trying to group promising issues in order to create momentum can be part of the tactics and strategies that were discussed in the previous sections.

Frequently monitoring progress of individual issues as proposed in this subsection should result in adjustments in tactics and strategies if necessary. If repairs have to be made in the context of the guidance schemes for managing out, managing in and managing up, it is helpful to keep in mind that the general categories in the toolbox that could make the difference are new actors, new cognitions, new motives, new arenas and facilitating with resources (see Chapter 2).

10.4 COPING WITH NATIONAL BORDERS

Across border boundary spanning is to some extent different from other forms of spanning scale boundaries such as between regions. If regions in two or more sovereign countries are involved the differences between regions will be many and substantial. Whether or not a difference can be considered as potentially critical depends very much on the context. In this section we present seven differences between the assessed regions across national borders that in our case proved influential. After introducing them some suggestions are given on how boundary spanners might cope with the difference.

1. The composition and structure of the public administration systems. The composition and structure of public administration tells a lot about how things work in a country. In the situation in which organizations from both sides start cooperating without enough knowledge of these systems there is a severe chance that participants show little empathy for positions and limitations brought to the attention of participants from the other side. Miscommunication can easily happen and be interpreted as lack of respect, which will lead to irritation and disappointment. Some suggestions to handle the issue:

    (a) Supply the participants with an overview of composition and structure of public administration systems at both sides of the border. This has to be discussed at an early stage in terms of chances and constraints for the cooperation.

(b) Participants should produce the overview for their own situation. However we have to signal that this commitment might also be expecting too much from the participants. Do not forget that it is not the participants' regular job to search for and structure this type of information. Still, for warming up the cooperation it is a great procedure, although some of the needed analysis and reporting should be done by experts.

(c) Ensure that the participants inform each other in a plenary meeting. Direct information and communication works best and participants can question colleagues from the other side directly. The downside is that it is often not that easy to understand colleagues that are not specialized in transferring this kind of knowledge. Also the language can play a crucial role; colleagues from the other side tend to prefer to present in their own language.

2. The specific organization of the water sector.
In case the initiators have little knowledge on how the water sector at the other side of the border is organized, there is a great chance that in the early stages of cooperation a lot of time will be wasted. This happens, for instance, by contacting and investing in organizations which in the end will not prove relevant and will not be participants in the cooperation. In addition, it can happen that essential organizations are only approached in a later stage and feel passed by. Or alternatively take a lot of effort to update and come alongside. Some suggestions:

(a) Supply the participants with an overview of the organization of the water sector. Let the actors involved correct and supplement the overviews.

(b) Let the participants inform each other. Direct information and communication works best and participants can question colleagues from the other side directly. A discussion helps to internalize information.

(c) Exchange of personnel. Involved personnel learn how water management at the other side is organized. This information can be shared with colleagues. An additional advantage is that people get to know each other's organizations.

3. Knowledge of the other participants' political affairs.
Regional political affairs from the other side of the border are often not picked up by the regular information channels. Therefore it is

not easy to be informed on political affairs and contemporary issues. Some suggestions to handle the issue:

(a) Establish new information channels. For instance, by reading regional newspapers from the other side of the border. The internet can be of great value, for instance, to follow the news and newsletters from organizations from abroad. Also getting on their mailing lists is relevant.
(b) Start networking at the other side of the border, attend meetings and get to know some people, just be present there.
(c) Start managing the relations. Keep in touch; in between the formal meetings expand the existing contacts on different levels. Informal contacts on the executive or board level can be very profitable.
(d) During official meetings colleagues from the other side tend to express themselves in words that reflect the contemporary political affairs at home. It is wise to be alert to this information.

4. Methods and techniques being used.
Measuring techniques, techniques for analysis and the interpretation frameworks at both sides of the border often do not match. This is hard to change because the organizations involved have to stay in line with their own national regulations. In such situations it may be difficult to compare standards and data from both sides of the border. Some suggestions:

(a) Try to straighten things out; what are the real issues and differences?
(b) Perhaps a shared pilot project can be carried out in order to assess relevant differences in methods and techniques and their implications.
(c) Sometimes certain locations at or near the border can be sampled, measured or interpreted in both systems, so that the data enable assessment of the real differences.
(d) Inform the responsible institutions about the different approaches and hope that in the longer term this will lead to harmonization.

5. Budgets available.
In case the budgets to be spent differ strongly at both sides of the border it may become difficult to develop a balanced cooperation. Some suggestions to handle the issue:

(a) Be transparent on the real differences in budgets. Take care that this issue is discussable, don't let it simmer.
(b) Think of and use possibilities to compensate budget differences. Let, for instance, the participant with the smallest budget compensate by investing more time. An organization with a small budget might, for instance, also pay a smaller amount for certain services. By finding the right arguments, differences in available budgets can sometimes be more acceptable and be overcome.
(c) Agenda setting at a higher level. See whether participants with the lowest budget can be helped by introducing the issue on the agenda at a higher level so that additional budget will become available for these participants.

6. Culture.
   Although the physical distances between regional organizations on both sides of the border can be very small, the cultural differences can still be substantial. Cultural differences are often very inflexible and can have a substantial negative impact on the cooperation process. Some suggestions to handle the issue:

   (a) Make cultural differences discussable at an early stage. Cultural differences are nothing special, they play a role whenever organizations cooperate and therefore also in the case of cross-border cooperation. Cultural differences are not only difficult to handle but can also be an incentive for innovation or a reason to laugh together.
   (b) Try to spot persons within the participating organizations that have a real interest in dealing with other cultures. This might, for instance, also become clear through their hobbies or through their holiday destinations.
   (c) As cultural differences can be very inflexible, the boundary spanner sometimes has no other choice left than to accept a solution that is very unpractical but which is acceptable to all participants.
   (d) There is a serious pitfall for the boundary spanner involved: focusing too much on cultural differences between organizations across the border, whereas cultural differences between organizations at the same side of the border can also have a substantial negative impact on the cooperation.

7. Language.
   Language problems can be the reason that people do not communicate and do not like to maintain the necessary contacts across the

border. Cooperating bilingually requires extra time and sometimes also extra money (translation cost). Some suggestions to handle the issue:

(a) To a certain extent language problems can be compensated; for instance, by spreading bilingual minutes and having translation facilities available during meetings.
(b) In border regions people tend to have some feeling for each others' language and the dialects on both sides of the border are often very similar. When this is the case the choice can be made that all participants speak their own language or dialect.
(c) In case language problems are hindering communication the boundary spanner should be aware. Is this really because of a language problem or are there other things going on? In case of a language problem the boundary spanner can easily assist to solve the problem.
(d) A person who is bilingual and thus speaks two languages. This does, however, not necessarily imply that this person can also think in both languages. This should also not be forgotten when a person is hired to manage the cooperation process. A combination of two process managers from both sides of the border might be a solution.

From the spanning directions presented above a strategy for the boundary spanner can be derived which can be summarized as follows: create transparency, neutralize the consequences of the critical difference and, if possible, span the difference concerned. So don't let the critical difference between the regions do its work in silence. First of all, try to create transparency, second, try at least to neutralize the consequences of the critical difference, and third, when possible span the difference concerned so that it will no longer be critical. Finally, it is stressed once more that these were the critical factors that played a role in the communal Vecht Vision. In other cases or in other non-water management fields the critical differences between regions due to national borders might to some extent be different. This being said, the list of seven might be the best reference available when starting regional cooperation across national borders.

10.5 CONCLUSIONS

In this chapter some guidance for boundary spanners was presented. In the first place this was done by introducing and explaining four guidance schemes. Four foci were introduced that were labelled managing out, the external perspective on boundary spanning, managing in, the internal perspective on boundary spanning, managing up, the political perspective on boundary spanning and the accounting perspective towards boundary spanning. The first three perspectives offer guidance for boundary spanners in terms of issues that require attention and can help to proceed. The fourth perspective introduced a scheme for typical patterns of interaction that forecast boundary spanning success. If progress is disappointing, some aspects within the management of the first three perspectives might be out of balance or otherwise not sufficient.

It is important to stress that none of the schemes are meant to be interpreted in a serial and deterministic manner. The guidance scheme should be used as tools to structure adaptive management. A case of boundary spanning across national borders was used to illustrate both the guidance schemes and how they could be used.

In addition, seven differences were described that proved to be influential in our case of regional cooperation across national borders. It was illustrated how boundary spanners might cope with each of these seven differences.

NOTE

1. Jan van der Molen and Kris Lulofs participated in the European Rivercross project that assessed cross-border cooperation within Europe at several borders (www.rivercross.nl). Jan van der Molen is practicing boundary spanner for the Dutch water board Velt and Vecht and was involved in development of the cross-border Vecht vision, which is used as a case that illustrates the presented principles of orchestrating boundary spanning.

11. Conclusions

Hans Bressers and Kris Lulofs

11.1 INTRODUCTION

The relevance of this volume was clear to us beforehand. We started this book with a broad outline of three eras of water management. We concluded that many of the urgent contemporary water issues on the agenda require boundary spanning. It is unlikely that water managers are able to cope with the challenges on their own. Overcoming barriers in society often implies seeking cooperation, searching for well-equipped coalitions that together possess the needed resources. And if such a coalition is willing to engage in a multi-purpose project that serves several functions in society, something splendid can be realized and the involved water management community can be proud of it.

This being said, we also conclude that craftsmanship of water management in the twenty-first century requires conscious consideration of whether boundary spanning is an effective and efficient strategy given the job to be done and the goals to be reached. Boundary spanning and the creation of coalitions inherently lead to dependency and complexity. What is acquired in terms of resources and power can easily be lost in terms of decisiveness and policy drift. The authors of this book tried to demonstrate that a careful reconsideration of strategies to realize water ambitions, together with more in-depth knowledge on the theories and practices of boundary spanning, could make solutions for contemporary water problems become feasible.

Some self-chosen guidelines were dominant for selecting chapters and case studies that are included in this book: any chapter included should deal with boundary spanning on significant water management issues. Any presented case should furthermore be informative on the applicability of one or more concepts and mechanisms in our frameworks. Taken together in a cumulative research perspective, the cases should enable statements about the status of the framework and suggest improvements. Therefore, also, suggestions to improve the framework based on empirical observations were applauded beforehand. Finally, we encouraged reporting on guidance for boundary spanning in practice. Now it is time to wrap things up.

In Section 11.2 of this synthesis we elaborate what Chapters 3–10 taught us with regard to the introduced conceptual and theoretical frameworks. In Section 11.3 of this synthesis we review our findings with regard to issues of importance for organizations and individuals that want to span boundaries.

11.2 THE SCIENTIFIC LENS ON BOUNDARY SPANNING

We were inquisitive with regard to uncovering the mechanisms for boundary spanning and the strategies and circumstances of influence that affect success or failure of such attempts of water managers to move beyond mediocrity. While developing conceptual and theoretical frameworks, we tried to be as clear and parsimonious as we thought we could be without oversimplifying. This concerns an effort to avoid unneeded theoretical diversity that often comes when social science theories and frameworks are integrated in order to understand phenomena that at first sight seem complex. The conceptual and theoretical frameworks are based on previous academic scholarly work as well as involvement in all research programmes and projects that the cases in this book were derived from. This implies that we had some global knowledge of cases before they were selected to be reanalyzed in the context of this volume. Nevertheless only the case studies presented in Chapters 5 and 6 were conducted with the explicit purpose of contributing to the development of conceptual and theoretical frameworks concerning boundary spanning. We do not perceive this as problematic since the nature and characteristics of the framework, being a social science and particular policy science framework, inherently imply that positivist testing of the complete framework cannot be achieved easily. Still, the framework is clear enough in its described patterns to be proven wrong or inapt, when this would be the case. The empirical cases and issues covered in this book were all pre-selected on the presence of boundary spanning efforts. So the presence of substantial boundary spanning efforts should not surprise anybody. The cases lined up in this volume support the theoretical framework although not all presented empirical material can be regarded as rigorous testing. Our work on conceptual and theoretical foci was deliberately mingled with empiricism.

Our theoretical model in Chapter 2 specifies and focuses upon the micro-process and its direct context as well as upon conditions from contextual layers that offer windows of opportunity or barriers to boundary spanners. In our model the specific context, the structural context and the wider contexts were distinguished within this contextual environment (see

Figure 2.4). Furthermore it was assumed that in micro-processes characteristics of actors are essential to understand the behavioural intentions and behaviour of actors: their motivations (values, interests), resources (creating capacity and power) and cognitions. The theoretical framework also assumes that among the latter actor characteristics the boundary judgements and receptivity are of crucial importance. As elements of the cognitions of actors these are considered essential targets for boundary spanning. According to the framework the boundary spanner in principle can influence diverging boundary judgements and exploit converging boundary judgements. However the boundary spanner also has to adopt their strategies to other actor characteristics and circumstances in the described contextual layers.

In order to synthesize what can be learned from Chapters 3–10 with regard to the support for the framework we use the list of issues and questions introduced in Section 2.5. These issues and questions are especially relevant for case studies that are structured by our theoretical framework. Therefore we also structure our synthesis by these issues and questions.

The first question introduced reads: *What is the initial issue the researcher wants to focus on?*

We ended up with a wide variety of cases and incorporated issues. On the long list of cases that could potentially produce insights in core mechanisms in our framework were:

- The case of flood risks management in long-term system perspective, a case covering boundary spanning developments in contextual perspective (Chapter 3).
- The case of droughts and the choice of crops, a case covering boundary spanning over agriculture and water policy and their associated time frames (Chapter 4).
- The case of flood risks management in the context of realizing water storing capacity for peak levels, spanning agriculture and nature in a river basin (Chapter 5).
- The case of digging a complete new water course involving ecological habitat creation, water policy and, among others, industrial estates planning (Chapter 6).
- The multiple cases of restoring wetlands involving other functions (Chapter 7).
- The cases of creating nature habitats in agricultural areas in the context of joined learning (Chapter 8).
- The case of restructuring of large creek systems linking to ecological and cultural considerations and attempting to integrate project phases (Chapter 9).

- The case concerning establishment of linkages between multiple sectors across national borders (Chapter 10).

Second, we take together four issues/questions that in Section 2.5 were introduced as four separate issues/questions. Summarized these concern: *the assessments of the emerged linkages (and failures), the involved actors and their relevant cognitions, motivations, and resources and the roles of boundary judgements and receptivity of actors.*

Taken together, these issues/questions represent the core of the theoretical framework. The vast majority of empirical data analyzed in the chapters address precisely these issues. The cases in Chapters 5 and 6 were analyzed exactly in line with the logics and steps that are inherent to the application of the framework. The case in Chapter 5 dealt predominantly with efforts to repair a stranded project while Chapter 6 reported a case in which boundary spanners strived for linkages to create added value to an ambitious project beforehand. Especially the differences between the two cases in terms of the characteristics of the linkages that were established and how the case stories unrolled in interaction with the contextual layers are convincing. Differences found in the receptivity of involved spanners played important roles as did the time horizons of the actors involved. In the case in Chapter 6 spanning of sectors was mingled with spanning of scales and time dimensions. In the case in Chapter 5 sectors were also spanned, or at least efforts to span sectors were observed. However this was not or very little mingled with spanning of scales and time dimensions.

This leads us unavoidably to a partial further elaboration of the framework initiated in Chapter 4. Chapter 4 introduced concepts that make the time dimension of boundary judgements more recognizable, tangible and applicable. By distinguishing concepts such as time horizon, temporal perception, temporal orientation and temporal discounting, a more parsimonious analysis of the role of the time dimension in boundary spanning was introduced. This fits in perfectly in our framework and makes it clearer without making it less parsimonious. Also the interrelations between the time dimension and the sector and scale dimensions of boundary judgements were deepened. It was described that any successful spanning of sector and scale boundaries always includes spanning of temporal boundaries. And also that if boundary judgements of actors converge with regard to time dimensions and this convergence includes taking longer periods into account, this will facilitate boundary spanning over sectors and scales substantially. This is indeed a valuable stepping stone that is offered that we gladly integrate in the framework in further research efforts. This line of theorizing is supported by the differences between the boundary spanning storylines in Chapters 5 and 6. Also the empirical findings on cross-national border cooperation as presented in Chapter 10 with regard to the communal vision on a river basin presents a strong case with regard to these arguments. The long time horizon under analysis enabled the boundary spanner to make progress and also influence other dimensions of relevant boundary judgements. The involved river basin is, to refresh, the same as was studied in Chapter 5 with regard to realization of retention capacity for peak levels, a case that was dominated by time pressure and short deadlines. Reviewing the basic three spanning dimensions as introduced in Chapter 1 (sectors, scales and temporal dimensions) the vast majority of empirical data confirmed that individual spanning efforts and individual linkages can very well be classified within this typology. Also the further specification of this typology by distinguished aspects and sub-aspects (see Table 1.2) does not raise any objections from a logical or empirical perspective.

Resuming our journey through chapters, the multiple cases that were analyzed in Chapter 7 add to the credibility of our framework. In this comparison the key differences between the patterns of success and failure were in line with the framework. The empirical analysis in Chapter 8 with regard to the use of beta knowledge in the policy process is also supportive for our framework. Overlooking the found patterns that were described in several chapters we feel it is safe to conclude that the applicability and preciseness of the theoretical framework for studying boundary spanning is convincingly illustrated. This being said, relatively less emphasis was placed on the role of receptiveness. In Chapter 2 we assumed that the receptiveness is a separate aspect of cognitions of actors that should be distinguished from boundary judgements. There might be a discussion whether this represents a reasonable assumption. Could it also be the case that actors showing large receptiveness just do so because they perceived converging boundary judgements? And could it be that actors showing little receptiveness just do so because they perceived diverging boundary judgements? Considerable support was found in several chapters that there is no straightforward relation between diverging or converging boundary judgements between actors and the variable receptiveness. Several examples illustrated that actors can be very receptive to the outside world and outsiders that actually show very diverging boundary cognitions. Especially Chapters 5, 6 and 8 were relevant with regard to this issue and include an essential third variable: dependency. Chapter 5 showed that actors that got themselves into severe problems and perceive severe time pressure became remarkably receptive to anyone who might be able to offer solutions, while in the same case individuals that believed they gained from slowing down progress showed little receptiveness. Also in Chapters 6 and 8 examples can be found of actors that are quite receptive without clear indications that the boundary judgements are converging. Receptiveness seems to be a state of mind rather than an effect of comparing boundary judgements. Here the importance is demonstrated not only of confining the analysis to actor characteristics of a cognitive nature, but also relating these to actor characteristics in terms of motivations and resources. Comparing boundary judgements and efforts to influence boundary judgements towards convergence can often probably be better considered as effects of the level of receptiveness that might be produced by motivation and resource position than the other way around.

We now proceed with the conclusions with regard to the interaction with contextual layers. The sixth issue as indicated in Section 2.5 consists of: *the interaction between the specific context, the structural context and the wider context.*

Wrapping up the presented empirical work on the contextual layers, the following observations seem relevant. The documented argument in Chapter 10 on cross-border cooperation made clear how multiform and decisive the differences in contextual layers can be. In Chapters 5 and 6 the contextual layers were scanned in a systematic manner, however the analysis was done in a hermeneutic manner in terms of selected variables. In analyses of the structural and wider contexts in other chapters often a small number of relevant variables were identified and included, incorporated in analyses that in most cases concentrated dominantly on the specific context. This being said, tracking relevant factors and developments in the contextual layers, such as the coherence of the structural or governance context (Bressers and Kuks, 2004), and assessing how they influence the micro-process is of significant importance to uncover why certain boundary spanning efforts succeed and others fail. It is evident that actor characteristics are strongly influenced by contextual factors and that these contextual layers change over time.

A second follow-up on our frameworks enables us to elaborate the multi-level and systemic aspect of analyzing boundary spanning and the question at what level to start. In Chapter 3 an alternative approach towards boundary spanning in flood policies was presented: analysis in a system perspective. Luhmanns's system approach was chosen as the strategy to structure a longitudinal assessment of boundary spanning in centuries of flood policies. It was illustrated how in a long-term perspective the wider circles are of essential importance and developments in these wider circles, or contextual layers in our language, channel the kind of boundary judgements that can be expected. By induction a typology of spanned boundaries was presented. In contrast, we emphasized the role of boundary judgements in interaction processes at the micro level, however we also included wider contextual layers that bridge to and specify characteristics of system levels (see Figure 2.4). We perceive the converging outcomes between the long-term analysis at system level and the outcomes of application of our conceptual and theoretical frameworks in several chapters as important support offered. The conclusion has to be that predominantly the problem statement and derived research questions have to be the point of departure to decide on this aspect of research strategy.

The seventh issue as indicated in Section 2.5 concerns: *the specific strategies used by actors to manage the boundary judgements of themselves or other actors and/or to cope with differences.*

The conclusions with regard to this final issue in this section concern the strategies that are included in the theoretical framework in Chapter 2. It was described that interventions to influence boundary judgements towards convergence could be classified into:

- adding new actors among which policy brokers;
- creating new arenas by adding new meeting points such as installing committees;
- creating new cognitions by introducing new information, spreading information, involving the media and so on;
- creating new motivations by creating salience among others by luring with resources;
- adding new resources and power bases.

In Chapters 5 and 6 the interventions used for influencing boundary judgements were described using these five categories. It proved not at all problematic to label concrete activities in these categories. Also in the other chapters a range of interventions fitting in different categories were described. Nevertheless in some chapters, for instance Chapter 9, it seemed that a very limited selection of strategies was applied. In this particular situation a rather high risk option was chosen that assumes that reliable estimates of the situation and the actors' boundary judgements and receptivity are available. Alternative low risk and step by step approaches can be imagined and should perhaps be preferred in uncertain situations, as, among others, Chapter 10 indicated. Imprecise estimates of the situation and what is needed to proceed can easily happen. In the next section some hints are given on how to maximize the protection level against such mistakes. This can be done by analysis and by careful selecting and planning interventions. This certainly does not imply that boundary spanning is a research activity that, when studied carefully, will lead to certain success. Boundary spanning also needs to be undertaken rigorously, to some extent a trial and error approach, carefully monitored and frequently adjusted, is as valuable as analysis. Preparation and analysis thus should be mingled with concrete action. This conclusion is in line with the principles of adaptive water resource management.

11.3 THE PRACTITIONERS' LENS ON BOUNDARY SPANNING

Boundary spanning comes with complexity and dependencies. We concluded that for relatively simple tasks, not using boundary spanning efforts is a serious option. Many chapters in this volume illustrated the emerging complexity and dependencies that accompany boundary spanning. In several chapters guidance was included for boundary spanning practitioners. The most prominent chapters in this regard were Chapters 4 and 10. We now add our observations to the offered toolbox.

In Chapter 4 it was concluded that the boundary spanning water manager needs to know the time dimensions of boundary judgements of relevant actors and that these time dimensions should be managed. Of course we have to add to this that identical attention should be given to the sector and scale dimensions of boundary judgements of relevant actors. When strategies for boundary spanning are considered, the lesson of Chapter 4 to the boundary spanning is that influencing diverging boundary judgements is more likely if actors' time horizons are longer. This being said, in many cases there might be converging boundary judgements that just need to be activated.

It all comes down to the first crucial strategy for the boundary spanner: *do everything needed to know your environment well, the environment includes the outside environment as well as the inside environment in your own organization, monitor continuously and learn by studying and doing simultaneously.*

In practitioners' language this implies getting to know what the plans and agendas of other governments on various levels are – at least that is what a reflexive practitioner should do. Invite yourself to consultations on the preparation of projects and policies at a regional and provincial level. Learn about the stakes and interests of various possibly relevant private and public organizations. This is in order to facilitate later attempts to find and formulate joint interests and to show understanding and tact in negotiations, issues that were also advised in Chapter 10 of this volume. A hands on approach is to start interacting; this comes with the risk of wasting time and efforts. If you seek for possibilities to cooperate in the wrong places or if you miss crucial actors and possibilities that have to be incorporated at a later stage, you missed some opportunities. The dilemma is not to stay stuck in analysis and not to be too hasty, greedy and imprudent. As usual, the 'good' is to be found in the balance between two extremes. Cooperating over boundaries will often also imply that some policy drift and drift of goals will be inevitable to motivate others to work together. This should be communicated and coordinated internally in your own organization sufficiently in order to proceed without the risk of losing legitimacy and support in your own organization.

The second crucial strategy for boundary spanners is: *to invest in good relations in the networks, also in redundant relations, for future linkages.*

Obviously boundary spanning requires persuading others to participate in your interaction processes or alternatively embedment of your interaction processes in those of others, all being undertaken with the intention of establishing linkages. This is not only a matter of rational analyses and knowing your environment well, it is also about investing in trust and long-term engagements. Purposeful activities in this context are, among others, initiating networks, activating and engaging individuals, managing the networks and working your way into settlements of coalitions that can deliver. You should also be aware that all kinds of goals and ambitions that today cannot be realized together with others might be attainable in the future, for instance, when some factors in the contextual layers change. So keep those ambitions on the agenda and communicate them frequently. It should also be noticed that engaging in a mutual project with others however insignificant these activities might be for your own organization could prepare the floor for the serious work. Who is relevant in the network and in a coalition might change over time. Keep track of that and realize that professionals and governors come and leave. So frequently the situation will become fluid and can develop for the better or worse. Invest thus also in relations that might become important in the longer term (under uncertainty enable serendipity). Welcome initiatives by others to establish contact. Create surplus value: *you scratch my back and then I'll scratch yours.* Boundary spanning will thus normally not be a hit and run activity but instead a conscious and consistent effort in long-term relations.

Therefore the third crucial strategy for boundary spanners is: *to fit up your own organization for boundary spanning.*

We already emphasized the importance of all kinds of dynamics in interaction processes, networks and the contextual layers. All such dynamics should be monitored and responded to. This implies that positions and stakes to some extent must be fluid. The internal organization of the hosting organization of a boundary spanner as well as the boundary spanners themselves should prepare for all of this. Create an organizational philosophy that is oriented towards external cooperation. Accommodate and adapt the staff: hire or exchange other types of people and give capable present staff the possibility to learn the necessary competencies. This holds true especially for the project manager, who should be communicative, flexible and entrepreneurial. Have the project managers regularly visit the meetings of each others' projects, so they can learn from each other and from the enlarged variety of situations they experience. As a representative of the organization, give confidence that your proposals are backed up by the responsible governors (which should, of course, also be true when necessary). Be honest and open to the governors about the risks of proposals, developments and the project as a whole – only then the support won't fail after a first disappointment. This implies a low threshold between the levels in the organization. The staff should be somewhat acquainted with each others' social networks so that problems can be solved through short lines. Try to add resources, for instance, by hiring a subsidy manager. Other advice is to group projects in bundles or programmes in the long-term financial projection so that a financial disappointment in one project can be compensated by good luck in another project, without disturbing the important long-term orientation. All in all, this could be hard to fit in to a normal structure, so sometimes it is therefore preferred to create a special unit. This strategy might work well in the case of boundary spanning that results in a concrete project, to realize that project, under the immediate supervision of the responsible governors. This being said, the lot of boundary spanning efforts might be better grounded in the internal normal organizations if they are not set aside from normal procedures. These normal procedures should accommodate boundary spanning and therefore should be revised.

The fourth crucial strategy for boundary spanners is: *to engage consciously in adding complexity.*

Note that new opportunities often come with new complexities. Do not span in order to just create many redundant linkages in one project. Also be aware that in cooperation every partner has to be kept aboard by carefully balancing the benefits and costs of participation. The transaction costs will increase when more actors and interests are involved. Consciously seek for shared and overlapping agendas, problem perceptions and solutions that could be compatible or adjustable for more than one problem. Be aware that there is a clear difference between keeping in touch and upholding redundant contacts in networks and activating partners and interests in concrete programmes and projects. At any time consider as well options to expand and options for thinning coalitions in concrete programmes and projects. Be aware of the constituencies of actors, for instance, do not allow agricultural representative organizations to take co-responsibility for issues that are generally neutral or irrelevant to regional agriculture, but might be regarded negatively by one or two individual farmers. The larger the coalition, the more difficult it becomes to monitor all these relevant aspects.

The fifth crucial strategy for boundary spanners is: *to show reliability, openness and determination during the entire process.*

Commissioning an external independent process manager, who shows that it is not just a water project, can help in this respect. But for the rest: avoid hiring interim personnel that after the project leave with all the knowledge learned. Take care that there is enough capacity attributed and the right responsibilities are given to the right person. Call in responsible administrators at strategic moments to prevent escalation by showing both determination and using their short lines to other organization leaders in the network.

Try to contain the risks of the indirect communication that always occurs when talks are held with individuals that participate on behalf of an organization. Watch whether everybody does their homework properly and keeps their organization well informed. Watch carefully whether the information is properly handed over when the representation of that (or the own!) organization is transferred from one individual to another.

Create open communication towards citizens with open access information markets and 'kitchen table' conversations with crucial individual households instead of general slide shows for an audience with questions afterwards. The latter way of communication can, in fact, be detrimental: the first critic sets the tone for the entire evening and the rest keeps silent because they do not feel at ease. It is a recipe for an 'us and them' feeling. As far as projects are not fully integrative, try to combine communication about all various projects and developments in the same geographical area together, enabling citizens to get the whole picture. They are not interested in the sector boundaries!

Boundary spanning is omnipresent in our complex society. It is one of the rare options we have to realize multiple ambitions in our complex society without creating excess conflict followed by the unbridled use of hierarchy and huge compensation costs. A careful reconsideration of strategies to reach out for water ambitions, together with more in-depth knowledge on the theories and practices of boundary spanning, could thus make solutions for contemporary water problems come closer to us. However not without energetic investments in the needed adaptive processes, keeping in mind that during these processes the manager continuously has to juggle in the context of boundary spanning dilemmas such as:

- boundary spanning enables more optimal solutions but also raises expectations;
- adaptive implementation and a consensual attitude of finding the way together can drift away from essential water goals;

- compromises are necessary but can decrease the legitimacy of the process within the represented organizations and groups;
- sharing responsibilities is essential, but can blur accountability;
- sharing resources creates dependencies.

All these items illustrate that while it is certainly possible to mention some do's and dont's, in dealing with complexity there will also remain dilemmas that can only be raised to awareness, but not solved. For some of those dilemmas the only honest advice is: take care.

References

Ainslie, G. (2005), 'Précis of breakdown of will', *Behavioral and Brain Sciences*, **28**, 635–50.

Andeweg, R.B. and G.A. Irwin (2005), *Governance and Politics of the Netherlands*, New York: Palgrave Macmillan.

Arquit Niederberger, A. (2005), 'Science for climate change policy-making: applying theory to practice to enhance effectiveness', *Science and Public Policy*, **32**(1), 2–16.

Bandura, A. (1997), *Self-efficacy in Changing Societies*, New York: Cambridge University Press.

Bardach, E. (1998), *Getting Agencies to Work Together*, Washington, DC: Brookings Institution Press.

Barnes, B. (1977), *Interests and the Growth of Knowledge*, London: Routledge and Kegan Paul.

Barrett, S.M. and C. Fudge (1981), 'Reconstructing the field of analysis', in S.M. Barrett and C. Fudge (eds), *Policy and Action: Essays on the Implementation of Public Policy*, London: Methuen, pp. 249–78.

Bausch, K.C. (2001), *The Emerging Consensus in Social Systems Theory*, Berlin: Springer.

Berg, B. L. (2001), *Qualitative Research Methods for the Social Sciences*, Boston, MA: Allyn and Bacon.

Berger, P.L. and T. Luckmann (1967), *The Social Construction of Reality: A Treatise in the Sociology of Knowledge*, Garden City, NY: Anchor Books.

Berkes, F. and C. Folke (2002), 'Back to the future: ecosystem dynamics and local knowledge', in L.H. Gunderson and C.S. Holling (eds), *Panarchy, Understanding Transformations in Human and Natural Systems*, Washington, DC: Island Press, pp. 121–46.

Bloor, D.M. (1976), *Knowledge and Social Imagery*, London: Routledge and Kegan Paul.

Borsuk, M., R. Clemen, L. Maguire and K. Reckhow (2001), 'Stakeholder values and the scientific modeling in the Neuse River Watershed', *Group Decision and Negotiation*, **10**, 355–73.

Bressers, J.Th.A. (1983), *Beleidseffectiviteit en waterkwaliteitsbeleid* (Policy effectiveness and water quality policy), Enschede: Universiteit Twente.

Bressers, H.T.A. (2004), 'Implementing sustainable development: how to know what works, where, when and how', in W.M. Lafferty (ed.), *Governance for Sustainable Development: The Challenge of Adapting Form to Function*, Cheltenham, UK and Northampton, MA, USA: Edward Elgar Publishing, pp. 284–318.

Bressers, H.T.A. (2007), 'Contextual Interaction Theory and the issue of boundary definition: governance and the motivation, cognitions and resources of actors', *External report ISBP EU-project*, January, available on website ISBP, http://www.tigress.ac/isbp/, accessed August 2008, CSTM series Studies and Reports, no. 323, pp. 1–31.

Bressers, H.T.A. (2009), 'From public administration to policy networks: contextual interaction analysis', in S. Nahrath and F. Varone (eds), *Rediscovering Public Law and Public Administration in Comparative Policy Analysis*, Berne: Haupt Verlag, pp. 123–42.

Bressers, J.Th.A. and P.J. Klok (1987), *Een voorlopige instrumententheorie van het milieubeleid* (A provisional instrumentation theory of environmental policy), Den Haag: VROM.

Bressers, H.T.A. and S. Kuks (2003), 'What does "Governance" mean? From conception to elaboration', in H.T.A. Bressers and W.A. Rosenbaum (eds), *Achieving Sustainable Development; The Challenge of Governance Across Social Scales*, Westport, CT and London: Praeger, pp. 65–88.

Bressers, H.T.A. and S. Kuks (eds) (2004), *Integrated Governance and Water Basin Management*, Dordrecht, Boston, MA and London: Kluwer Academic Publishers.

Bressers, H.T.A. and K.R.D. Lulofs (2004), 'Industrial water pollution in the Netherlands: a fee based approach', in W. Harrington, R. Morgenstern and T. Sterner (eds), *Choosing Environmental Policy: Comparing Instruments and Outcomes in the United States and Europe*, Washington, DC: Resources for the Future Press, pp. 91–116.

Carstensen, L.L., D.M. Isaacowitz and S.T. Charles (1999), 'Taking time seriously: a theory of socioemotional selectivity', *The American Psychologist*, **54**(3), 165–81.

Cash, D.W. and S.C. Moser (2000), 'Linking global and local scales: designing dynamic assessment and management processes', *Global Environmental Change*, **10**(2), 109–20.

Chapman, G.B. (1998), 'Sooner or later: the psychology of intertemporal choice', in D.L. Medin (ed.), *The Psychology of Learning and Motivation*, vol. 38, San Diego, CA: Academy Press, pp. 83–113.

Dawes, R.M. (1980), 'Social dilemmas', *Annual Review of Psychology*, **31**, 169–93.

Dente, B., P. Fareri and J. Ligteringen (1998), 'A theoretical framework for case study analysis', in B. Dente, P. Fareri and J. Ligteringen (eds), *The Waste and the Backyard*, Dordrecht: Kluwer Academic, pp. 197–223.

Deutsch, K.W. (1966), *The Nerves of Government: Models of Political Communication and Control*, New York: The Free Press of Glencoe.

Dryzek, J.S. (1997), *The Politics of the Earth: Environmental Discourses*, New York: Oxford University Press.

Easton, D. (1966), *Varieties of Political Theory*, Upper Saddle River, NJ: Prentice Hall.

EC (European Commission) (2007), *European Directive on the Assessment and Management of Flood Risks* (2007/60/EC).

Evers, J.G. (2007), *Naar Interactieve Uitvoering. Actoren, Interacties en Context*, Tussenrapportage uitvoering project Eperbeken, Enschede: CSTM / Universiteit Twente (unpublished).

Frederick, S., G. Loewenstein and T. O'Donoghue (2002), 'Time discounting and time preference: a critical review', *Journal of Economic Literature*, **40**(2), June, 351–401.

Geldof, G.D. (2001), *Omgaan met complexiteit bij Integraal Waterbeheer*, Deventer: Tauw bv.

Geldof, G.D. (2004), *Omgaan met complexiteit bij integraal waterbeheer: Op weg naar Interactieve Uitvoering*, Deventer: Tauw B.V.

Gieryn, T.F. (1983), 'Boundary-work and the demarcation of science from non-science: strains and interests in professional ideologies of scientists', *American Sociological Review*, **48**, 781–95.

Gonzales, A. and P. Zimbardo (1985), 'Time in perspective: the sense we learn early affects how we do our jobs and enjoy our pleasures', *Psychology Today*, **19**, 21–6.

Gunderson, L.H. and C.S. Holling (2002), 'Resilience and adaptive cycles', in L.H. Gunderson and C.S. Holling (eds), *Panarchy, Understanding Transformations in Human and Natural Systems*, Washington, DC: Island Press, pp. 25–62.

Guston, D.H. (1999), 'Stabilizing the boundary between politics and science: the role of the Office of Technology Transfer as a boundary organization', *Social Studies of Science*, **29**(1), 87–112.

Hajer, M. (1995), 'Discourse coalitions and the institutionalization of practice: the case of acid rain in Britain', in F. Fischer and J. Forester (eds), *The Argumentative Turn in Policy Analysis and Planning*, Durham and London: Duke University Press, pp. 43–76.

Hajer, M. and D. Sijmons (2006), *Een plan dat werkt*, Rotterdam: NAi Uitgevers.

Hendrickx, L., A. van der Berg and C. Vlek (1993), 'Concern for tomorrow? The factor "time" in the evaluation of environmental risks', *Tijdschrift voor Milieukunde*, **8**, 148–52.

Hendrickx, L., W. Poortinga and R. van der Kooij (2001), 'Temporal factors in resource dilemmas', *Acta Psychologica*, **108**, 137–54.

Hill, M. and P. Hupe (2002), *Implementing Public Policy*, London: Sage Publications.

Hobbs, R.J. and J.A. Harris (2001), 'Restoration Ecology: repairing the Earth's ecosystem in the new millennium', *Restoration Ecology*, **9**(2), 239–46.

Hoppe, R. (2002), *Van flipperkast naar grensverkeer: veranderende visies op de relatie tussen wetenschap en beleid*, no. 25, Den Haag: Adviesraad voor het Wetenschaps- en Technologiebeleid.

Intergovernmental Panel on Climate Change (IPCC) (2007), 'Climate change 2007: Mitigation. Contribution of the Working Group III to the Fourth Assessment Report of the Intergovernmental Panel on Climate Change', in B. Metz, O.R. Davidson, P.R. Bosch, R. Dave and L.A. Meyer (eds), *Summary for Policymakers*, Cambridge and New York: Cambridge University Press, pp. 9–18.

IRMA programme (2007), http://www.irma-programme.org/a_about/objectives.htm (accessed 14 September 2007).

Jasanoff, S. (1986), *Risk Management and Political Culture*, New York: Russel Sage Foundation.

Jasanoff, S. (1990), *The Fifth Branch: Science Advisers as Policymakers*, Cambridge, MA: Harvard University Press.

Jasanoff, S. (2003), 'Accounting for expertise?', *Science and Public Policy*, **30**(3), 157–62.

Jeffrey, P. and R.A.F. Seaton (2003/4), 'A conceptual model of "receptivity" applied to the design and deployment of water policy mechanisms', *Environmental Sciences*, **1**(3), 277–300.

Johnson, B.L. (1999), 'The role of adaptive management as an operational approach for resource management agencies', *Conservation Ecology*, **3**(2), available at http://www.consecol.org/vol3/iss2/art8/, accessed November 2008.

Joireman, J.A. (2005), *Understanding Behavior in the Context of Time – Theory, Research and Application*, Mahwah, NJ; London: Lawrence Erlbaum Associates.

Joireman J.A., T.P. Lasane, J. Bennett, D. Richards and S. Solaimani (2001), 'Integrating social value orientation and the consideration of future consequences within the extended norm activation model of proenvironmental behavior', *British Journal of Social Psychology*, **40**(1), March, 133–55.

Joireman, J.A., P.A.M. Van Lange and M. Van Vugt (2004), 'Who cares about the environmental impact of cars? Those with an eye toward the future', *Environment and Behavior*, **36**, 187–206.

Jones, R.V. (1972), 'Temptations and risks of the scientific adviser', *Minerva*, **10**, 441–51.

Juuti, P.S. and T.S. Katko (2005), 'Historical development of water and sanitation services', in P.S. Juuti and T.S. Katko, *Water, Time and European Cities: History Matters for the Future*, Tampere: Tampere University Press, pp. 25–51.

Kaats, E.A.P., P.J. van Klaveren and W. Opheij (2005), *Organiseren tussen organisaties; Inrichting en besturing van samenwerkingsrelaties*, Schiedam: Scriptum.

Kearney, J., F. Berkes, A. Charles, E. Pinkerton and M. Wiber (2007), 'The role of participatory governance and community-based management in integrated coastal and ocean management in Canada', *Coastal Management*, **35**(1), 79–104.

Keetman, W. (2006), 'Grensoverschrijdend Vechtwerk: op naar betere Nederlands-Duitse samenwerking met de KRW?', *H twee O*, **39**(21), 17–19.

Kingdon, J.W. (1984), *Agendas, Alternatives and Public Policies*, Boston, MA: Little Brown.

Kingdon, J. (1995), *Agendas, Alternatives and Public Policies*, New York: Harper Collins.

Klijn, E. (2006), 'Networks as perspective on policy and implementation', in S. Cropper, M. Ebers, C. Huxham and P. Ring (eds), *Handbook of Interorganizational Relations*, Oxford: Oxford University Press, pp. 118–46.

Klijn, F., P. Baan, K. de Bruijn and J. Kwadijk (2007), *Overstromingsrisico's in Nederland in een veranderend klimaat. Verwachtingen, schattingen en berekeningen voor het project Nederland Later*, Delft: WL Delft Hydraulics.

Klok, P-J. (1991), *Een instrumententheorie voor milieubeleid* (An instrumentation theory for environmental policy), Enschede: Universiteit Twente.

Kloprogge, P. and J.P. van der Sluis (2006), 'The inclusion of stakeholder knowledge and perspectives in integrated assessment of climate change', *Climatic Change*, **75**, 359–89.

Knorr-Cetina, K.D. and M. Mulkay (1983), *Science Observed: Perspectives on the Social Study of Science*, London: Sage.

Korringa, H. and J. van der Molen (2005), *Het dualiteitenkabinet; Over bestuurders, kaders en stoeptegels*, Assen: Koninklijke van Gorcum.

Kortenkamp, K.V. and C.F. Moore (2006), 'Time, uncertainty, and individual differences in decisions to cooperate in resource dilemmas', *Personality and Social Psychology*, **32**(5), 603–15.

Kuks, S.M.M. (2004), 'Water governance and institutional change', PhD thesis, University of Twente.

Lasswell, H.D. (1971), *A Pre-view of Policy Sciences*, New York: Elsevier.

Latour, B. and S. Woolgar (1979), *Laboratory Life, The Social Construction of Scientific Facts*, Beverly Hills, CA and London: Sage Publications.

Lee, K.N. (1993), *Compass and Gyroscope: Integrating Politics and Science for the Environment*, Washington, DC: Island Press.

Leven met Water (2007), available at http://www.levenmetwater.nl, accessed September 2008.

Lewin, K. (1951), *Field Theory in Social Science*, New York: Harper & Brothers.

Liberatore, A. and S. Funtowicz (2003), '"Democratising" expertise, "expertising" democracy: what does it mean and why bother?', *Science and Public Policy*, **30**(3), 146–50.

Lindblom, C.E. (1959), 'The science of "muddling through"', *Public Administration Review*, **19**, pp. 74–88.

Loewenstein, G. (1998), 'Frames of mind in intertemporal choice', *Management Science*, **34**(2), 200–14.

Luhmann, N. (1984), *Sociale Systeme: Grundriß einer algemeine Theorie*: Frankfurt am Main: Suhrkamp Verlag, English Translation (1995): *Social Systems*, Stanford, CA: Stanford University Press.

Lulofs, K. (2003), 'Evaluatie realisatie retentiegebieden Noord en Zuid Meene' (Evaluation realisation retention areas north and south Meene), Report to the water authority of Velt and Vecht, Enschede: CSTM.

Lulofs, K. and F. Coenen (2007), 'Cross border co-operation on water quality in the Vecht river basin', in J. Verwijmeren and M. Wiering (eds), *Many Rivers to Cross, Cross Border Co-operation in River Management*, Delft: Eburon, pp. 71–93.

Lulofs, K. and R. Hoppe (2006), 'Het pleitcoalitiemodel geëvalueerd: suggesties uit Europese toepassingen', *Beleidswetenschap* (Policy Science), **20**(2), 22–40.

Lulofs, K., F. Coenen, and S. Kuks (2004), 'Positionering planfiguren "Water in de Stad"' (Position of various plans for the 'water in the city' programme), Report for the Ministry of Transport, Public Works and Water Management, Enschede: CSTM.

MacRae, D. Jr. (1976), 'Technical communities and political choice', *Minerva*, **14**, 169–90.

Mannix, E.A. (1991), 'Resource dilemmas and discount rates in decision making groups', *Journal of Experimental Social Psychology*, **27**, 379–91.

March, J.G. and J.P. Olsen (eds) (1976), *Ambiguity and Choice in Organizations*, Bergen, Norway: Universiteits forlaget.

Medd, W. and S. Marvin (2007), 'Making water work: intermediating between regional strategy and local practice', *Environment and Planning D: Society and Space*, advance online publication doi:10.1068/d3205.

Messick D.M. and M.B. Brewer (1983), 'Solving social dilemmas: a review', in L. Wheeler and P. Shaver (eds), *Review of Personality and Social Psychology*, vol. 4, pp. 11–41.

Messick, D.M. and C.L. McClelland (1983), 'Social traps and temporal traps', *Personality and Social Psychology Bulletin*, **9**, 105–10.

Milfont, T.M. and V.V. Gouveia (2006), 'Time perspective and values: an exploratory study of their relations to environmental attitudes', *Journal of Environmental Psychology*, **26**, 72–82.

MNP (2007), 'Nederland Later: tweede Duurzaamheidsverkenning', *Fysieke Leefomgeving Nederland*, Bilthoven: Milieu- en Natuurplanbureau.

Nelkin, D. (1979), *Controversy, Politics of Technical Decisions*, Beverly Hills, CA and London: Sage Publications.

Nooteboom, S. (2006), *Adaptive Networks: The Governance for Sustainable Development*, Delft: Eburon Academic Publishers.

Nuttin, J.R. (1985), *Future Time Perspective and Motivation: Theory and Research Method*, Hillsdale, NJ: Lawrence Erlbaum, as appeared in Zimbardo et al. (1997).

Ostrom, E. (1999), 'Institutional Rational Choice: an assessment of the institutional analysis and development framework', In P.A. Sabatier (ed.), *Theories of the Policy Process*, Boulder, CO: Westview Press, pp. 35–71.

Otto, M.M. (2000), 'Het besturen van veranderingsprocessen', College voor de postdoctorale opleiding voor Management Consultant (PDO-MC), Vrije Universiteit Amsterdam.

Owens, K.A. (2008), *Understanding How Actors Influence Policy Implementation: A Comparative Study of Wetland Restorations in New Jersey, Oregon, the Netherlands and Finland*, Enschede: University of Twente.

Pellow, D. (ed.) (1996), *Setting Boundaries: The Anthropology of Spatial and Social Organization*, Westport, CT: Bergin & Garvey.

Pols, L., P. Kronberger, N. Pieterse and J. Tennekes (2007), *Overstromingsrisico als ruimtelijke opgave*, NAi Uitgevers Rotterdam, Ruimtelijk Planbureau Den Haag.

Price, D.K. (1967), *The Scientific Estate*, Cambridge, MA: Harvard University Press.

Quade, E.S. (1980), 'Pitfalls in formulation and modeling', in G. Majone and E.S. Quade (eds), *Pitfalls of Analysis*, Laxenburg: IIASA, pp. 23–43.

Ravetz, J. (2001), 'Science advice in the knowledge economy', *Science and Public Policy*, **28**(5), 389–93.

Reeze, A.J.G., A.D. Buijse and W.M. Liefveld (2005), *Weet wat er leeft langs Rijn en Maas: Ecologische toestand van de grote rivieren in Europees perspectief*, RIZA rapport 2005.010, Lelystad: Ministerie van Verkeer en Waterstaat, Rijkswaterstaat.

Roth, D., J. Warner and M. Winnubst (2006), *Een noodverband tegen hoog water: Waterkennis, beleid en politiek rond noodoverloopgebieden*, Wageningen: Wageningen UR.

Sabatier, P.A. and H.C. Jenkins-Smith (1999), 'The advocacy coalition framework: an assessment', in P.A. Sabatier (ed.), *Theories of the Policy Process*, Boulder, CO: Westview Press, pp. 117–68.

Samuelson, P. (1937), 'A note on measurement of utility', *The Review of Economic Studies*, **4**(2), 155–61.

Scholz, J.T. and B. Stiftel (eds) (2005), *Adaptive Governance and Water Conflict: New Institutions for Collaborative Planning*, Washington, DC: Resources For the Future Press.

Schon, D.A. and M. Rein (1994), *Frame Reflection: Toward the Resolution of Intractable Policy Controversies*, New York: BasicBooks.

Schooler, D.J. (1971), *Science, Scientists and Public Policy*, New York: The Free Press.

Siegel, D.S., D.A. Waldman, L.E. Atwater and A.N. Link (2004), 'Toward a model of the effective transfer of scientific knowledge from academicians to practitioner: qualitative evidence from the commercialization of University technologies', *Journal of Engineering and Technology Management*, **21**, 115–42.

Smith, A. and A. Stirling (2006), 'Moving inside or outside? Positioning the governance of sociotechnical systems', University of Sussex, Science and Technology Policy Research, SPRU electronic working paper series, no. 148.

Snow, C.P. (1951), *The Two Cultures*, Cambridge: Cambridge University Press.

Star, S.L. and J.R. Griesemer (1989), 'Institutional ecology, 'translations' and boundary objects: amateurs and professionals in Berkeley's Museum of Vertebrate Zoology 1907–39', *Social Studies of Science*, **19**(3), 387–420.

Strathman, A., F. Gleicher, D.S. Boningen and C.S. Edwards (1994), 'The consideration of future consequences: weighing immediate and distant outcomes of behavior', *Journal of Personality and Social Psychology*, **66**, 742–52.

Svenson, O. (1979), 'Process descriptions in decision making', *Organizational Behavior and Human Performance*, **23**, 86–112.

Svenson, O. and G. Karlsson (1989), 'Decision-making, time horizons and risk in very long term perspective', *Risk Analysis*, **9**, 385–99.

Swart, J.A.A. and J. van Andel (2007), 'Rethinking the interface between ecology and society. The case of the cockle controversy in the Dutch Wadden', *Sea Journal of Applied Ecology*, **45**(1), 82–90.

Teisman, G. R., J. Edelenbos, E. Klijn and J. Verbart (2001), 'Ruimtelijke Ontwikkelingsprocessen', in G.R. Teisman, A. Klijn and W.J. Oosten (eds), *Besluitvorming en Ruimtelijk Procesmanagement; Studie naar eigenschappen van ruimtelijke besluitvorming die Realisatie van meervoudig ruimtegebruik remmen of bevorderen*, Delft: Eburon, pp. 29–43.

Ulrich, W. (1996), *A Primer to Critical Systems Heuristics for Action Researchers*, Hull: Centre for Systems Studies, University of Hull.

Ulrich, W. (2000), 'Reflective practice in the civil society', *Reflective Practice*, **1**(2), 247–68.

Van Ast, J.A. and S.P. Boot (2003), 'Participation in European water policy', *Physics and Chemistry of the Earth*, **28**, 555–62.

Van der Meij, S. (2006), *Plan van Aanpak: Ontmanteling depot Wiemanstraat te Emst*, Apeldoorn: Waterschap Veluwe, afdeling projecten.

Van der Molen, J. (2001), 'Mag het ITCI meer zijn? Van customer intimacy naar omzetgroei', Scriptie postdoctorale opleiding voor Management Consultant (PDO-MC), Vrije Universiteit Amsterdam.

Van Leussen, W. and K. Lulofs (2009), 'Governance of water resources in the Netherlands', in H. Folmer and S. Reinhard (eds), *Water Problems and Policies in the Netherlands*, Washington, DC: RFF Press, pp. 171–85.

Van Leussen, W., G. Kater and P.P.M. van Meel (2000), 'Multi-level approach to flood control in the Dutch part of the river Meuse', in A.J.M. Smits, P.H. Nienhuis and R.S.E.W. Leuven (eds), *New Approaches to River Management*, Leiden: Backhuys Publishers, pp. 287–305.

Van Stokkom, H.T.C. and A.J.M. Smits (2002), 'Flood defence in the Netherlands: a new era, a new approach', in B. Wu, Z. Wang, G. Wang, G.G.H. Huang, H. Fang and J. Huang (eds), *Flood Defence 2002*, New York: Science Press, pp. 34–47.

Van Vugt, M. (1999), 'Concerns about the privatization of public goods: a social dilemma analysis', *Social Psychology Quarterly*, **60**(4), 355–67.

Vechtvisie (Outlook on river Vecht) (1997), Report of the working group Vechtvisie, prepared by Arcadis.

Verwijmeren, J. and M. Wiering (eds) (2007), *Many Rivers to Cross: Cross-border Co-operation in River Management*, Delft: Eburon.

Vlek, C. and G.B. Keren (1992), 'Behavioral decision theory and environmental risk management: assessment and resolution of four "survival" dilemmas', *Acta Psychologica*, **80**, 249–78.

Von Bertalanffy, L. (1968), *General System Theory: Foundations,*

Developments, Applications, New York: George Braziller.

Weingart, P. (1999), 'Scientific expertise and political accountability: paradoxes of science in politics', *Science and Public Policy*, **26**(3), 151–61.

Weiss, C. (1973), *Evaluation Research in the Political Context: Annual Meeting of the American Psychological Association*, Montreal: Bureau of Applied Social Research, Columbia University.

Weiss, C.H. (1979), 'The many meanings of research utilization', *Public Administration Review*, **39**(5), 426–31.

Westley, F. (2002), 'The devil in the dynamics: adaptive management on the front lines', in L.H. Gunderson and C.S. Holling (eds), *Panarchy, Understanding Transformations in Human and Natural Systems*, Washington, DC: Island Press, pp. 333–60.

Westley, F., S.R. Carpenter, W.A. Brock, C.S. Holling and L.H. Gunderson (2002), 'Why systems of people and nature are not just social and ecological systems', in L.H. Gunderson and C.S. Holling (eds), *Panarchy, Understanding Transformations in Human and Natural Systems*, Washington, DC: Island Press, pp. 103–19.

Whetten, D.A. (1982), 'Issues in conducting research', in D.L. Rogers and D.A. Whetten (eds), *Interorganizational Coordination: Theory, Research and Implementation*, Ames, IO: Iowa State University Press.

White House (2006), *The Federal Response to Hurricane Katrina: Lessons Learned.*

Williams, P. (2002), 'The competent boundary spanner', *Public Administration*, **80**(1), 103–24.

Winder, N. (2007), 'Innovation and metastability: a systems model', *Ecology and Society*, **12**(2): 28.

WRD (Waterschap Regge en Dinkel) (1997), *Reggevisie*.

Yan, A. and L.R. Meryl (1999), 'The migration of organizational functions to the work unit level: buffering, spanning, and bringing up boundaries', *Human Relations*, **52**(1), 25–47.

Zahariadis, N. (1999), 'Ambiguity, time, and multiple streams', in P. Sabatier (ed.), *Theories of the Policy Process*, Boulder, CO: Westview, pp. 73–93.

Zaleski, Z. (ed.) (1994), *Psychology of Future Orientation*, Lublin, Poland: Scientific Society of KUL, as appeared in Zimbardo et al. (1997).

Zimbardo, P. (1997), *Psychology*, New York: Longman.

Zimbardo, P. and J.N. Boyd (1999), 'Putting time in perspective: a valid, reliable individual-differences metric', *Journal of Personality and Social Psychology*, **77**(6), 1271–88.

Zimbardo, P.G., K.A. Keough and J.N. Boyd (1997), 'Present time perspective as a predictor of risky driving', *Personality and Individual Differences*, **23**(6), 1007–23.

Index